Joycean Temporalities

The Florida James Joyce Series

Florida A&M University, Tallahassee
Florida Atlantic University, Boca Raton
Florida Gulf Coast University, Ft. Myers
Florida International University, Miami
Florida State University, Tallahassee
University of Central Florida, Orlando
University of Florida, Gainesville
University of North Florida, Jacksonville
University of South Florida, Tampa
University of West Florida, Pensacola

Joycean Temporalities

Debts, Promises, and Countersignatures

Tony Thwaites

University Press of Florida

Gainesville · Tallahassee · Tampa · Boca Raton
Pensacola · Orlando · Miami · Jacksonville · Ft. Myers

06 05 04 03 02 01   6 5 4 3 2 1

Library of Congress Cataloging-in-Publication Data
Thwaites, Tony.
Joycean temporalities: debts, promises, and countersignatures /
Tony Thwaites.
p. cm.—(Florida James Joyce series)
Includes bibliographical references (p.) and index.
ISBN 0-8130-2114-6 (cloth: alk. paper)
1. Joyce, James, 1882-1941—Criticism and interpretation. 2. Joyce,
James, 1882-1941—Views on time. 3. Time in literature. I. Title.
II. Series.
PR6019.O9 Z829 2001
823'.912—dc21 2001034076

The University Press of Florida is the scholarly publishing agency
for the State University System of Florida, comprising Florida A&M
University, Florida Atlantic University, Florida Gulf Coast University,
Florida International University, Florida State University, University
of Central Florida, University of Florida, University of North Florida, University of South Florida, and University of West Florida.

University Press of Florida
15 Northwest 15th Street
Gainesville, FL 32611–2079
http://www.upf.com

Guy d'Esprit Thwaites

16.7.1921–3.5.1993

Eileen Margery Thwaites

20.10.1917–16.5.1999

*The Muse who has gathered up everything that
the more exalted Muses of philosophy and art
have rejected, everything that is not founded upon
truth, everything that is merely contingent,
but that reveals other laws as well, is History.*

Proust, XI 335

Contents

Foreword

Tony Thwaites sees Joyce's works as providing no definitive answers, but possibilities for speculation; in short the works speculate on themselves and a future outcome or resolution that is not achieved in any convincing way in the works themselves. They are self-referential, bearing the signature of Joyce, but depending on tentative speculation to answer the problems they pose. For Thwaites, the meaning of Joyce's texts is found on the periphery of the fictions—correspondences yielding a variety of tentative conclusions about an outcome that is yet to come when the last page is read. The process purposely invites such an interpretation of inconclusiveness as its hallmark by offering tantalizing clues about how it works within the texts themselves, and inviting a variety of interpretations as possibilities. In their celebration of their own uncertainty the works ultimately provide the close reader a source of playful joy in their interpretation.

Using a technique of speculative, extremely close reading à la Fritz Senn, but informed by Derrida, psychoanalytic theory, and a host of Joyce commentators, Thwaites develops a unique logic for meaning in Joyce. The book is written in deceptively clear prose. But the complicated, sometimes convoluted, paradoxical logic regarding the meaning of non-meaning in what is described as the fragmented purposeful incompleteness of Joyce's narrative, as it exists on the border of comprehension outside totally understandable intent or meaning, makes Thwaites's text as well as the texts of Joyce consist of tantalizing possibility rather than providing definitive answers.

Paradoxically it is Thwaites's splendid glosses and insightful interpretations of Joyce's texts that make the book exceptionally worthwhile. Thwaites revisits a lot of the old Joyce conundrums, like the throwaway and U.P.:Up, giving new and particular insights into every aspect of their serialized appearances in the text. His analysis of Gerty's section of Nausicaa, with its own internal inconsistencies and contradictions, is equally brilliant, and his culminating rationale for the *Wake* is certainly one of the best explanations of Joyce's intent to date. It makes a perfect conclusion to a book based on inconclusiveness.

Zack Bowen
Series Editor

Promissory Note

This book is about time in Joyce's work. Immediately, there are two aspects, linked but not the same, and for each of them we shall immediately have to speak of times in the plural, for they each include all sorts of things. On the one hand, there are the ways in which Joyce's work treats, or treats of, time: what it says and shows about time through its narration, characters, and events, from the individual experience of time passing to the large questions of the history in which those events are immersed. This is time as a theme. On the other hand, there are the times set up by Joyce's work itself, as a series of events in the world: the complexities of writing and revision, publication and reception, criticism and commentary.

Joycean Temporalities seeks to straddle those two aspects of the question, to see how the one informs the other. Its starting point is the signature, and the temporalities it introduces. At its simplest, when I sign my name, I affirm a debt or responsibility: *I am the same person as the one who last made this signature, I once more take up what he or she owes.* And I do this in the mode of a promise: that I *will be* that person, which is to say that I will continue to take up that debt in the future. The signature is a temporal eddy. Countersignature, debt, and promise provide a way of looking at some of the complexities of Joycean temporalities, both in and across the texts. In the course of this book, I shall be using these ideas to return to a number of familiar passages and critical issues in Joyce's writing, with the idea of reframing them in order—I hope—to reveal something new about their workings: questions such as narration and the putative figure of the narrator, free indirect speech and interior monologue, autobiography and the subject, mythopoeia and the Gilbert and Linati schemas.

In developing these ideas, this book draws on the work of a number of critics and theorists, but without trying to claim that it provides any sort of overall synthesis of them. On the contrary, I want to emphasize instead a certain irreducible conceptual multiplicity. Everywhere, Joyce puts together differences without totality, staging their meetings in fortuitous, tactical, and perhaps only momentary collisions, over which we should not be too hasty to make the magic and reconciling gesture of synthesis. Joyce's writing does not so much resolve the tensions and dissonances these collisions set up as accentuate and exploit them: they are behind much of the richness and fascination, not to mention difficulties, of his work. In Joyce, criticism inevitably finds itself faced with the problem of a writing which asks for intricate, careful, and patient reading and argumentation, but which insistently poses the issue of conceptual framework as a problem. This is why I prefer to begin not by outlining a theoretical framework, but by opening up a set of problems; the book tries to be guided by Joyce's writing and the complex ways in which it stages and thinks through these problems, rather than see Joyce as a fertile source of exempla.

The eclecticism of this book, then, is an attempt to keep some of those tensions open, and to stay for a while at the stage before some of the more ready critical syntheses have taken place. In particular, it is an attempt to slow things down to look at what happens before, as *Finnegans Wake* has it, "the traits featuring the *chiaroscuro* coalesce, their contrarieties eliminated, in one stable somebody" (*FW* 107.29–30). What happens if we refuse to take the integrity of personality or the self for granted, if we no longer quite know what such staples of narratology as character and narrator might be, and see them instead in what amount to the radically *im*personal terms of the multiplicity of collisions I have been suggesting?

The conceptual work I draw on all tends, in various ways, to thematize explicitly such multiplicity. I can name some of the main strands here, briefly, leaving the documentation for later; other threads will become obvious in the course of the argument. Derrida's work on the autobiographical, on responsibility, and on the signature has been important throughout; so too have Lacanian analysis and Žižek's developments of it, particularly on questions of the formation of the subject and the logic of the symptom; across these, a third strand in the braid is provided by Benjamin's meditations on history and the rupture of the Messianic; and though the substance of his work is perhaps not to be seen in these pages, my argument is everywhere informed by the work of Michel Serres, whose ability to link the most disparate things to the illumination of all continues to excite and inspire me.

And of course, this study has clear links and debts to a wide, though far from exhaustive, body of Joyce criticism, which it both continues and marks itself off from. This book traces the ways in which problems which are opened in Joyce's earliest writing are continually explored and rewritten throughout his work; but if it looks back to find *Finnegans Wake* in

Dubliners, it differs from Kimberly J. Devlin's *Wandering and Return in "Finnegans Wake"* in that the repetition it is concerned with is not thematic, but at a level logically prior to theme and representation; the same could be said of its invocation of debt and the economic in relation to Mark Osteen's *The Economy of "Ulysses."* Though this book is concerned at times with the reception of Joyce's work and the critical commentary on it, it is not a history of these (like Joseph Kelly's *Our Joyce*), but focuses instead on the ways in which one inhabits the other. Concerned with history, it is not an attempt to situate Joyce in his own historical and cultural moment (as in Vincent Cheng's *Joyce, Race, and Empire*, James Fairhall's *James Joyce and the Question of History*, Cheryl Herr's *Joyce's Anatomy of Culture*, or Dominic Manganiello's *Joyce's Politics*), but to think through ways in which, without falling back on sentimental reassurances that Art transcends History, Joyce's work opens itself out to the unforeseeable. I do not share the suspicions of "poststructuralism" with which a number of recent accounts of Joyce begin (such as Robert Spoo's *James Joyce and the Language of History* and Margot Norris's *Joyce's Web*), and where it is seen as a diversion of the critic's energies from the real of history into a specular labyrinth. Instead, I see the Derridean moment of dehiscence and the Lacanian irruption of the Real as differing descriptions of the very possibility of history itself. And in that, the questions I am asking of Lacan are different from those asked by Sheldon Brivic in *The Veil of Signs:* my concern is not with structures of mind so much as with the ways in which a radical impersonality of writing works itself out everywhere in Joyce. Joycean language everywhere speaks in tongues other than the user's, whatever the user, even if one of them should sign itself "Joyce"; and this is where the subject is—from the very beginning, before it is even a subject—historical. In this, what I am trying to investigate here is thus close to what Eloise Knowlton characterizes in *Joyce, Joyceans, and the Rhetoric of Citation* as a quotational regime, within which something like a subject can become established (10). All of these are debts to work admired, not refutations or corrections: what you offer back is always something different from what you received.

This book has other debts, for which a note like this can only be scant repayment. The first is the one marked in the dedication. As always, it is also for my family, with all love: Jennie, Lauren, and Sam, who put up with it for a long time. It is also for Brian Sager and Lyndon Walker, who put me up to it a long time ago.

Abbreviations

D   James Joyce, *Dubliners,* with an introduction and notes by Terence Brown (Harmondsworth: Penguin, 1992).

E   James Joyce, *Exiles,* in *A James Joyce Reader,* ed. Harry Levin (Harmondsworth: Penguin, 1993), 527–626.

FW   James Joyce, *Finnegans Wake* (London: Faber and Faber, 1964).

JJ   Richard Ellmann, *James Joyce,* new and rev. ed. (New York: Oxford University Press, 1982).

L1   *Letters of James Joyce,* vol. 1, ed. Stuart Gilbert (New York: Viking, 1957).

L2   *Letters of James Joyce,* vol. 2, ed. Richard Ellman (New York: Viking, 1966).

L3   *Letters of James Joyce,* vol. 3, ed. Richard Ellman (New York: Viking, 1966).

P   James Joyce, *A Portrait of the Artist as a Young Man,* ed. Seamus Deane (Harmondsworth: Penguin, 1992).

SH   James Joyce, *Stephen Hero: Part of the First Draft of "A Portrait of the Artist as a Young Man,"* rev. ed., edited and with an introduction by Theodore Spencer, with revisions and foreword by John J. Slocum and Herbert Cahoon (London: Jonathan Cape, 1956).

SL   *Selected Letters of James Joyce,* ed. Richard Ellmann (London: Faber and Faber, 1975).

U   James Joyce, *Ulysses: A Critical and Synoptic Edition,* 3 vols., ed. Hans Walter Gabler (New York and London: Garland Publishing, 1986).

U:P   James Joyce, *Ulysses,* ed. Declan Kiberd (Harmondsworth: Penguin, 1992).

U:S&Co   James Joyce, *Ulysses,* ed. Jeri Johnson, World's Classics series (Oxford: Oxford University Press, 1993).

Opening Accounts

Signatures and Countertimes

I live on my own credit, the credit I establish and give myself: it
is perhaps a mere prejudice that I live.
Nietzsche, 1899 Preface to *Ecce Homo*

Il se promène, lisant au livre de lui-même.
Mallarmé, as cited by Mr. Best in the Library, *U* 9.114

It seems to be Joyce himself who famously declared, "I've put in so many
enigmas and puzzles that it will keep the professors busy for centuries,
arguing over what I meant" (*JJ* 521). And from that authorial pronounce-
ment on, it is as if the legacy includes not only the enigmas and puzzles, but
also that statement itself, to be cited by Joycean scholars along with the
enigmas and puzzles. It is a hint, encouraging and authorizing: *Look for
the enigmas and puzzles: they* are *there, I put them there.* But at the same
time it is a disparagement. Its definite article lumps "the professors" into
a familiar and parodic aggregate, engaged in their harmless busyness and
endless argumentation: we can easily hear Stephen facing the dean of studies, or A.E. and the librarians. This alone gives it a slightly odd, indirect,
and even paradoxical address: *You, whom I am not addressing, do what
this statement is not bidding you to do.* And this is Joyce as reported years
later to Richard Ellmann by Jacques Benoîst-Méchin, once Joyce's trans-
lator. Joyce—if indeed it is Joyce, and not just apocryphal, or an inter-
viewee's elaboration for an inquiring professor—addresses the professors
across another's voice; or perhaps that other addresses them across
Joyce's. Everybody is eavesdropping, addressing as if not addressing, being addressed as if not being addressed, listening in on a huge echoing
party line, and from the outset silent countersignatories to a still-circulat-
ing letter.

Joyce commentary may be second only to Shakespearean in its sheer size and proliferation, and Joyce fostered it in all sorts of ways. By the time the Shakespeare and Company edition had gathered together and often elaborately reworked the individual episodes which had appeared to date, *Ulysses* was already immersed in commentary, much of it initiated by Joyce, or with his full approval, or even tacit collaboration. Within or behind or beyond or above Stuart Gilbert, Valéry Larbaud, and Frank Budgen, as Kenner says, "the artist disappears, nail-file in hand" (*Joyce's Voices* 63). Gilbert's study of *Ulysses*, on which Joyce was indeed virtually a collaborator, reached most English-speaking audiences well before legal copies of the novel itself did; and by that time, the novel was well known in translation—that other form of commentary—to a number of non-English-speaking audiences. *Finnegans Wake* was preceded by the collective *Exagmination*, and was meant to be accompanied shortly after its publication by another collection. Joyce's texts are not so much followed by commentary as swathed in it, from the outset.

Of course there is an obvious pragmatism in all this. If we content ourselves with the crude measure of the number of published pages, Joyce is hardly a prolific writer. Two books occupied almost his entire working life for more than a quarter of a century, and directly or indirectly provided most of his income during that time. Moves such as the serialization of *Ulysses* and the sale of the Rosenbach manuscript are then at very least canny means of making the one project pay in as many ways as possible.[1] They are essentially (and essential) speculations on a future: on a book not yet completed, and a reputation which, while hardly minor at the time, promises even more. As it is being produced, Joyce's work pieces itself out into a number of commodities which play the market in different ways: the serialized episodes of *Ulysses;* the slim limited editions of parts of the *Wake,* aimed at the collector; the manuscripts with their apparent but constantly revised uniqueness and authoritativeness. These are all incomplete objects. Their fascination and meaning lies in part somewhere outside of them, in what has not yet arrived but to which they nevertheless point alluringly. They are promises of the future, taking on their meaning in this incompleteness. Even at the height of Joyce's celebrity, this promise says that there is something to come, something not yet there, something which above all is unpredictable from what is already there and cannot be extrapolated from what has already been published. These tantalizing objects in front of us are only hints, teasers for everything they are not and which will not yet be revealed. Even the very title of the *Work in Progress* is withheld to the last minute, the object of a Joyce-inspired guessing game

(*JJ* 720–21, *SL* 395). And no matter how safe the speculation may seem, there is always the possibility that the promise will not be honored, that the check will bounce. Like any investment, these writings must be underwritten, carry a guarantee of their worth.

This promise is attached above all to the signature, and the peculiar way in which the signature places these objects to which it is attached into an economy of speculations and sureties. We could say of Joyce what Derrida says of the Nietzsche of *Ecce Homo:* that the identity to which he lays claim "has passed to him through the unheard-of contract he has drawn up with himself. He has taken out a loan with himself and *has implicated us in this transaction through what, on the force of a signature, remains of his text*" (*Ear of the Other* 8). Joyce's entire oeuvre is an immense and complex implementation of the signature and its promissory effects.

All this goes much further than the banal question of whether or not Joyce's work *fulfills* a promise (is *Finnegans Wake* the crowning masterpiece of a career, or a decline into hermetic obsession?). My argument in this book is that Joyce's work is structured *as* promise. That is, its everescalated remortgaging of itself does not affect only those things easily put to one side as externalities—the circumstances of its composition, publication, circulation, and reputation, say—but is from beginning to end at the unstable heart of these texts' meaning. The signature draws on the future: not only for those puzzles to keep professors busy, the teasing fragments of works in progress, the serializations and the collectors' items, the unique manuscripts, but no less for the completed published works themselves. It plays on what is to come, and on what remains still to come even after publication. What the name *Joyce* comes to mean is still open. We have poststructuralist Joyces, feminist Joyces, postcolonial, centennial and millennial Joyces, as if the name has *not yet* received its content. One could, of course, say something similar about any author who remains the object of critical or popular attention. In Joyce, though, this *not yet* is forever spilling over any boundaries between what is, on the one hand, "inside" the text and belonging to it as genuinely textual, and what is, on the other, "external" and incidental. Forever raising the ante, the signature marks that margin on which there comes to be such a thing as a text.

In an article on "Silence in *Dubliners,*" Jean-Michel Rabaté asks, "in what sense does this book offer a theory of its own interpretation, of its reading, of possible metadiscourses about its textuality?" (*Joyce upon the Void* 46). It is a familiar question. Joyce studies have been concerned with it long before those meetings between Joyce studies and what for want of a better term I will simply (with some misgivings) call "poststructuralism."[2] (We hardly need to elide the two to appreciate as entirely appropriate Fritz Senn's reported comment after Jacques Derrida delivered his "Two Words for Joyce" at the Centre Georges Pompidou in 1982: "But this is not so different from what we've been doing for years.")[3] From the outset, Joyce's texts have been seen as commenting on themselves, prefiguring themselves within themselves, or providing suggestions on how they might be read. We could make a sizable library of critical work which pieces together an aesthetics from Stephen's fragments of Aquinas and Aristotle; *Finnegans Wake* figures within its own pages as a letter scratched up from a dungheap by a hen.

All of which is familiar enough to be truism. But we need to take that logic of speculation seriously here. It is not enough to see this as a matter of mirrors held up to themselves, lost in the infinite hall of reflections of their own making. It is, at very least, a *speculation* which wagers on what is irreducibly outside it. Speculating on ideas it ponders, thinks through, or plays with, it also speculates on its own future, on a career. Stephen's aesthetics are not necessarily the key to what is done in the *Portrait* or *Ulysses,* but they are certainly a complex move in them. In the Library, Stephen is trying desperately to impress A.E., and secure an invitation into the older writer's coterie and forthcoming anthology of younger Irish poets; it is a party turn he has done before, something Mulligan even advises the Englishman Haines to put on his itinerary of Things to Do and See While in Dublin (*U* 1.487, 555–57). Stephen's famous and prompt "No" to Eglinton's question whether he believes his own theory (*U* 9.1065–67) reminds us that *theory* and *speculation* run together etymologically. Further back, Stephen's theorizing on the beach at Sandymount inverts itself once those old women come down the steps from Leahy's terrace, and the "midwife's bag" one of them carries (*U* 3.32) triggers his guilty and unresolved thoughts of his mother: behind the self-consciously learned meditation on the limits of the visible, we start to glimpse the limits of what Stephen himself wishes not to see, and which until now Aristotle has kept at bay: his philosophizing may be a way of "getting on nicely in the dark" (*U* 3.15). And further back again, this time to *Portrait,* Stephen's theories of art are again peripatetic, working also, and for all their importance to the novel, as a surface which will only gradually reveal the sexual longings they deflect. These theorizings may not be primarily—or even at all, in the case of the Library episode—about giving us the spectacles which will let us see clearly how to read the book they seem to know they inhabit; they are about pushing and pulling, making do with what is available, making things bearable even if that involves keeping them from sight, laying a wager on outcomes, altering the odds.

The metalingual is never just self-reflexivity, as if a text could know itself thoroughly and completely. It is a constitutively open moment of the text, speculating on an outcome it cannot guarantee. If no text can govern its own reception, it can lay a bet on it. Indeed, there is almost a subgenre of *Wake* criticism addressing this, and one of its most fruitful. We could call it, after Bernard Benstock, "What we don't yet know about *Finnegans Wake*."[4] Its illustrious exponents would include Fritz Senn and, perhaps despite himself, Roland McHugh. John Bishop's *Joyce's Book of the Dark* shows how this not-knowing actually structures the *Wake* itself, as a book about mostly dreamless sleep written in a "natlanguage." McHugh is confident that once we know what all the words mean, we'll know what the *Wake* means. Yet it's not just the gaps where his *Annotations* offer no readings that bother me: it's the extent to which his identifications, in their very accuracy and copiousness—and I say this with no disparagement of a truly invaluable resource—*do not help*. Senn writes of the "linguistic frustrations" with which, after three decades of patient and exemplary scholarship, he still feels that the opacities outnumber what is known, that by far the greatest number of passages resist explanation ("Linguistic Dissatisfaction" 211–12). This raises the serious possibility that *Finnegans Wake* may not be a book which is ever to be known. I do not mean this in a trivial or mystical sense: that is, not because it is without meaning or because its meaning is hidden away from mortals behind divine veils. If anything is the problem, it is that the *Wake* has *too much* meaning: that its proliferating and at the same time hypotactic organization is far from random, is instead merely relentlessly unhierarchical. What happens inevitably in this proliferation of meanings is also a necessary proliferation of blind spots, where the rub is not that there is not meaning there, but that we have no way of telling if there is or not. McHugh envisages a book which at some distance in the future will be completely known and mapped. However, it may be that the reality is a book constructed so as to make such a completeness impossible: Klaus Reichert speaks of a Wakean *sublime* ("Towards the Sublime"). There may be no general theory of Joyce's writing, only a multiplicity of incompatible but complementary theories between the global and what Senn calls the "hypolectic" ("Linguistic Dissatisfaction" 213).

Because the signature has the force and structure of a promise, it always looks ahead to find its meaning in what is not yet, and indeed carries no guarantee of ever being simply present.[5] But the signature also, and at the same time, looks back: a signature is a signature only because it is already a *countersignature*, the repetition of something which is already recognized as signature. The people at the bank accept my signature because it is like the samples of it they already have on their records. Even then, there is strictly no first signature: what I gave the bank when I opened my account cannot function as signature if it does not correspond to what I will produce in the future when asked to sign something. The first signature is first only provisionally, as long as it measures up to all those signatures which have not yet even been produced, and in relation to which it is thus second. There are no signatures, but there are countersignatures, and only countersignatures. In the very moment of its *being* a signature, the signature reaches forward and back to other times. At the heart of the present, the signature opens up the serial temporality this book will explore.

Something new arrives, for signature. Which is to say that the only things I sign are those which are not already mine: if it is already in some sense mine, it is already in some sense signed. I write, and the words I use and the concepts I draw on are not mine until that writing countersigns them. *What I sign comes to me from elsewhere:* my signature is a countersignature on what may have been signed elsewhere, for other purposes. Even as it affirms me as signatory and marks what I sign as mine, the signature marks an intrusion of something profoundly other, and it does that at the very moment I claim it. We can go further: what arrives from elsewhere and what gets made mine in that event of signing is also the very "I" that signs. Just as what I sign only becomes mine in the signing, there is a sense in which the "I" that signs arrives with the signature too: it's only in the signing of *Ulysses* that there is now, in the world, that James Joyce, author of *Ulysses,* scandalous writer, major figure of European letters, subject of biography, distant employer of busy professors.

And if what arrives for my signature is something other than mine, something which breaks unforeseeably from what has gone before, then there is something quite *inconsistent* about signature. Or rather, signature is exactly the way inconsistencies get articulated. Signature works by being inconsistent: it brings together two quite heterogeneous and autonomous regimes, and does so by marking and preserving that heterogeneity. By its very nature, in what makes it possible, it is always partial, impure, mixed with other things: never quite enough to ensure its felicity, it has to repeat and reaffirm itself, over and over. This means signature is always close to forgery, from which it can never separate itself enough.

Signature is the boundlessness of connection. It marks the text on the outside, as it were, certifying it as commodity, property, literary object, part of an oeuvre, in the quite mundane world in which it makes its way. There is an entire pragmatics bound up with this aspect of the signature, and Joyce himself was a particularly canny player of that market. At the same time, the signature necessarily marks the text with an internal seriality. This is what is at work when we recognize a text as "Joycean" for, say, its encyclopedism, its technical virtuosity, or its particular comedy, whether or not the text is by Joyce. It is at work in all the plays on his name and person which Joyce scatters through his texts: from the "J.J." by which the narrator calls O'Molloy in Barney Kiernan's pub, or Molly's invocation, "O Jamesy let me up out of this" (*U* 18.1128–29), or a multitude of wordplays on *joy* throughout *Ulysses* and the *Wake;* to the Stephen of three books, or the "lankylooking galoot in the macintosh" (*U* 6.805) who strides through the pages of *Ulysses,* or Shem in the "inspissated grime of his glaucous den" deep in the *Wake* (*FW* 179.25–26). In order for it even to be signature, the signature necessarily and incessantly crosses that apparent boundary between text and world which it is all too easy to model on the closure of the covers of a book.

To sign something is to make some sort of claim on it, and that claim of property is carried in the signature. In other words, the signature is a performative: it is not the mark of a claim which has already been made elsewhere, it *is* that claim. I claim what I sign, in the very act of signing. After I sign, the claim is in place; before I sign, my claim is simply not there. The signature is an *event.* In it, something happens: something which was not there before, but which arrives in this window which the signature and its promise open up to past and future. This arrival is everywhere in Joyce: a shout coming through the window of the schoolroom as Stephen is arguing with Mr. Deasy in *Ulysses,* but also that book's unprecedented and radical reinvention of itself as it progresses.

"The Sisters" is of course Joyce's first published story, and over a decade later it was to open his first book of fiction, *Dubliners,* though in a considerably revised form on which Joyce worked while writing the last of the *Dubliners* stories, "The Dead." In the meantime, *Dubliners* had been through its own remarkable and protracted story of delays, rejections, canceled contracts, revisions, concessions, and overbiddings. The first chapter looks at this in terms of the logic of speculation and signature I have just outlined, which it argues is also internal to the stories themselves. The hinge here is the word "paralysis." In a frequently cited letter to his publisher Grant Richards, Joyce famously invokes paralysis as a diagnosis of the moral state of Dublin itself; and in the first paragraph of "The Sisters," in the version that was eventually to open *Dubliners,* it is one of the three words which notoriously fascinate the boy narrator. By paying attention to the contexts of the word on each occasion, it is possible to see that even at this far-from-simple inaugural point of a career, Joyce's writing already breaks significantly from a moral naturalism, in ways which prefigure the concerns of *Ulysses* and even *Finnegans Wake.* At the very beginning of Joyce's oeuvre, "The Sisters" brings into play a complex temporality in which the very idea of beginning is itself posed as a question.

The second chapter inverts that figure of promise, to begin with a consideration of Eliot's famous comment that "we are all indebted" to *Ulysses.* Signatures mark out debts, and this enables us to reconsider the Gilbert and Linati schemas for *Ulysses* in terms of list and symptom, rather than in terms of mythic parallels or archetypal symbols. For psychoanalysis, the symptom is a small and in itself inconsequential detail, which takes on significance only when it is transplanted into the right interpretative framework. The symptom means only by being in some sense out of place, displaced; it signifies a prior state only by being achronic, out of time. A term borrowed from Benjamin and echoing the first chapter's discussion of *paralysis* will be fruitful for the later discussion of Stephen's aesthetics in the *Portrait:* the symptom is an *arrest.* A particularly telling figure of the symptom in *Ulysses* is the "shout in the street," the cry from the hockey field which Stephen and Garrett Deasy hear through the study window as they argue history and the ways of the world. It will in turn allow us to look at one of the more enigmatic aspects of the schemas, the suggestion that the end of the book sees a union between Bloom-Odysseus and Stephen-Telemachus.

Chapter 3 turns the argument towards a consideration of subjectivity and the temporalities of narrative which arise out of these logics of promise and debt. A discussion of the opening pages of *A Portrait of the Artist as a Young Man* develops the earlier idea of the *arrest.* The infant Stephen makes his appearance in a whirl of others' discourse, as an empty point traversed by words he does not even yet understand. This suggests that the real Joycean innovation is not interior monologue (which in itself remains psychologistic and realist) but the quite unprecedented instability of a *free indirect discourse.* More: interior monologue is itself fruitfully approached as a subcategory of free indirect discourse. The chapter examines a classical critical version of Joyce's use of free indirect discourse (Hugh Kenner's "Uncle Charles Principle"), and the "Nausicaa" chapter of *Ulysses,* in which indirect discourse is no longer strictly locatable as the characteristic expression of a character. The signature is always first of all a countersignature, on a found object.

In this light, chapter 4 turns to the final chapter of *A Portrait of the Artist as a Young Man,* and returns to the earlier question of the autobiographical. Rather than try to derive a coherent aesthetic theory from Stephen's soliloquizing and his dialogues with the Dean and Lynch—one which could then more or less be applied to the *Portrait* or Joyce's work in general—it looks at that aestheticizing in its novelistic and narrative context. It follows Stephen on the two walks he takes in the final chapter of *A Portrait of the Artist as a Young Man,* to layer together Stephen's aesthetic theory with the richly mundane and contingent world through which he moves. If Stephen insists that art should have a properly aesthetic stasis, that context is forever immersing him and his theorizing in the improper and the kinetic; though he shuns the goods and language of the marketplace in favor of the aesthetic, the logic of signature means that he can never make that separation as clearly and cleanly as he would wish. In this traversal of the art and the life, and the complex qualification of Stephen offered by the novel's use of free indirect discourse, the *Portrait* offers an aesthetic of the contingent which is quite different from Stephen's aesthetic.

The subject is something which is invoked: by a rhythm, a call, the incessant rain of words in which an infant is bathed, a shout in the street. This invocation returns in *Finnegans Wake* in what may be its purest form, offering some of Joyce's most complex uses of the logics of the event and the signature. The final chapter focuses on ALP, whose presence in *Finnegans Wake* is so frequently one of invocation and countersignature, and on the sigla, which have a radically different function from that of a shorthand for characters. In this retrospective mirror, one can see quite clearly Joyce's development of these processes from their earliest appearances in his writings.

|

Paralysis

Consider *Dubliners*. The story of the collection is well known. In July 1904, Joyce told Con Curran that he was writing "a series of epicleti—ten—for a paper. I have written one. I call the series *Dubliners* to betray the soul of that hemiplegia or paralysis which many consider a city" (*SL* 22). The paper, the *Irish Homestead,* was to run three of these stories. By late 1905, when Joyce first approached Grant Richards with the stories he was eventually to publish, they had grown to twelve. Richards accepted them on February 17, 1906, and signed a contract in March (*JJ* 219). It was to this point, at least, a piece of good fortune for a relatively unknown minor writer, one who had previously published only three stories and a few reviews, articles, and poems. But what happened in the mere couple of weeks *between* these close dates of acceptance and contract would delay publication for another eight years. Though this is often read as a drama of artistic integrity, in which even as a young man one of the century's great innovators refuses to compromise his work, we may also suspect there is more than a touch of perversity in the whole affair.

On February 22—the timing is important: this is only days after Richards's acceptance, and before any contract has been set—Joyce sent Richards another story for inclusion. This was "Two Gallants," and Richards passed it on directly to the printer, perhaps with enough evident trust in his new writer not to need to read it for himself. But the printer refused it as laying both himself and Richards open to prosecution for obscenity, and he returned the story with the offending passages marked up to make them unmissable. Newly sensitized, he also marked what he now thought had been dangerous passages after all in two of the stories he had earlier passed.

Richards broke the news to Joyce in late April. Joyce's immediate response was to refuse all changes, but this modulated into a rather risky defense, coupling concessions with what is almost a dare:

You cannot say that the phrases objected to are gratuitous and impossible to print and at the same time approve of the tenor of the book. Granted this latter as legitimate I cannot see how anyone can consider these minute and necessary details illegitimate. I must say that these objections seem to me illogical. Why do you not object to the theme of *An Encounter,* to the passage "he stood up slowly saying that he had to leave us for a few moments &c . . ."? Why do you not object to the theme of *The Boarding-House?* Why do you omit to censure the allusions to the Royal Family, to the Holy Ghost, to the Dublin Police, to the Lord Mayor of Dublin, to the cities of the plain, to the Irish Parliamentary Party, &c? As I told you in my last letter I cannot understand at all what has been admired in the book at all if these passages have been condemned. What would remain of the book if I had to efface everything which might give offence? The title, perhaps? (*SL* 86)

You approve of the book, the letter says, *so how is it possible for you to argue that these phrases are offensive?* But this so easily inverts itself into something else: *You find these phrases offensive, so how is it possible for you to approve of the book to which they are essential? Was your initial admiration of the book wrong after all? Look, here are some more things you seem to have missed.* What presents itself as a counter to the printer's work of sensitization is indistinguishable from a continuation of it. *Dubliners* is already haunted by the phantom of an unpublishable book.

By June, Joyce was conceding with protests to some of Richards's demands. Nevertheless, in the midst of these he mentions a new, fourteenth story, "A Little Cloud," which he would be sending back with the others—one which Richards had not yet seen, but in which "I do not expect you will find anything . . . to object to" (*SL* 89). Richards does not appear to have objected, but because of Joyce's evident fondness for it—he was to tell Stanislaus that "A page of *A Little Cloud* gives me more pleasure than all my verses"—it became a bargaining point for the changes the publisher wanted to force: "I wrote to Grant R—to know had he decided to refuse definitely my concessions: namely deletion of 'bloody' from 3 stories and deletion of paragraph in 'Counterparts' against inclusion of *Two Gallants* and *A Little Cloud*" (*SL* 121, 120).

Two footnotes. The first: in 1909, the collection having been long since rejected by Richards, Joyce contracted the book with Maunsel of Dublin, who this time did indeed want to "censure the allusions to the Royal Family" in "Ivy Day in the Committee Room," where Mr. Henchy makes a too-familiar reference to Edward VII (*D* 129). And the second: *Chamber Music,* whose modest title is both "too complacent" ("I should prefer a title which to a certain extent repudiated the book without altogether disparaging it" [*SL* 121]) and mildly scatological,[1] also manages to enter the game. Before it was at last published by Elkin Mathews in 1907, the manuscript was to be mislaid twice, once by Joyce and once by Richards, and then rejected in quick succession by Richards, John Lane, Constable, and Heinemann (*JJ* 192, 219).

Each time, Joyce is on the verge of closing the deal; and each time, this is the very moment the bid is raised and everything is once more thrown back into jeopardy. Sometimes this is openly Joyce's doing: ("It was I, again, who pointed out to you the 'enormity' in ['An Encounter']" [*SL* 87]). Sometimes—even better—it is *something which just happens,* not at all his doing but *as if in answer* to a suggestion he has already made. It would be too easy to suggest that this is Joyce playing the Hegelian Beautiful Soul (Hegel 400), decrying the cruel world which has brought his good intentions to nothing, and all the while working under the surface of things to make sure that cruel world continues its work as the best possible excuse for failure. In the National Library of "Scylla and Charybdis," Stephen will dismiss Eglinton's assertion that Shakespeare's marriage to Anne Hathaway was a mistake he "got out of . . . as quickly and as best he could": "Bosh! Stephen said rudely. A man of genius makes no mistakes. His errors are volitional and are the portals of discovery" (*U* 9.226–29). Not mistakes, says Stephen, but errors. The Latin root, *errare,* covers being mistaken, but also wandering, straying, roaming, wavering, as indeed the English word itself still did in Shakespeare's time[2]—and to err willfully in that sense may be to open the door to something genuinely new and unforeseen. This is volitional in that you accede to what happens, even though it may not be of your making. Indeed, whether or not you made it happen is irrelevant: the volition is not in the making, but in the affirming it *as if* you had made it happen all along. So this volition is a curious thing: yours in the affirmation, other than yours in its causes, it is poised somewhere on very margins of the one who wills; not something which emerges from the depths of a self in order to assert that self on the world outside it, but something which takes place on a very thin membrane between *in* and *out*—a portal perhaps, through which one discovers what lies on either side of it, including this tenuous willing self. The drama the Beautiful Soul plays out is quite different: it holds itself apart from the world and seeks above all to maintain its own purity as a self; as a result, the only self it encounters is one which fails in this impossible task; and blaming this failure on the world rather than on the impossibility of the task, it denies its own complicity in that world. In a word, hysteria. But the drama played out here is one of the *subject*, thrown from the outset into a world of which it is not the measure, and affirming that abandonment as its own constitutive impossibility. In this sense, subjectivity is exactly what the Beautiful Soul seeks to protect itself against; conversely, the only authentic subject may be one which refuses to distance itself from that "failure" with the ruses of the Beautiful Soul. Subjectivity is a destitution, no doubt, and one which, as Lacan recognized, courts psychosis in affirming itself *as* symptom. Joyce's achievement is to show its profound and unsettling comedy: *Joyce le sinthome* (Lacan et al. 37–48, 49–67).

And each time, everything is suspended: everything, including those things which are most important, hangs without resolve, open to the future as a speculation. The drama of mortgaging and remortgaging spills out everywhere.

On its most obvious level, we have a clash over money, where neither party really has much room to move. Richards had just recently been discharged from bankruptcy,[3] and had made his return to publishing only by putting the new business in his wife's name (*JJ* 191, 220, *SL* 43–44). And Joyce, as always, was impecunious: the paragraph offering Richards the collection concludes that "Unfortunately I am in such circumstances that it is necessary for me to have either of the books [*Dubliners* and *Chamber Music*] published as soon as possible" (*SL* 78). But even when things are at their most pecuniary, they play out the claims on the future made by a number of other more symbolic forms of capital, over and over. Joyce is risking a reputation which exists only in this speculation, one he does not yet have but which can certainly be jeopardized in the present: "You tell me in conclusion that I am *endangering my future* and your reputation," he retorts to Richards (*SL* 84, emphasis added). Literature itself will be called in to underwrite this line of credit: "I know very little of the state of English literature at present . . . [b]ut I suspect it will follow the other countries of Europe as it did in Chaucer's time." (*SL* 83). So too will the integrity of the artist, whose duty to the role requires a certain veracity:

> I have written it for the main part in a style of scrupulous meanness and with the conviction that he is a very bold man who dares to alter in the presentment, still more to deform, whatever he has seen and heard. I cannot do any more than this. I cannot alter what I have written. (*SL* 83)

Such an argument is already calling on the very morality which both Richards and the printer fear underwrites the possibility of legal action. Far from being immoral, Joyce will claim repeatedly, these stories are morality itself:

> My intention was to write a chapter of the moral history of my country and I chose Dublin for the scene because that city seemed to me the center of paralysis. (*SL* 83)

This passage is often read as an authoritative comment on what the stories mean, rather than as a speculation in which Joyce is trying to take over the very terms which are being used against him. We should, at very least, let it become colored by the calculation of interest he offers:

> from the point of view of financial success it seems to me more than probable than [*sic*] an attack, even a fierce and organized attack, on the book by the press would have the effect of interesting the public in it to much better purpose than the tired chorus of imprimaturs with which the critical body greets the appearance of every book which is not dangerous to faith or morals. (*SL* 88)

And this is present from the very first occasion on which Joyce wrote to Richards about the collection: "I think people might be willing to pay for the special odour of corruption which, I hope, floats over my stories" (*SL* 79).

Taken one at a time, the arguments are all reasonable enough in their own terms; but when put together, there is more than the faintest odor not so much of corruption as of Freud's famous "kettle-logic."[4] They are simply inconsistent with each other. On the one hand,

> Your suggestion that those concerned in the publishing of *Dubliners* may be prosecuted for indecency is in my opinion an extraordinary contribution to the discussion. I know that some amazing imbecilities have been perpetrated in England but I really cannot see how any civilized tribunal could listen for two minutes to such an accusation against my book. I care little or nothing whether what I write is indecent or not but, if I understand the meaning of words, I have written nothing indecent whatever in *Dubliners*. (*SL* 89)

On the other (and this some six weeks earlier),

> All these objections of which the printer is now the mouthpiece arose in my mind when I was writing the book, both as to the themes of the

stories and their manner of treatment. Had I listened to them I would not have written the book. I have come to the conclusion that I cannot write without offending people. (*SL* 83)

Dubliners is a thoroughly moral book; that it's dangerous to morals is all the better for sales. I knew people would say exactly this about the book when I was writing it; it comes as a surprise to me that people can even say such things about it. As Freud suggests, such kettle-logic may function as an accession to and displacement of guilt. We do not have to invoke some sort of personal guilt here, an authentic interior truth of what Joyce *must really have felt.* There is an errancy involved in this, after all, that volition which is never just personal. What is happening has instead the structure of an accusation. It arrives from elsewhere, from a diffuse and vast other which always regresses beyond and behind the particular bearer of the message. The objections are not first of all Richards's, it would seem, but the printer's; not the printer's but the law's; and then not even the law's but that "English opinion" of which the printer and the law alike would seem only to be the barometer (*SL* 81), a "public morality" which is not so much outraged as *in danger* of being outraged—before the outrage has ever taken place, and as a preempting of its ever taking place, as if the very danger itself constituted the outrage (*SL* 84).

And paradoxically these objections are already *also* Joyce's, before the event, before Richards or the printer even raised them, and they even already form part of the book: "All these objections of which the printer is now the mouthpiece arose in my mind while I was writing the book." On the one hand, the only thing to be done with these objections is to put them to one side and ignore them. *If I had listened to them, I would not have written the book; I cannot afford to consider whether what I write is indecent or not; to court that tired chorus of imprimaturs by striving to write something which runs no risk of being found dangerous to faith or morals would be the death of my writing; if that writing offends people, so be it.* But on the other hand, *Dubliners* has already listened to them and done their bidding. The book is itself a "moral history," quite "scrupulous" in its presentment of what it has seen and heard, with "nothing indecent whatever in it." It is already just what the promptings of morality are asking for, a thoroughly moral response. What's more, it is more thoroughly moral than the tribunals which call for morality, the "amazing imbecilities" of which have already shown them incapable of listening to the very call in whose name they have carried out their prosecutions. If "I cannot alter what I have written," this is not out of pride, but out of the modesty which listens scrupulously and with conviction to what it hears, and refuses to "deform it": "he is a very bold man who dares" do otherwise. Joyce is even such a faithful and moral listener he can give lessons in it, going out of his way to point out possible objections which Richards can then dutifully take up:

> While I have made concessions as to the alteration of a word in three of the stories you are simply allowing me to use it in a story where, not having noticed it until I pointed it out to you, you had not objected to it. Moreover, you now say that you wish to leave out altogether the story 'An Encounter.' You said nothing of this in your first letter and it was I, again, who pointed out to you the 'enormity' in it. (*SL* 87)

Who is leading, who is following? I ignore; I take to heart. I do not listen to a word of it; I listen to every word of it. I am deaf; I hear. *And* I hear *in being* deaf, and am deaf in my very hearing. In ignoring, I take to heart, in a way which mere taking to heart cannot begin to understand; listening faithfully, I put it all to one side. Listening and not listening are not opposed to each other here, they are each other's impossible condition. The accusation comes from the future, in the name of something which has not yet happened. We can no longer tell what is being asked, of that future or of us, or whether that future something is what *must not be allowed to happen* or what *must be made to happen*. Its incessant, agitated hold on the present lies solely in that *must*, which slips between the *must* of law and the *must* of ethical obligation. Everything lies open. We have, in short, another form of credit. Its addressee is already its debtor, under the obligation to answer—and because we can never be sure of who is being addressed and who addresses, or of who is being addressed and who is not, this is an obligation with no clear bounds. An accusation like this can never be something one silences by answering: response is exactly what it demands in the first place, and to respond is to accede to the position the accusation has already prepared. As Jean-François Lyotard points out, silence is not a refusal of this language game, but is itself a phrase in the exchange, a way of responding (Lyotard, *Differend* xii). Structurally, one can never answer from the position of innocence. In these letters we already glimpse—as if they were themselves already answering an unforeseeable call from the future—the burgeoning guilt which patterns so much of *Finnegans Wake*. Because response itself is to affirm, no amount of denial will ever be enough. Everything HCE can say will just be a stammer writ large, getting him nowhere; as the first meeting with the Cad shows so well (*FW* 35–36), the very fact of utterance marks him as guilty. To speak is to say both too little (nothing he can say will be enough to exculpate him) and too much (the very act of speaking is to accede to the accusation). It is already to respond to a prior call, and thus to speak in a language which is already Babelized: as exile, foreigner, Jew, Greek, Norse, the inconceivable polyglot of *Finnegans Wake* (Derrida, "Two Words" 152–57). One is no longer simply what one is, but finds oneself always and already scattered across the intersections and traversals of a vast language machine.

Here—in passing, and in order to return to it later on, in the final chapter—we would have to note the massive *thematics* of the call throughout Joyce's work, and the figures of prosopopoeia and apostrophe it so often involves.[5] But this could not be *just* a thematics, not just what Joyce's writing is *about*, because it is also what that writing itself inhabits and is made possible by. When Beckett argues in the *Exagmination* that "His writing is not *about* something: *it is that something itself*" (14), he is not saying that Joyce's writing is *about itself*, which would confine us once more to a thematic. It is a matter of what this writing *is*, the very possibility of its existence in the world. Thematization always points to what is outside, on the margins, edges between in this case the work and the life, in this work which swallows up the life.

Similarly, speculation is never simply extraneous to the disputed stories of *Dubliners*, an accident happening to them somewhere after their composition, on the way to the printer's. The sexual prurience of the two gallants of the story which precipitated the objections turns a most literal and monetary profit in its final line; and surely the perceived offense of the three passages of "Counterparts" which the printer originally marked lies in the ways in which they speak of sexual behavior as a cunning calculation, a profit to be turned:

> "a man with two establishments to keep up, of course he couldn't
> . . ."
> "Farrington said he wouldn't mind having the far one and began to smile at her . . ."
> "She continued to cast bold glances at him and changed the position of her legs often; and when she was going out she brushed against his chair and said 'Pardon!' in a Cockney accent" (*SL* 82)

—and after her going out, Farrington "cursed his want of money" (*D* 91). All this speculation over the limits of morality focuses on specific passages of the book in which we find—speculation. Even the "scrupulous meanness" of the narration enters the game in its very refusal to adjudicate on the side of moralism. Is any of this accidental? The concerns of the passages marked for excision are themselves those of the entire exchange over their excision: if they were not, they would not have been marked out. What would the accidental be in such a case, where speculation itself feeds on the unforeseeable, the unnecessary, the fortuitous, the contingent? The Beautiful Soul knows just what is accident and what is not: the problem is that events do not seem willing to observe what *should*—if the world were a fair place—be that clear and moral distinction between self and other.

Sometimes the stories of *Dubliners* do seem to invite us to read them as expressions of that devastated and morally empty *unfair* modern world. At least, this is the way Joyce invites Richards to read them, and through Richards an army of commentators. But there may be other things at stake here, things which are prior to that reading and which it does not exhaust. Eveline's indecision, the snow which blankets Gabriel Conroy's realization of his distance from his wife, Greta, Little Chandler's tears of remorse, Mr. Duffy's aloneness: before all these are examples of personal failure, they are errancies, in the sense suggested earlier. Something is coming unraveled, and suddenly, instead of the smooth fabric of a life, there is only a gap. Without any necessary continuity, let alone narrative resolution, what opens out is a sometimes scarcely bearable field of possibilities. In *Dubliners,* certainly, what these errancies may lack is the volition: we may feel that very few of them will individually turn out to be portals of discovery for the characters involved (*that* will be Stephen's discovery about destitution, later). Collectively, though, they are the arrival of something new in Joyce's work, which in these stories only gradually and incompletely disengages itself from the familiar claim to moral diagnosis. This involves a different conception of the subject, certainly, but also *a new sort of writing.* It no longer easily lets itself be called diagnosis, or satire, or parody—the gods of which, after all, are neither invisible nor refined out of existence nor indifferent, but quite immediately and distinctly superior to their handiwork. In diagnosis, we would also have to include claims that Joyce's writing "is capable of an ideological self-correction" (Norris, *Joyce's Web* 7), or that the "belief that genuine creativity drives out the false gods, that honest, expressive fictions defy and subvert dominant discourses, is the basis of Joyce's historiographic art" (Spoo 5). In saying that, my own aim is not to correct or subvert these particular studies, let alone historiographical work on Joyce in general. It is to point out that since diagnosis is inevitably a process of recognition of what one already knows (the ideological in need of correction, the false gods to be driven out), what it has to miss—and *in its very necessity*—is that discontinuity and rupture which is the very possibility of historicality. In that deliberate overbidding which is never quite distinguishable from perversity, Joyce's work is capable of surprising and disconcerting even the most admirable politics, in a risk which cannot be calculated. We may read the emergence of this other writing in the famous "paralysis" Joyce wrote of to Curran and Richards: what *Dubliners* discovers behind or before the diagnosis is a radical temporal discontinuity which may be constitutive of the possibility of there being such things as subjects and histories. *Stephen Hero,* written at much the same time as *Dubliners,*[6] will call the irruption of such discontinuity an epiphany; the Stephen of the *Portrait,* an arrest. In *Dubliners,* this is a subtle internal dislocation across which the entire book realigns itself; between *Stephen Hero* and the *Portrait,* it is a rift, even a mythical conflagration, something the one work can no longer contain. With *Ulysses,* this discontinuity becomes a radical principle of structuring the book: "each successive episode," Joyce famously explained to Harriet Shaw Weaver, "leaves behind it a burnt up field," like "the progress of some sandblast" (*SL* 241). These discontinuities and uninhabitable faultlines are precisely where one finds the Joycean artist.

There is Stephen at the end of the *Portrait,* preparing gleefully to strip himself of family, country, and religion, and going "to encounter for the millionth time the reality of experience" (*P* 275–76). There is Stephen at the beginning of *Ulysses,* falling ineluctably through the *Nebeneinander* (*U* 3.14–15) now that he has realized that all of this cuts far deeper than the adolescent of the *Portrait* could have suspected, but still not giving in. And there is Stephen at the end of *Ulysses,* now with three homes he refuses to go to (the Dedaluses', the tower, and 7 Eccles Street—and this in the very Nostos!), no closer to resolving the guilt over his mother's death than he was when the book began. In part, this opens the possibility for reading both books as satire on Stephen and his aestheticism (Joyce rewriting *Patience*). Everyone knows it is hard to like Stephen, after all. But what if the *Portrait* and *Ulysses* are not arguing that this is a diversion or a stage he must put behind him if he is to be the artist who can truly sign and be worthy of the works in which he appears? What if in this destitution Stephen is already on the way, if still very uncomfortably? We do not have to invoke the familiar willed self-destruction which haunts so many romantic accounts of the creative artist (driven, demonic, drug-using, alcoholic, schizophrenic), or a quasi-Nietzschean overcoming of the morality of the herd in order to follow a higher calling. Rather, the space the Joycean artist inhabits is one which is always marked by an incompletion, a vanishing. When the God of creation disappears within or behind or beyond or above his handiwork, what we are left with is not the final signature which would endow everything with the unity of the Grecian urn. What we find ourselves with is a creation in which everything leads out elsewhere, in a dense weave of connections whose convergence can no longer be guaranteed. "Signatures of all things I am here to read," muses Stephen on the beach at Sandymount, amid the waves' calligraphy and its "fourworded wavespeech," where "[t]hese heavy sands are language tide and wind have silted here" (*U* 3.2, 3.456–57, 3.288–89). A gap opens up in the world, between the absolute and infinite density of its signs and the meanings it yields, and in which everything is yet to be done, or made, or meant, awaiting its own arrival. This is the space, or non-space, inhabited by the Joycean artist. Joyce is not the repudiation of Stephen so much as his acceleration.

And again, this is not just a thematic, one which Joyce would come across early in his career and choose to expand on as a suitable topic for fiction. It is not a thematic for the reason that it refuses to remain internal to the text, as its representation of what lies outside or incidental to its essential textuality. What is at stake here is again, and quite precisely, the very limits of the text, a performativity which is not to be confused with self-referentiality: again, we recall Beckett. *Dubliners* and all of the subsequent writings will be enmeshed on all levels in a series of debts and credits, unpayable and gratuitous: what we have is not so much a credit or debt which is due to or owing one particular person or another, but a generalized credit, a system of exchanges in which all sorts of things take place.

In November 1913, Joyce began *Exiles* and wrote a curt letter to Grant Richards recapitulating *Dubliners'* sorry history with Maunsel: "I think that perhaps the time has come for my luckless book to appear" (*SL* 208). An apparently conscience-stricken Richards gave in, and in January agreed to publish it. It appeared in June 1914, by which time Joyce had finished *Exiles* and started *Ulysses*. In *Exiles,* Robert Hand and Bertha will all but fall into an affair, and this will leave a "deep, deep wound of doubt" (*E* 626) in the hero Richard Rowan's soul which even Bertha's reassurances cannot heal. Like Bertha, we may suspect this has been all but arranged by Richard, as the real aim of the exercise. "You urged me to it," she points out, and the stage direction is *"threateningly"*: "Not because you love me. If you loved me or if you knew what love was you would not have left me. For your own sake you urged me to it." To which Richard can only concur: "I did not make myself. I am what I am" (*E* 616).

We can conjecture about the displacements involved in that name *Richard* over these few months.

We recall Stephen's argument about displaced names in "Scylla and Charybdis": out of the "trinity of black Wills," "two bear the wicked uncles' names," Richard and Edmund (*U* 9.911–12), in an act of revenge against the adulterous brothers. Stephen foresees the obvious objection: "You will say those names were already in the chronicles from which he took the stuff of his plays. Why did he take them rather than others?" (9.983–84). That the name is already there in the sources is the perfect alibi. There are also two Richards closer at hand, in *Ulysses*. The most immediate, and the most harmless, is librarian Best: "That is my name, Richard, don't you know. I hope you are going to say a good word for Richard, don't you know, for my sake." *Laughter,* says the stage direction (for at this point "Scylla and Charybdis" is pretending to be a play) (*U* 9.900–905). The laughter marks a dismissal: *Oh no, Richard, no one would say a word against you*—a far from unambiguous reassurance as Best has already been set up as a figure of fun. What events are those which need to be marked as dismissals? Those, perhaps, whose ultimate triviality we need to be assured of, because there is always the uneasy possibility that what we would like to dismiss may not be trivial and may otherwise stay around and hurt. Or perhaps—and perhaps indistinguishable from these—those events to which a dismissal draws subtle attention, ensuring that they do linger on after all, with the suspicion of a small revenge enacted: we recall *H. Rumbold, Master Barber,* at whose letter no one laughs (*U* 12.430–31). Whether his worry is genuine or self-deprecation, Best himself raises the possibility that this found name may provide the occasion for unflattering comment on the person who happens to bear it. The other Richard of *Ulysses* is genuine betrayer rather than mere aesthete, and Stephen will bring him to mind shortly: "nuncle Richie," the abuser of his own daughter, from "Proteus" (*U* 9.1039, 3.76–88). Stephen's first mention of the Shakespeare brothers as "wicked *uncles*" is already colored by the relationship this Richard has to Stephen rather than to Shakespeare. All of this sets up a tiered set of relationships. If the name *Richard* in Holinshed provides the screen or support which allows the implication of Shakespeare's treacherous brother, and if the name *Richard* in Shakespeare in turn provides the screen for Stephen's implication of his own treacherous uncle, then the name *Richard* in "Scylla and Charybdis" and *Exiles* may by exactly the same logic act as screen to another perceived act of treachery. And here we have another overdetermination of that phrase "wicked uncles": an *uncle* is also since the mid-eighteenth century the word for a pawnbroker: someone who has your future in hock. *Exiles* gives the name of the betrayer to its hero rather than to his betrayer; as Bertha knows, this is a hero who is his own best betrayer.[7]

And it is a system of debts and credits in which Joyce begins with nothing. In 1904, from the very beginning of the ten-year period between the earliest sketches for the stories and their publication, there is an autobiographical essay called "A Portrait of the Artist." Like *Stephen Hero,* the early essay renders its third-person subject as a sensitive soul among the philistines; like *Dubliners,* its diagnosis is paralysis. The title, like Joyce himself, draws on the future: the Artist this young man is determined to become does not yet exist except as the subject of the Portrait which performatively brings him into existence. The title reaches into the future, to grasp and bring back what does not yet exist. The essay's entire project makes sense only proleptically, as a wager on the future: *this is what I become in the very stating.* Joyce signs it as "Stephen Daedalus." The fictitious name of an actual writer will become the name of a fictitious writer, both of whom are drawing on credit, gambling on what is not yet written. Stephen, as we all know, is not Joyce. But they nevertheless *correspond:* it is impossible to tell whether "A Portrait of the Artist" is a letter to or from the future. Let the *a* stand for that, the undelivered letter which marks the difference between *Dedalus* and *Daedalus.* The career of the writer and the writer of the career write (to) each other.

Beginning is a limit, a paper-thin membrane pressed on from both sides, past and future. There is more to it than a point on a chronology, even if it should be a hidden or secret point. In chapter 5, we shall look at how this very figure of the wellspring, the *Wake*'s ALP, never functions as stable source (some sort of variation on the mythopoeic Earth Mother), but as a complex and involuted limit which is always in part constituted by its being *after* the event. Such a beginning is more like what Deleuze calls an *aleatory point,* one which traverses and is scattered out over an entire series which it makes possible (Deleuze, *Logic* 100–108; *Difference* 283). *From the beginning,* we might say, beginning is scattered out across a corpus which need not yet exist. Each successive chapter of *Ulysses* alters what has gone before it, both for the reader and, as Michael Groden's *"Ulysses" in Progress* shows, for the writer. The process is potentially endless. *Ulysses* and *Finnegans Wake* are not so much completed (indeed, the term hardly has meaning here) as called to a halt at an arbitrary deadline, Joyce's birthday.

That deadline signs the text, in a way which is rather different from all of those other Joycean signature effects which abound in both *Ulysses* and the *Wake*. In *Ulysses,* some of the most obvious of these would be the shared details of Stephen's and Joyce's past, 7 Eccles Street, a pub conversation in which a "J. J." [O'Molloy] is frequently addressed, the Man in the Macintosh, Molly's "O Jamesy let me up out of this" (*U* 18.1128–29), and, of course, Bloomsday itself. All of these have some meaning within the represented events of the novel. But whereas Miss Dunne clicks "16 June 1904" on the keyboard of her typewriter, there is no February 2 in the novel. In this sense, it seems quite external to the novel's events; but it governs the entire composition of the novel and where its potentially endless revisions stop. It is both nowhere and everywhere in the text: outside it as a fact which has no significance for anyone or anything in the novel, and inside it as the horizon of its meanings; between the life it inaugurates and the writing it concludes, it marks a space of *autobiography.*

There are two familiar ways in which Joyce's writing is autobiographical. On the one hand, "Joyce" is the name for an *object* of these texts: what they are *about* (Stephen is Joyce), even if that "about" should be circuitous, indirect, and disguised (Stephen is not Joyce). On the other hand, "Joyce" is also the name of an *addresser,* one who signs, consigns these texts into the world and in doing this marks himself off as their source, or proprietor, or legal owner. In a commonsensical way, "autobiography" is what is marked out at the intersection of these two, when object and addresser overlap to a greater or lesser degree. But a third point follows from these, and it is the aspect of the autobiographical Derrida identifies as so important to Nietzsche's *Ecce Homo.* If "Joyce" marks an addresser, it also marks an *addressee,* a place these texts address themselves *to.* If the addresser is the conferring of a certain name on the texts, as their author or proprietor, then the texts also necessarily in this same movement *confer those roles on that name.* The name has these attributes only through the bestowal of the texts, and there is no addresser which is not simultaneously addressee, no message which, in Lacanian terms, is not received in reverse at its origin—that is to say, at the point which it marks as its origin in this very movement. Addressing this text, signing it and sending it out to circulate, "Joyce" becomes also the point it addresses, called into being by it, even if, again, that calling-into-being should be by indirection, from afar, and under the address of this Stephen Dedalus and his "silence, exile and cunning," withdrawn within or behind or beyond or above. That Joyce calls Stephen into being is banal; far more interestingly, it is Stephen who calls Joyce into being. Joyce does not exist outside of this indefinite line of credit he extends to himself. Stephen is autobiographical in this sense of the complex effects of address, even—or perhaps even most particularly—where he is clearly *not* autobiographical in the sense of an object of the texts.

To ask the question of autobiography as living on credit—that is, in terms of addressee and what Derrida calls "destinerrance" ("Of an Apocalyptic Tone" 30)—is to pose *institution* as a problem: the processes and effects of a vast postal machinery by means of which the name of the author becomes the destination of a history yet to play itself out. Such a machinery is never just internal to the work, a matter of its correspondences and representations. It traverses the work, but also machineries of publishing, dissemination, commentary, teaching, the clearance of checks, the circulation and occasional burning of commodities, laws and their various incompatibilities and struggles. This is not an unlimited machinery: it is even a machine *of* limits, constituted by and on limits. (These would be errors only in the sense in which Stephen spoke of them earlier; not the "nets flung at [the soul] to hold it back from flight," but the errancies by which one flies by them [*U* 9.226–29; *P* 220].) But as a machinery *of* limits, it is not something with an outside beyond the scope of the machine: constructing outsides is precisely one of the things the machine does in its functioning. To be destined is not to be fated: the emblem of destination is that resonating silence between the last and first words of the *Wake,* where everything is yet again to be decided: that gap which is the very possibility and space of invention and intervention.

And of intention. But what might that mean when this speculating and speculated, addressed and addressing subject is destitute?

Kant famously describes the work of art as characterized by a "purposiveness without purpose."[8] What distinguishes the work of art from something produced by natural forces or, say, that "image of a cow" made by "a man hacking in fury at a block of wood"—Stephen's conundrum from *A Portrait of the Artist as a Young Man,* which Lynch declares to have "the true scholastic stink" about it (*P* 232)—is that we attribute a purposiveness to the genuine work. We take it as the product of an intention to mean, though we may not have any idea of what that intended meaning might actually be. The distinction which is being made here is crucial to Kant's argument. We take the work *as if it were* produced by an intention, and this *as if* is its purposiveness. It is quite distinct from the claim that the work is actually and ascertainably produced teleologically, a claim Kant will spend much energy refuting in the Third Critique. First of all, it implies that this intention to mean is essentially empty—as empty as that destitute subject of the intention. Such purposiveness attributes nothing whatsoever to the object; what it gives us is a *stance* towards it, a way of addressing it (Kant 23). It is of no consequence at all whether we can ascribe a specific intention to the work. Such an intention may happily be empirically unknown, or even in principle quite unknowable (and surely it is far from accidental that the two proper names which lie behind so much of *Ulysses* should be those of writers for whom the attribution of intention is particularly problematic: Homer and Shakespeare). A specific content of intention is not necessary for the whole thing to work. All that is needed is the ascription of an intentionality, which thus remains in some sense necessarily fictive: it is the ascription rather than the content which starts the whole process going, the stance one takes to the object. The empty space of intentionality is that of Stephen's nail-paring God of creation, famously "within or behind or beyond or above his handiwork, invisible, refined out of existence" (*P* 233). This is not a doctrine of masks behind which the real Joyce could hide, and neither is it an opposition of surface appearances and deeper realities on which that would rest; far from being a deeper cause, it is a genuine indifference. This is a writing whose intention, if you like, is to be without intention, in the sense of a writing whose meaning-to-say increasingly reduces itself as much as possible to an empty intentionality. Few writings will go as far in this as *Finnegans Wake.*[9]

Secondly, as it is empty, this space of an intention marks not so much the informing source of a text as one of its limits. Intention belongs to the work, in that it is posited as being the very gateway to its intelligibility; but at the same time it does *not* belong to the work, which remains supremely indifferent to it, and to which it adds nothing. Such intention is something like a point of spillage: essential to the very possibility of there being a work and yet never seeming to come to it from outside; not quite its own and yet not quite mine, a sort of never-quite-internalized margin between the work and an "outside" which would include the various possibilities of any "I" who might come to it as reader. It is there to meet us as we approach the text, the very thing which allows us passage into the text. It ensures that a text is always written elsewhere: its signature is always multiple, by other hands. The text is not signed at its heart by a creator-author, but on its edges, by many names, as the condition of its circulation and exchange. It is only on this field of names that the particular proper name of the author can emerge. Thus we find, structurally and as its very condition of legibility *as* aesthetic text, the empty place for the burgeoning countersignature. Empty, it is already inhabited by others, and echoes with other voices: in everything from Joyce's use of documentation to free indirect speech, from mimicry of established styles to the juxtaposition of voices. Joyce's work will be incessantly concerned with questions of the signature, of authorization, claim, filiation, inheritance, right: not as things which are to be defended against others, but as claims which the signature can make only *in* this detour of and through the other.

As a limit of the text, then—third point—this space of intention and signature is not really a space at all, but an unstable boundary which is both and neither within nor outside the text. The limit is that mobile, fractal point by which we can speak of a work and a life, and by which we can trace out the necessary distinctions between them, to which it however owes nothing. At the limit, series of meanings traverse both work and life, distinguishing them only by a necessary shuttling across the boundary they determine, the same series traversing both, in a way which has nothing to do with representation (the work's faithful reflection of a life). Those questions with which Joyce's work is so concerned—signature, authorization, claim, filiation, inheritance, right—are not just themes, the work's *internal* representations of itself or its history. They are all in one way or another concerned with the very possibilities of representation: with drawing boundaries between inside and outside, with determining the proper, and what belongs where and by what right.

And fourth and last, that this intention remains structurally open means that it is a point at which the text opens to a future. That is, its meaning arrives not simply from a future which has not yet become present (that would be the teleology Kant is at such pains to refute), but from *an absolute future* which can never become present or find its place on any timeline: the possibility of a future *as such*. What it opens is the possibility of a history. And given the liminal nature of such an intention, that very future is not exterior to the text itself. At bottom of the possibility of a text's meaning—that is, of its meaning anything at all—there is what has not yet (and not yet ever) arrived at it. The text is already its history, but in a sense which has nothing whatever to do with determinism. At the very beginning of the work in its classically Kantian dimensions is a sort of speculation, the drawing up of credit. And as such, this Kantian purposiveness is precisely economic in that it takes its place in a system of exchanges, one whose boundaries are yet to be known and established, and which includes—though it is not exhausted by—the narrower sense of the commodity and the market. Neither is it a matter of the market forces overdetermining the aesthetic in the last instance. It is again the operation of a *generalized credit* which traverses and makes possible both the commodity and the aesthetic speculation, which are thus both more intimately related and more profoundly autonomous than either an aestheticism or a determinist materialism can conceive. And again, we shall see this thematized and performed through Joyce, in an intense and ever-renewed remortgaging of the promise.

The boundaries of *Dubliners* are far from clear. In many ways, the debacle of its publication suggests that it is a book which simply cannot be finished, or finished with: which Joyce, that is, no less than we or Richards, could finish with. It overlaps with and even seems to encompass much of Joyce's later work. One of the projected stories was never to appear in *Dubliners:* the tale of the Dublin Jew Mr. Hunter, which turns *Ulysses* into a sort of monstrous supplement to *Dubliners*. We can flick through the imaginary pages of this supplemented *Dubliners* as we approach its new and unfamiliar continuation. "A Mother," one of the longer stories, is followed by "Grace," which is over half as long again; "Grace" is followed by "The Dead," which is in turn twice its length; and the final story, *Ulysses,* burgeons out into something like four times the length of all the other stories put together. It rewrites what has gone before it, too: some twenty-eight or so of the earlier stories' characters appear or are mentioned in *Ulysses,* brought together now by their relationships to the Blooms or the Dedaluses. In Stephen, *Ulysses* also absorbs and rewrites *A Portrait of the Artist as a Young Man,* which was never part of the *Dubliners* series but now finds itself closely juxtaposed with it. And as the drafts of *Ulysses* show, Joyce's method of writing is accretion and elaboration rather than cutting: each successive draft grows far beyond the boundaries of the previous, just as the later chapters far outstrip the earlier in size. In the later parts of the book, each chapter also rewrites all the others, the whole lot to be capped off arbitrarily on Joyce's birthday. And *Finnegans Wake* will rewrite these yet again, in the figure of Shem the Penman and its own formal circularity.

And so "The Sisters" comes to stand as an opening to the Joyce opus. Though it is hardly his first published work, it is his first published story and then—after those delays—the first story in his first published book of fiction. Written in July 1904, it appeared next month in the *Irish Homestead,* but the version which was eventually to appear in *Dubliners* is the result of thorough revision almost two years later, in May and June of 1906. Taken by completion dates, then, "The Sisters" is also one of the later stories of the collection: of the fifteen, the only stories postdating it are "The Dead" and possibly revisions to "A Little Cloud," "A Painful Case" and "Clay."[10] What stands as "Joyce's first story" is already, in its very structure, a matter of revision. Something which has not yet arrived already returns to it from the future, to endow it in retrospect with its firstness. It must both know and not know what will arrive, and say and not say what it already knows, or will know, or—because this knowing arrives only from the future and can be installed only in retrospect—will have known. The logic of prefacing will tie this story into a complex tangle of (not-)knowing, (not-)saying.

It is hardly surprising, then, that the very opening—of this story whose function is to open—should stage such a situation. It opens as a complex series of folds:

> There was no hope for him this time: it was the third stroke. Night after night I had passed the house (it was vacation time) and studied the lighted square of window: and night after night I found it lighted in the same way, faintly and evenly. If he was dead, I thought, I would see the reflection of candles on the darkened blind for I knew that two candles must be set at the head of a corpse. He had often said to me: *I am not long for this world,* and I had thought his words idle. Now I knew they were true. Every night as I gazed up at the window I said softly to myself the word *paralysis.* It had always sounded strangely in my ears, like the word *gnomon* in the Euclid and the word *simony* in the Catechism. But now it sounded to me like the name of some maleficent and sinful being. It filled me with fear, and yet I longed to be nearer to it and to look upon its deadly work. (*D* 1)

That first sentence withholds both the referent of that "him" and its situation: suspended, it waits for its meaning, just as the next sentence has the boy waiting for the message which will be the end of his suspension. "Hope"—and no less when it is "no hope"—sets up a line of communication from events which have not yet happened. The only words of the old man, *I am not long for this world,* remember a past occasion, so they refer to two times, a time of their utterance and a time of recollection, in both of which they draw on the future in exactly the same way as that "There was no hope for him this time." The boy reads the light in the window as a simple message, almost the simplest possible: a minimal sign system of two options, faint lighting for life, candles for death; one or the other, nothing else possible. But this is immediately set up as a false choice by that "no hope": the sign *will* sooner or later be that of death, even if on those many occasions the boy has passed by the window it has always still had that "faint and even" lighting. There is not really a possibility other than death: the choice is not really between death and life, but between a death which has not yet occurred and one which has already occurred. The window opens onto both past and future.

This "not yet" and "already" comes to structure much of the story and its reticences. Old Cotter's recollection, for example, is said "as if returning to some former remark of his"—which is to say as if recollecting another recollection, recollecting recollection itself:[11]

> —No, I wouldn't say he was exactly . . . but there was something queer . . . there was something uncanny about him. I'll tell you my opinion . . . [. . .]
>   —I have my own theory about it, he said. I think it was one of those . . . peculiar cases . . . But it's hard to say. . . .
>   He began to puff again at his pipe without giving us his theory. (D 1–2: all ellipses Joyce's, except for that in the square brackets)

There is the *already* of what the old man might or might not have done, and of Cotter's opinion on that, his "own theory"; and there is the *not yet* of Cotter's promise to reveal all ("I'll tell you my opinion"); but all he gets around to saying is these hesitations, delays, and promises, and instead of that promised content only the assurance that there is "something queer" beyond all possibility of telling, whose only trace in the present is an uncanniness. Telling nothing, Cotter is putting on a performance, drawing all eyes and ears towards himself, and then lighting his pipe for dramatic pause. He is playing the role of storyteller, commanding its address without actually having a story to tell, in a way which has long since become an empty speculation:

> He began to puff at his pipe, no doubt arranging his opinion in his mind. Tiresome old fool! When we knew him first he used to be rather interesting, talking of faints and worms, but I soon grew tired of him and his endless stories about the distillery. (D 1)

Cotter's hesitations are echoed at the other end of the story, in Eliza's recounting of the priest's collapse:

> —Mind you, I noticed there was something queer coming over him latterly. Whenever I'd bring in his soup to him I'd find him with his breviary fallen to the floor, lying back in the chair and his mouth open. (9)

and:

—Wide-awake and laughing-like to himself. . . . So then, of course, when they saw that, that made them think that there was something gone wrong with him. . . . (10)

There was something queer; there was something queer; there was something uncanny; there was something gone wrong. The echo is important. In it, the two ends of the story join up in a non-narrative web of partial interconnections.[12] The space between the repeated assertions of "something queer" is not governed by the gradual unraveling of a mystery, but by the repetition of the ellipses, silences, and refusals which constitute that queerness. Before this is the failure of a project to speak the truth and speak it all, it is a matter of refusal, of deflection, turning aside.

In its structure, form, and subject matter, the very first sentences of "The Sisters" present a temporal eddy, in which meaning is at the same time both deferred and arriving back from the future. The text shuttles rapidly back and forth, in a rhythm which is unstable and forever repeated. *Dubliners* initiates the Joycean project of a *writing structured on deferral,* rather than a *writing about loss.* What will emerge from it is the profoundly comic atonality of writing of *Ulysses* and *Finnegans Wake.* But even here, even in the first story's very first mention of that key word of stern moral diagnosis and loss of integrity, that *paralysis* on which Joyce tried to sell Richards, the writing is already distancing itself from the tragic and playing out an uncanny and unsettling sort of comedy.

The old priest "had often said to me: *I am not long for this world,* and I had thought his words idle." Now, however—gazing up at the window in which there is still only that faint, even light saying that there is no hope even though death has not yet come—"Now I knew they were true." The window opens onto a message; the light says something, addresses the boy, and each time, "every night," the boy responds to this, as he gazes, with "the word *paralysis.*" *No hope,* says the light; *paralysis,* says the boy. Call and response. It is easy to see this in quite naturalistic terms: looking up at the window, the boy knows that there is no hope *because of* the severity of this third stroke and the paralysis it has brought. It is easy also to turn this into a moral metaphor for the spiritual paralysis which seems to have seized the old man long ago. There is even the ominous suggestion of another sort of paralysis, faint but with its echoes elsewhere in the story and later: "General paralysis of the insane," Mulligan will laughingly diagnose Stephen's glumness at the beginning of *Ulysses,* using the current medical term for the ravages of tertiary syphilis and a clear peg on which to hang a moral allegory. Walzl, for example, states that studies show that the three mysterious words of the story "project emblematically three main themes of the book, paralysis—the inability of the characters to act meaningfully; the gnomon—their stunted development and incompleteness as individuals; and simony—their selling of themselves and others for mercenary reasons" (117). But this is to take morality—or perhaps moralism—as the clear and fixed measure of everything the stories speculate on, not as something which itself enters into the speculation everywhere in and out of the stories; it is to know already what it is to "act meaningfully," as though there were a possibility of acting without meaning; to see individuals as things which not only can but should, at the risk of moral dereliction, be completed; to imagine that there is a clear distinction of kind between the monetary and any other kind of speculation. It is also to read the story as essentially unchanged from its *Irish Homestead* version, with its generic sentimentalism and moralism.[13] As Walzl says, it is to deal with themes. Paying attention to the structures of this folded opening and its looping temporalities of speculation may suggest other things at work here.

And in particular the deadly work of the word:

He had often said to me: *I am not long for this world,* and I had thought his words idle. Now I knew they were true. Every night as I gazed up at the window I said softly to myself the word *paralysis.* It had always sounded strangely in my ears, like the word *gnomon* in the Euclid and the word *simony* in the Catechism. But now it sounded to me like the name of some maleficent and sinful being. It filled me with fear, and yet I longed to be nearer to it and to look upon its deadly work. (*D* 1)

Let us underline the careful use of the word *word* here. What we are dealing with, it says, is not the *concepts* of paralysis, gnomon, and simony and their ability to stand as themes, but—and the text emphasizes this in its repetition—"the word *paralysis*," "the word *gnomon*," "the word *simony.*" Senn argues that this is a mistake the boy makes: in awe of paralysis, the boy confuses thing and name, so this becomes "probably the first intentional and meaningful error in Joyce's works"—a line which will include Martha Clifford's "I do not like that other world" of *Ulysses* and the *hesitency* motif of *Finnegans Wake*. "It is as though," Senn suggests, "in the first paragraph of his first story, Joyce made it subtly clear that *his* words are neither empty of meaning nor inactive" ("'He Was Too Scrupulous'" 67–68). But then, whether the boy knows it or not, he is not simply making a mistake. The *words* have "always sounded strangely" in his ears, before or regardless of whatever they might signify. This is a process of designification: whatever these words are doing here is not reducible to what they mean. Running repeatedly through his head, they *fascinate* before they signify—like the rhyme the chastised infant Stephen will later make, not in defiance or acquiescence, just captivated by the sound of the words:

Pull out his eyes,
Apologize,
Apologize,
Pull out his eyes.

Apologize,
Pull out his eyes,
Pull out his eyes,
Apologize. (P 4)

Words can do this only to the extent that they lose signification, repeated until they are drained of meaning ("Every night . . . I said softly," "It had always sounded strangely"). Only then does the word start to function as the object of a fascination, filled with a perverse and even somewhat nauseous enjoyment. But now it is barely a word anymore, for it no longer takes part in any semiotics. It is instead something like *voice* in its purest form, as Lacan defines it: the "objectal leftover of the signifying operation" which exceeds any purely conceptual weight assigned it.[14] We find this objectal, abject voice repeatedly associated with the old man, and particularly—the paradox is no more than apparent—at just those moments when the text is silent about what he says, or even when he says nothing. Falling asleep, the boy imagines he sees "the heavy grey face of the paralytic" murmuring a confession to him; but we do not know what is confessed, and are left with only the physicality of the voice itself, uncomfortable in extreme close-up and detached from any person (the pronouns are important: this is not the priest who murmurs, smiles, and salivates, but "it," the face, leaden and deathly in its materiality):

It murmured; and I understood that it desired to confess something. I felt my soul receding into some pleasant and vicious region; and there again I found it waiting for me. It began to confess to me in a murmuring voice and I wondered why it smiled continually and why the lips were so moist with spittle. (D 3)

In a long paragraph two pages later, the boy will detail some of the things the two spoke about and all the things he learned from the old man. They fascinate him still, where Cotter's "endless stories" about other matters of spirit palled very quickly, and at the end of the long enumeration, the paragraph separates that fascination from any content; it returns to the smile and the overwhelming close-up physicality of the very organs of voice only when speech is emptied to silence, or a stammer, or mechanical repetition:

> Often . . . I could make no answer or only a very foolish and halting one upon which he used to smile and nod his head twice or thrice. Sometimes he used to put me through the responses of the Mass which he had made me learn by heart; and, as I pattered, he used to smile pensively and nod his head, now and then pushing huge pinches of snuff up each nostril alternately. When he smiled he used to uncover his big discolored teeth and let his tongue lie upon his lower lip—a habit which had made me feel uneasy in the beginning of our acquaintance before I knew him well. (*D* 5)

At this point, let us note that there is at least a *fourth* such word in the story, one which like the others was added after the *Irish Homestead* version, and whose work exceeds its literal meaning. It is far less frequently commented on than the other three, as its context and placing make it a small joke late in the piece rather than an opening enigma, but what it plays with is precisely voice:

> —If we could get one of them new-fangled carriages that makes no noise that Father O'Rourke told him about—them with the rheumatic wheels . . . (*D* 9)

The malapropism substitutes one word for another with a different meaning on the basis of a similar sound. From *pneuma* to *rheuma*, πνεῦμα to ῥεῦμα: from breath or spirit to the physicality of bodily flow or discharge. The spirit of the signified is precipitated—should we say *rheumatized?*—into the physicality of voice: swollen, stiffened, *paralyzed*. It is a substitution *of* the voice, *by* the voice: Eliza substitutes a word for one which *sounds* familiar. *Rheumatic* hides *pneumatic,* and by a rheumatic act.

In this objectality, there is an obdurate and perverse kernel which both fascinates and repels, an enjoyment which floats freely without being caught in the nets which structure meaning. But then neither can it be reduced to fantasy, whose scenarios aim to hide just such gaps, inconsistencies, and impossibilities at the heart of those structures. It would be easy to turn "The Sisters" into a story which revolves around fantasy sustained or dispelled: we could have the priest and boy as master and disciple, for example, so that on the master's death the disciple discovers a vocation, or is disabused by the revelation of his master's true nature when he overhears old Cotter, or realizes a human dimension which does or does not compensate for the old man's loss of faith, or finds a new and more genuine religiosity in that loss of faith, . . . Indeed, the *Irish Homestead* version of the story is close to doing such a rewriting for us already. Fantasy attempts to answer the question of what the other really wants of me: what precious and secret treasure (the Lacanian *agalma*) may be in me that the other may desire me, and which gives me my consistency (Žižek, *Plague* 8); and how I may best know and be true to this true self and this desire from elsewhere. But what disturbs in the story is how little of this there is to be found, just where it is generically to be expected. Encountering the card with the death notice on the old man's door, the boy is curiously unmoved, and a bit bothered by that:

> I walked away slowly along the sunny side of the street, reading all the theatrical advertisements in the shopwindows as I went. I found it strange that neither I nor the day seemed in a mourning mood and I even felt annoyed at discovering in myself a sensation of freedom as if I had been freed from something by his death. I wondered at this for, as my uncle had said the night before, he had taught me a great deal. (*D* 4–5)

What is expected of the one who survives, what does the other really want of him? Mourning. What is expected of a story in which a boy loses a mentor? Mourning, or if there is none, an explanation of why this should be so. Instead, we get a character and a story which both refuse those expectations, and which both refuse to explain that refusal. "Scrupulous meanness," Joyce described the style of the stories: we should recall that for the church, scruples are overnice distinctions which may lead to moral perplexity. "He was too scrupulous always," says Eliza of her brother. "The duties of the priesthood was too much for him" (*D* 9). Scruples paralyze, and produce indecision; the scrupulous meanness of the story produces an extraordinary destitution in which the narrator is not character so much as empty narrating instance—the forerunner, indeed, of the Beckettian narrator. There is no treasure, no consistency, no fantasy to paper over the gaps or be projected onto the figure of the old man. On the contrary, the queasiness of those extreme close-ups (lips, a tongue, the cavernous nostrils; flecks of snuff and swirls of smoke; stains on a jacket—

all of them huge, as if filling a movie screen) comes from their massive and senseless materiality: they hide nothing and stand for nothing, and yet force themselves forward uncomfortably, even obscenely.

In this excess, it is the word beyond concept whose work is deadly, and which fills the boy with fear even as he longs to be nearer to it. Important as they may be for the young boy, it is not the signified illness and the *incumbent* death of the old priest which produce these effects of dread fascination. The word itself, become inarticulate voice and obscene flesh in its designified strangeness, takes on some sort of uncanny agency, and the general and grammatically passive import of "it had always sounded strangely" crystallizes into specific time and place and active sentence construction: "now it sounded to me," "it filled me with fear." In its strangeness, it sounds like "the name of some maleficent and sinful being," and performs as if it is itself such a being. If paralysis, the condition signified by the word, is an incapacity to act or a suspension of activity (*Oxford English Dictionary*), then the uncanniness of *the word "paralysis"* is that on the contrary it acts, works, *performs* work as only a word can, and does this intense and deadly work only where a conceptual, thematizable meaning *no longer* holds sway over it. Its work is not that of a signified meaning, the *real meaning* of "paralysis," "gnomon," and "simony" in the story. The deadly work of the word *paralysis*—the work of a death which has always just or not yet occurred, and by which everything is other than where it is—is to escape (its) meaning. Which is to say, to escape meaning in general, and in particular its own specific meaning, which is after all paralysis. The deadly work of the word *paralysis* is to escape paralysis. Paralysis is exactly what cannot be confined to the thematic.

What of those other paralyzed words which so fascinate the boy? We should not expect to find in them a coherent thematic. What all of them do, in a number of different ways which are not all versions of the one thing, or for that matter even necessarily compatible with each other, is suspend the thematic; in the halt or arrest they produce there is the irruption of a certain fascination and unease. *Gnomon* invites particular attention for several reasons: it would appear to be the most recondite and inexplicable of them, and the least grounded in its immediate narrative context; it is the only one which is not overtly repeated and expanded upon in the text (the old man is described elsewhere as a paralytic [*D* 3, and possibly 9 and 10 as well, where Eliza talks of that "something queer coming over him latterly . . . I'd find him with his breviary fallen to the floor, lying back in the chair and his mouth open," and of the breaking of the chalice] and simoniac [*D* 3]); it is perhaps the most widely polysemous of the three; and it is also the one which is the most resistant to the standard interpretation in terms of moral turpitude. The *Oxford English Dictionary* suggests at least three irreducible yet overlapping areas of meaning for it.

Let us move quickly: all of this is familiar from the abundant criticism on the story. "The word *gnomon* in the Euclid" describes a bit of geometry which is deceptive in its simplicity—what's left from a parallelogram after a similar parallelogram is taken away from one of its corners.[15] Simple as the instance may be, it raises in yet another form those questions of meaning and its blockages which have recurred in the story and—particularly important in a story which leaves considerable doubt about what it is the priest might have done and why everyone is so wary of him—of reconstruction. The gnomon sets a problem: given a current state of affairs, and the rule by which it has developed from an initial state, how do we reconstruct that initial state?[16] "I puzzled my head to extract meaning from [Cotter's] unfinished sentences," says the boy (*D* 3). What is more, the solution is barred: what you need to know *in order to* solve it (the shape of the missing piece) is already the solution itself; the rule which one uses in reconstructing the initial state can be defined only in terms of that initial and still-unknown state. The only way to know it is to know it already. The gnomon sets up a discontinuity between problem and solution, and an odd looping, proleptic temporality across that. But then the gnomon *is* also, precisely, "a rule, canon of belief or action" (*OED*)—a rule of omission, indirection, occlusion, *incompleteness of the rule itself*. Reading gnomonically would be to pay attention to what escapes, slips away, slides between meanings in their instability: to listen, like the boy, to the uncanny underweave of sense, and to look for the places where the stories invert themselves from moral tales which "betray the soul of that hemiplegia or paralysis which many consider a city" to the unfolding of an ambivalent and fascinated enjoyment which can be traced in the silences and slippages among senses, in a tenuous, broad, and loose web of interconnections without center, which catch in their speculation the faint echoes from a future not yet written.

A third possibility: what remains points to what has been left out, like the gnomon of a sundial, which occludes light and in that occlusion lets what cannot be observed directly make itself known indirectly. The gnomon makes visible not by shedding light on what would otherwise remain in darkness, but by casting shadow on what would otherwise remain blinded in light. As the narrator uses it, the very word *gnomon* works gnomonically. What fascinates the boy is not the properties of parallelo-grams and the shapes you can make from them, but that odd-sounding *word,* repeated so often it has become drained of meaning and reveals itself in a queasy fleshiness once it is unilluminated by sense. A rheumatic act: now, instead of the attenuated bearer of the spirit, *pneuma,* we hear what has always been there, the rheumatic whisper of matter.

Simoniacal, the *Oxford English Dictionary* notes, refers not only to the guilt of simony, but also to merely being "tainted with or marked by si-mony," as though accusation itself were enough. Old Cotter asserts that "I wouldn't like children of mine . . . to have too much to say to a man like that," but twice simply repeats the assertion when the narrator's aunt asks him what he means (*D* 2–3). What we are left with is even less than accu-sation: nothing has been named, the mere repetition of the innuendo does the tainting. Reconstruction of what actually happened is not the point here. The accusation's deadly work is in the act of speaking, not in the existence or truth of what is spoken about, just as in *Finnegans Wake* the trial and various attempts to exonerate HCE will not stop the cloud of rumor and speculation about what may or may not have happened in Phoenix Park, but only add to it. That gnomonic bar does not prevent but multiplies hypothesis. Simony is a speculation, and an illicit one, but it is also uncontrollable. Just as "the word *gnomon* in the Euclid" may screen other things than geometry, so too may "the word *simony* in the Cat-echism" suggest more than the ecclesiastical, as if there are other things to hear in it if we let ourselves be carried by that objectal, persistent signifier rather than the concepts it bears—sounds, perhaps, such as the very words *similar* and *similarly.* A gnomon, we recall, is "that part of a parallelogram which remains after a *similar* parallelogram is taken away from one of its corners," and to read gnomonically is to hear similarities across what is systematically unsaid. Various voices assert that there was "something queer" about the old man (*D* 1, 9); Cotter refuses to elaborate on his insistence that "it's bad for children" (*D* 2, 3); the boy dreams or imagines the priest confessing to him, and feels his soul recede into a "pleasant and vicious region" (*D* 3). All of these suggest that there is another word behind *simony,* a small missing piece whose shape will be that of the story itself, and whose very silence is an oblique, insistent, and troubled coun-terpoint throughout the text: *sodomy.* To an extent, the possibility of a pedophilic relationship between old man and boy has long been recog-nized in the criticism,[17] even if one of the most frequent modes of recogniz-ing it has been to deny it. Nevertheless, if I want to stop just *short* of claiming that this is the secret of the story, it is not to deny the nature of the relationship yet again, but because we need also to listen also to the story's reticence. It resists too hasty a filling in of the missing piece of the gnomon, and in that, it also resists becoming a moral tale centered on fantasy, where the question would be whether the boy does or does not come to grips with the truth of his relationship to his old master. The gnomonic may not be simply a shape to be put aside once the solution has been found; like the words *paralysis* and *simony*, it continues to fascinate in excess of whatever it might signify. As Bernard Benstock points out, it is important to read what old Cotter says as innuendo rather than truth ("'The Sisters' and the Critics" 34). Precisely: to be simoniacal is to be "tainted or marked by" simony, regardless of its commission, and in this the status of the word *sodomy* is precisely that of the word *incest* in the *Wake*. This elaborate simoniacal verbal game is not so much a matter of the concealment of a hidden and repressed act as a *staining* of the visible to produce the suspicion of such an act, whether or not it has occurred in fact. What is significant about this stain is that it spreads, marks, and is absorbed by everything with which it comes into contact. "It's bad for children," says old Cotter, "because their minds are so impressionable" (*D* 3). So many of the boy's memories of the priest's person are of something spilling over: the lips "so moist with spittle" (*D* 3), the old man's invariable spilling of the snuff the boy would bring as a present, the "little clouds of smoke" which "dribbled through his fingers over the front of his coat," the resultant fading of his clothes and the blackening of the handkerchief with which the old man tries ineffectually to brush away the grains (*D* 4). There is an insistent emphasis on ingestion and the cavities of the face here, fascinated and ill at ease: the lips and smile, the "big discolored teeth," the habit of lying the tongue upon the lower lip which "had made me feel uneasy in the beginning of our acquaintance" (*D* 5), the snuff-taking, the "black cavernous nostrils" of the corpse (*D* 6). Even the very placing of "The Sisters" within *Dubliners* serves to taint it by proximity: Father Flynn shares those discolored teeth, his smile, his greenish black suit and the epithet *queer* with the pedophilia of the next story, "An Encounter" (Benstock, "'The Sisters' and the Critics" 34).

These worries find their echoes in both *paralysis* and *gnomon*. Sounding strangely as "something queer," *paralysis* echoes in hiding the very cluster of words hidden in *simony*. If *simony* is *similarly*, then *paralysis* may also be *parallel*, like those similar parallelograms. Similar or parallel to *simony, paralysis* suggests the blocked, gnomonic process by which one is to read. Paralysis blocks, prevents movement or passage; but it does this by a parallel loosening (*lyein*, loosen: λύειν) whereby what is blocked can, as it were, pass by to one side (*para-*: παρά-); *paralipsis* is a figure in which something is emphasized precisely by passing over it without notice (*OED*).

And once three, or four, words work in this way, we are led with the suspicion of the quiet unraveling of others. During the day, the boy's thoughts return to the previous night's dream in which the old man confessed to him. Something else happened in it, he knows, in that "pleasant and vicious region" (*D* 3) where "the customs were strange," but it seems to be blocked from him:

> As I walked along in the sun I remembered old Cotter's words and tried to remember what had happened afterwards in the dream. I remembered that I had noticed long velvet curtains and a swinging lamp of antique fashion. I felt that I had been very far away, in some land where the customs were strange—in Persia, I thought. . . . But I could not remember the end of the dream. (*D* 5–6: ellipsis Joyce's)

"Old Cotter's words" seem to both trigger and block the remembrance of the dream, as if actually germane to it. Listening to it as to the earlier words, we might hear in the word *Persia* echoes of *perverse,* or *persecution.* We might also hear another dream, one Stephen will have almost ten years later in 1904, round about the time Joyce is writing the first draft of "The Sisters"; Stephen too will recall the dream later the next day, again triggered by the repetition of another's warning of a danger which is this time explicitly sexual:

> After he woke me last night same dream or was it? Wait. Open hallway. Street of harlots. Haroun al Raschid. I am almosting it. That man led me, spoke. I was not afraid. The melon he had held against my face. Smiled: creamfruit smell. That was the rule, said. In. Come. Red carpet spread. You will see who. (*U* 3.365–69)

> A man passed out between them, bowing, greeting.
> —Good day again, Buck Mulligan said.
> The portico.

> Here I watched the birds for augury. Aengus of the birds. They go, they come. Last night I flew. Easily flew. men wondered. Street of harlots after. A creamfruit melon he held to me. You will see.

> —The wandering jew, Buck Mulligan whispered with clown's awe.

Did you see his eye? He looked upon you to lust after you. I fear thee,
ancient mariner. O, Kinch, thou art in peril. Get thee a breechpad. (*U*
9.1203–11)

These are tenuous relations, gnomonic links and hypotheses of the kind
Joyce's later writing will increasingly ask us to make, but which we find
also here, at the outset, in the scrupulous meanness of *Dubliners*. *Dubliners looks* so much like realism, but these words which intercept us on the
way into the collection do not work on that plane at all. They haunt the
story from somewhere just beyond or behind what it means, off on the
edges of the field of vision, like the "wayward and flickering existence" (*D*
224) of those figures of the dead which haunt the ending of the last story—
a story which, we remember, Joyce was writing at the same time as *paralysis, gnomon,* and *simony* were finding their way into the revision of the
first. They occupy a liminal position, neither fully inside the story nor
simply outside it but a disturbance of its edges, here at the very edges of the
Joyce oeuvre, this first story in a first book which is neither a first story nor
of a first book.

We shall follow these figures further.

2

The Debt, the List, and the Window

So: let us backtrack.

Joyce's writing comes to us already read. We know of it long before reading it: its reputation, its stature, its density, its endless commentary, even its seeming need for endless commentary. We read it through dust-jacket blurbs which tell us that "'*Ulysses* is a novel to end all novels'" (as Jeri Johnson's 1993 edition for Oxford University Press's The World's Classics quotes Harry Levin), or that "'It is a book to which we are all indebted and from which none of us can escape'" (as Declan Kiberd's 1992 Penguin edition quotes T. S. Eliot). Wherever we first—but is there ever really such an occasion?—meet Joyce's writing, it is at a place already busy with voices, individual, corporate, and institutional. We enter as eavesdroppers to a conversation which has already been going on, in other rooms elsewhere, and find to our disconcertion that we are somehow already caught up in what is being discussed, and have been even before we made our entry, before our even knowing about it. The beginning of our involvement begins by being pushed back, and away.

We are all indebted to *Ulysses,* says Eliot: not surprisingly, then. And while that "we" may certainly refer quite specifically to the modernist avant-garde of the time, the pronoun's lack of specificity suggests the wider grouping to which we, the readers about to start reading or reread-ing *Ulysses,* are being invited to recognize ourselves: that is, as *already* belonging, *already* in debt, before we know it, even—in the same sense in which ignorance is deemed no excuse in the eyes of the law—whether we know it or not. The debt works away behind our backs. It does not require us to have contracted ourselves to it, as, for example, in a conscious deci-sion we might make to read Joyce. It is not a contract between parties who are taken to exist before the transaction, and who freely submit themselves and a part of their future in it, in full knowledge and out of a calculation of interest—*I will read this book because of the pleasure it will afford me.* Eliot is speaking of a far more paradoxical debt, which is in some sense there *before* we start reading: its action is to evert things, and to show something of what they have already been in order to be what they are now, to show us a preexisting indebtedness which we can only acknowledge—if not pay off—in that reading.

It is as if what we owe for is that very state of not-having-yet-read-Joyce. The debt is not for what has already been done, but for what has not yet taken place: for what makes it possible to read Joyce. Eliot is suggesting a debt for something which predates us, and which provides a sort of matrix into which any of our possible readings will fit. It addresses us, calls on us to recognize ourselves as indeed indebted, even if until then we had not been aware of ourselves as indebted, and to repay it in the only way possible: by reading Joyce. Rather than being a debt for pleasure gained, this debt comes before the pleasure, and thus the pleasure which may result can never be unalloyed. Derrida speaks of the resentment which necessarily accompanies reading Joyce ("Two Words" 146–48), resentment that this writing is never that impossibility, the pure gift, but something which demands response. The very possibility of pleasure binds us in advance, to all sorts of things which are not pleasure. The debt is thus a sort of stain, like the *simony* of "The Sisters," and the pleasure is a pleasure in that staining, in what from the beginning, from before the beginning, is already sullied. It is part of a long series which begins before the first page of *Dubliners,* in the Richards letters, and continues through Stephen's fascination with sin, the bodily and the abject, to Bloom's masturbation and voyeurism and the hallucinatory confession of his pleasures, or to the multiplying sins of *Finnegans Wake,* already committed even before the advent of HCE, in a book in which every event is both before and after every other.

This suggests a light by which to see the famous Homeric correspondences of *Ulysses.* In two related and well-known essays,[1] Wolfgang Iser argues that there are two frequent ways of answering the questions of just what those correspondences are doing in the book and how the events of the *Odyssey* might be related to those of Dublin of June 16, 1904. They are, says Iser, "the 'tried and tested' ideas of the recurrence of archetypes, or the analogy between the ideal and the real" (Iser 196). That is, the correspondences function as parallels which can work in two directions: either they ennoble Bloom as brave Odysseus in modern dress, or they point out the sad gap between an age of heroism and a humdrum urban modernity. As Iser says, both of these flounder rather quickly. It is not a problem that the parallels are incomplete: even the most rigorous allegory must be that. The real difficulties lie in the multiple and insistent inconsistencies of the parallels. This is nowhere flaunted more than in "Wandering Rocks," an entire episode whose tenuous connection to the *Odyssey* is that of a route *not* taken. It is as if it were grafted onto the Homeric table of the Gilbert or Linati schemas from Apollonius Rhodius, the *Argonautica Orphica*, Herodotus, Pliny, or Apollodorus: an interpolation from elsewhere. The number of episodes in "Wandering Rocks," nineteen, both suggests and muddies a parallel to the eighteen chapters of the book: one episode for each chapter (but which is which?) plus an interpolation (but which episode would that be?), as if its emphasis is always on the excess to any parallel or allegory. And of course each of the first eighteen of these episodes contains at least one interpolation of its own, either from other episodes in the chapter or in a couple of cases from other chapters. At the center of *Ulysses,* as the ninth and tenth chapters of the eighteen, we have not two successive episodes of the *Odyssey,* but a single choice: is Odysseus to go by Scylla and Charybdis, or by the Wandering Rocks? The route taken, and the route not taken. And "Wandering Rocks," the route not taken, is itself full of routes not taken: not taken by characters (episodes 4 and 13 are the last glimpses we will get of the siblings from whom Stephen has all but cut himself off) and, more importantly, not taken by the narration itself (we will never find out more about young Dignam's day [18], or the very reverend John Conmee's [1], or the success or otherwise of Tom Rochford's machine [9]). At the center of the book, a chapter of largely peripheral trajectories.

To see the Homeric correspondences as parallels—the decline of the present, or the rebirth of the heroic—is to take them as a direct translation of a past model into a present. One way approves, the other disapproves: both of them keep the model intact, as a yardstick, even if to deplore its corruption by circumstances and history. But what if the idea of *transmission* does not and cannot itself remain intact? It is, after all, made intensely problematic on every level in *Ulysses,* with all those little bits of paper bearing cryptic and misunderstood messages, the incessant cross-purposes of its characters, its focus on issues of paternity, inheritance, authorship, and authority, and, throughout, the ever-reinvented questions of style. Let us stick with "Wandering Rocks": where the first six chapters of *Ulysses* offer us the continuing presence of Stephen or Bloom as an apparent guarantee of narrative continuity, "Wandering Rocks" faces us with a number of quite independent and heterogeneous series of events, taking place sometimes at several miles' remove from each other, and involving characters who are generally not in contact with one another and do not know of each other's actions. Nevertheless, the entire chapter is crisscrossed with correspondences, of a very different sort from those made possible by the single gaze of a character. The path of the vice-regal carriage across Dublin in the final section ties many of the previous events together, without unifying them. This is an empty gaze from the carriage, one which does not know what it is seeing or the connections it is making: *we* know that the owner of these "sturdy trousers swallowed by a closing door" (*U* 7.1282) was not long ago having a conversation with the son of the man who on Ormond street "brought his hat low" in returned salute (*U* 7.1201); we even know their names, because the text freely tells us them, Almidani Artifoni and Simon Dedalus; but no one in the carriage knows any of this. What links everything together in this last section is a subjectless, empty, and purely fortuitous trajectory. And even the apparent continuity of a trajectory is shattered in the many interpolations which provide internal links among the sections; if some of these links appear to work by thematic similarity (Boylan's selection of a basket of fruit for Molly is interrupted by a glimpse of the cuckolded husband some quarter of a mile away, a "darkbacked figure under Merchants' arch scann[ing] books on the hawker's cart" [*U* 7.315–16]), others seem to be connected by nothing more than their implied simultaneity. For all the heterogeneity and autonomy of the various sections, they are incessantly and extensively in correspondence with one another, but it makes no sense to talk of this correspondence in terms of the transmission of a message or model. Noise plays a very different role here. Rather than something which merely interrupts the real business of transmission—an accident which is in principle removable if only we take the proper care, and therefore something which is ultimately no more than a trivial detour—it becomes a sort of matrix out of which rises a hubbub of tenuous and multiple interconnections. Communication without transmission. We could doubtless say similar things about any number of episodes or aspects of *Ulysses*—and of course *Finnegans Wake* forces us to grapple in every sentence with what eludes our reading, and with the possibility that its blank spots, reticences, and refusals are not simply there to be overcome in order to get to meaning, but essential to that meaning itself.

If Bloom is indeed in some sense a metempsychosis of Odysseus, the very word *metempsychosis* undergoes metempsychosis in the course of the book with Molly's "Met him pike hoses" (*U* 4.331–43) and the variations which will be made on this during the day (*U* 8.112, 8.1148, 11.500, 11.1062, 11.1188, 13.1280–81, 16.1473, 17.686, 18.565). The very title of the book suggests that it may be concerned with the vicissitudes of transmission before exactness to an original—it is *Ulysses*, after all, not

Odysseus: Latin rather than Greek, and Virgil and the *Aeneid* before Homer and the *Odyssey*. (And what would such an original be? An apocryphal figure, a tale already told.)[2] In pointing to the *Odyssey*, *Ulysses* points to one side: not to an origin, but from what has followed on yet is in no sense predictable from that origin. To call the book *Ulysses* is to point to what the *Odyssey* itself could never know, the vicissitudes of its own future: to point not only to the wanderings of Odysseus, but also to the wanderings of the *Odyssey* in the course of Western history. To see the correspondences in terms of allegorical or mythopoeic parallels, then, is to miss two things: what is *not* Homeric in the Homeric, in these very correspondences between a book and its history which arrive at us from somewhere after an origin, too late for origin and thus utterly without nostalgia; and what is Homeric in the non-Homeric, the ways in which these apparently external, later facticities of the *Odyssey* are themselves quite precisely wanderings and encounters like those of Odysseus, and pose the same questions of chance, origin, and destination as the *Odyssey* itself.[3] This is not the archetypal necessity of a pattern which constrains the characters and events of one story to follow those of another, even in ironically inverting them. What the correspondences pick up on is instead their sheer, external, contingent facticity: everything that has happened to the *Odyssey after* Homer, its existence as tradition, corpus, canon. This is not what is *transmitted* to form an imaginary continuity which lets the age-old patterns be read intact under a thin veneer of the modern, it is what *accretes* for all sorts of reasons undreamt-of by the original; what *remains*, irreducible to such continuities; what one is *left with*, a remainder which is at the same time a patrimony, the very possibility of patrimony. *Ulysses* is about the weight of what one does not contract with, but is simply left with to find one's way around as best one can: religion, nationality, family, history, language itself.

So *Ulysses* marks its debt to Homer, which is at the same time a debt to Virgil, to Shakespeare, to a history which is Irish and a language which is Bloom's and Stephen's only by imposition; and in this writing which marks the debt, Joyce draws out a complex demand for response. Eliot marks his debt to *Ulysses*, which is also, he says, our debt as readers of *Ulysses*, even not-yet readers. Because the heart of the debt is what remains rather than what is annulled by reversal, one does not repay debts so much as pass them on. I owe you; and even if I pay you back exactly what I owe you, nothing more and nothing less, in that very equity you are now beholden to me because I have honored the promise of the debt. In refusing to escalate the debt, I escalate it, automatically and irrevocably.

Even when there is nothing left to pay, there is something left over; in paying back exactly what I owe, there is more debt than ever before. Eliot pays back a debt by placing us all in arrears: not only to Joyce, but also to Eliot as the intermediary who invoices us for his client. Signatures—countersignatures—mark the passage of the debt, whose inception is always prior to any act of signing; in contracting myself, what I inherit in the act and sign myself as having received is already a system of conventions, legalities, and behaviors which make such an act possible.

So Eliot takes up, affirms, and passes on, affixing his signature. It is passed on to us, because we are already in its debt, though we may not know it. Eliot's statement of the debt is an *announcement* of what is already there: in a sense it adds nothing, after the announcement there is no new relationship that was not already there before; all it does is affirm, and pass that affirmation on to us for our signature. But if we are already in debt, we have already signed from the beginning, from before the beginning: it comes to us already signed with our signatures, which we can only affirm by countersignature. This letter which has arrived at its destination finds us already accounted for, and in the very place where we now read that the letter has always, in retrospect, said we would be. If—as Eliot had argued in 1919, "the historical sense involves a perception, not only of the pastness of the past, but of its presence" (*Selected Prose* 38)—this is not because it survives like a rock or a shard of pottery, an object across which time washes in an eroding and one-directional stream. The past is present as an already redoubled affirmation of what has already taken place. The past event can be placed in the linear succession of a history only because it can first of all be taken out of it, affirmed in its pastness from a present, as something which was itself once present. In the same movement, what this reaffirmation affirms must also be *affirmation itself*: an absolute past which was never present, in which I have always and already signed.

So: before they can be either archetypes or parody (the endless banality of the "human nature" in myth criticism, or the point of leverage for critique) the Homeric correspondences of *Ulysses* necessarily affirm the difference between the two layers, Odysseus and Bloom, Telemachus and Stephen, *as a problem:* an insistent relationship that never quite seems to be exhausted by any particular parallels it generates.[4] For all its elaborated detail, the correspondence leaves us none the wiser about just *how* we are to read Bloom and Stephen as homecoming Odysseus and Telemachus, and what it tells us about them. We know from the various notebooks that while Joyce's process of composition was in almost every case one of accumulation and expansion, the Homeric titles by which the episodes are universally known, and under which many were first published in serial form, were deleted from the final version at a comparatively late stage. It is as if once a sufficient density of correspondences had been achieved, Joyce chose to remove all of the obvious pointers to their existence except for the bare title. Once we put aside the sheer familiarity of the Homeric correspondences, we can see how extraordinarily attenuated they are in their very frequency and density. Indeed, the question has often been asked: if it were not for the title and the Gilbert and Linati schemas, would we read Homeric parallels here at all?[5] Once the hint *is* taken up, of course, an entire framework of possibilities appears, from Mulligan's sardonic citing of Yeats, to the suggestive webs of meaning that now, in that same chapter, seem to link both Stephen and his ostensible topic, Shakespeare, to Homer.[6]

This attenuation keeps open the gap between the Homeric events and Dublin on this June day in 1904. On the one hand, the correspondences are never less than insistent; once seen, they cannot be ignored. But on the other hand, they are never allowed to gain the consistency or coherence of allegory, and remain fragmented with the various levels at which they work refusing to come together into a single pervasive principle of organization. On the broadest level, we have the familiar assignment of roles by which Bloom is Odysseus, Molly Penelope, Stephen Telemachus. But when we look more closely, these correspondences appear atomized, even incidental: they flicker out of the text to surprise us, then disappear; for a moment, two distant things coalesce, at the next moment only to find themselves as distant as ever. In this attenuation, *Ulysses* manages both to suggest that the correspondences function as an underlying principle and to thwart any precise statement of what that principle might be. It takes great care to remain an accumulation of things which do not quite add up—or rather, it is much more accurate to say, of things which are so disposed in the text as to suggest all sorts of ways in which they could be added up, but to leave all of them partial and incomplete and to confirm none. This accumulation suggests a principle somewhere before the text, on the basis of which the text would have received its present shape; but that principle remains a hypothesis after the fact, partial and leaving much of the text unaccounted.

Perhaps, then, we should pay attention not only to the content of the Homeric correspondences, but to the form in which they are offered in the Linati and Gilbert schemas alike: a list. It is hardly accident that the list should be such a significant textual figure in *Ulysses* and, above all, in *Finnegans Wake*—or rather, the list is exactly that figure which raises the very question of accident, as a problem: just what *is* the connection between any two contiguous entries? Is it just a collocation, a disjunct set of elements whose only property in common is that they are members of the set? Or is it structured according to a strict principle which is never stated as such but of which all of the elements and their interrelationships would be precise and even predictable examples, if only we knew the principle?[7] The list plays a complex game between the specific and the general, the coherent and the incoherent: lists are not simply incoherent, in that they suggest an order, but neither are they quite coherent, except as a provisional hypothesis which stands to be overturned with the next term in the series. The figure of the list is *asyndeton,* the absence or omission of conjunctions: lists are haunted by the gnomonic possibility that what is at work may be more, or no more, than fortuity and juxtaposition.[8]

The schemas present the Homeric correspondences to us as a doubled list: the hour and scene of the Dublin day, and the Homeric titles and personages. Each of these lists suggests a narrative sequence, but for all the sequence and causality implied in narrative—and the basic narratological distinction between story and discourse will always remind us how much the process of reading narrative is a matter of hypothesis—the relationship between series is not narrative, but persistently asyndetic. There are always remainders, things which find no counterpart in the other series. None of the other series which make up the schemas are narrative, and their predominance suggests that even the Homeric and Dublin series may function not primarily as narrative, but more like those others surrounding them: a massive, dense, and asyndetic system of echoes scattered over the surface of the text, not yet its principle of continuity so much as the repeated invitation to hypothesis. Classical narratology has no real terms of description for what they do: if narratological kernels and satellites are linked together consequently and consecutively, these textual events are strewn at apparent haphazard. Read the Scene and Hours columns downwards together, and you certainly get the shell of a narrative: 1 pm, the Lunch; 2 pm, the Library; 3 pm, the Streets . . . But read the Technic, Symbol, or Color columns, and you learn nothing of the story (Enthymemic, Editor, and red; Peristaltic, Constables, and no color at all; Dialectic, Stratford and London, and no color . . .). Narratological kernels respond to each other with a certain symmetry over the extent of a narrative, opening up enigmas and generally—eventually, ideally, after the delay occasioned by all those subsidiary satellite functions—leading them to their answering closure; the categories of the schemas are aleatory points which multiply out across the narrative to link instantaneously occurrences which may be separated by many hundreds of pages. They do not even really work at the level of what Barthes calls indices, as they give neither explicit information about the time and place represented nor implicit information about "an atmosphere, a philosophy, a feeling, a personality trait" (Prince 43). On the contrary, as *Ulysses* progresses these categories tend to drift sometimes quite far from the ostensible matter of the narration.[9] Indices work to name and concretize as part of a "reality effect," but to do that they also need to slip back into a quiet and obedient instrumentality immediately after. The categories of the schemas, though, are forever derealizing these data; they force aspects of that background up into a prominence which is not due first of all to the demands of narrative but simply to insistence and repetition.

Everywhere throughout the Linati and Gilbert schemas we have the juxtaposition of independent series, just as we do on the level of narrative in "Wandering Rocks." Each of these series might—but need not—have its own causalities and sequentialities, but regardless, its encounters with all the others will not be governed by any of those. The shorthand term for this, as Pierre Bourdieu is fond of quoting Cournot, is *chance* (80). The fascination *Ulysses* and *Finnegans Wake* have for the chance encounter (the crossing of paths on a June day, the movement of a throwaway down the Liffey, a hen's scratching up a letter from a rubbish heap, the random marks of a professor's fork) is mirrored in the schemas, which multiply and arrange such collisions. The schemas are machines for exploring the ways in which meanings are generated *out of* the meetings of independent series: "chance" is always more than a thematic in Joyce.

Yet while they generate meanings, the schemas also block it. The grid they place over the top of the narrative assigns to each section a number of non-narrative elements which assert themselves, before it is clear what they may come to mean, purely by their insistent, repetitive presence. And such a repetition can work to a certain extent just as it did for the boy of "The Sisters," to *designify*. When certain words and forms repeat themselves according to a demand which is not wholly that of the narrated events, the text may seem marked everywhere with the traces of frequent tiny intrusions, irreducible to their context. These can come to embody a disruptive and fascinated enjoyment, as we find above all in "Circe," the place at which every recurrent object and theme in the book returns again with garrulous and hallucinatory insistence. "Sirens" plays with words as sound material; it constructs a continuum between speech and pure bodily noise ("Imperthnthn thnthnthn," sniffs the bootboy, pertinently throwing back Miss Douce's accusation of *impertinent insolence* to her [*U* 11.97–

100]), and even removes words entirely from their context to replay them as audible motifs in the two-page overture. The chapters often characterized as stylistically parodic ("Cyclops," "Nausicaa," "Oxen of the Sun," and "Eumaeus")[10] do not work on the distance on which parody classically relies, but on the collapse of any such distance, and the instability of any positions from which they can be inhabited, as we shall see in chapter 3.

It is not only within each chapter that the categories of the schemas make asyndetic fissures; it happens increasingly from one chapter to the next. The Technic column in particular sets up increasingly severe and problematic disjunctions from one chapter to the next: the progress of the book, as Joyce remarked, "is in fact like the progress of some sandblast . . . each successive episode . . . leaves behind it a burnt up field" (SL 241). The closer the narrative takes us to the obvious (narrative) resolution of a homecoming—at least in the case of Bloom: Stephen's resolution is, after all, *not* to return to the tower at which his day began—the further the Technic takes us from where we began as readers: an effect which is only emphasized by the symmetry which in the Gilbert schema has the Technics of the first three chapters reflecting those of the last three (narratives new and old, catechisms personal and impersonal, monologues male and female). Against the *nostos* of the narrated events, it is as if we have an accelerated stylistic diaspora: "Jewgreek is greekjew" (U 15.2097–98). The continuities of narrative structure give way to an increasingly asyndetic relationship between successive chapters.

Hence the significance of the list in Joyce, as the figure which comes increasingly to implement this juggling act between coherence and incoherence. Lists are at their most obvious in the *Wake*, of course, with its monstrous and sometimes pages-long catalogues (one of which we shall be looking at in more detail in chapter 5), and in the later episodes of *Ulysses*, with the gigantism of "Cyclops" and the catalogues of "Ithaca." But we also find the asyndetic elsewhere than in literal lists. We find it, for example, in the relationships of the *Wake*'s personages to each other, and the ways in which a single figure will appear to split up into an indefinite number of others: Glasheen's lists of these in her three censuses are invaluable here, and particularly in their admitted and necessary ambiguities or incompletenesses; instead of the single myth Campbell and Robinson leave us with in their *Skeleton Key*, we have a proliferation of stories whose relationship to the basic HCE narrative is both insistent and yet far from clear. And before any of these, almost every word of the *Wake* provides an example of the asyndetic: the portmanteau *Wake*-word, with its clash of languages enacting the clashes and migrations of human history itself, is the very figure of the contingent meeting of independent series. As well as in the increasing stylistic disjunctions between successive chapters of *Ulysses*, we see it in the granulation and ellipticality of the interior monologues, in the ways in which chapters may structure themselves internally according to processes of juxtaposition (the overture to "Sirens," the bar scenes and interpolations of "Cyclops," the apparent division down the middle of "Nausicaa," the free association of "Penelope"). *A Portrait of the Artist as a Young Man* works in a series of juxtaposed blocks, and the stories of *Dubliners* hint at a patterning throughout the book; whatever else it is, the epiphanic moment is also that "most delicate and evanescent of moments" (*SH* 216) in which the unexpected and independent run together.

Asyndeton is always a figure of *what remains:* of what, despite the possible monstrosity of the list, has not yet been said, and which will still remain to be said no matter how far one might actually continue the list. Bloom turns on the tap, and the gush of words which comes out (*U* 17.163–228) is both far too much and at the same time oddly too little. What we learn of the capacity of the Roundwood reservoir, the initial cost per yard of the pipe system, the name of the borough's waterworks engineer, and the recent conviction of a charitable institution for its waste of water under drought conditions—none of which we need to know in order to appreciate the all-important phatic qualities of that cup of tea Bloom will offer Stephen—only points out the arbitrariness of that information, and how little it has actually told us about that system. For all its concreteness, the list remains haunted by something which is not present, and which its indefinite extension will not be able to make present either: what the list looks to is the possibly infinite number of things it does not say, which it perhaps indicates with the trailing-off of an "etc." or a typographical ellipsis. . . . It opens up the space of a problem which, unlike the hermeneutic enigma of classical narratology, is not to be closed off: it is fitting that the penultimate chapter of *Ulysses*, then, should be an insistent, obsessive listing, not only of the accoutrements of the real which surround Bloom, but of his position within them, his fantasies, his desires, his past; and that the final chapter should be so carefully constructed according to self-contradiction, and—as the retrospective source for much of our knowledge about the Blooms' early life together—at the same time exquisitely implausible in the background it gives Molly.[11]

Like the figure of the gnomon, then, asyndeton is logically incomplete, though in different ways (it is inductive rather than abductive). What is at work in asyndeton is what Slavoj Žižek describes as the logic of the *symptom:*

> Symptoms are meaningless traces, their meaning is not discovered, excavated from the hidden depths of the past, but constructed retroactively—the analysis produces the truth; that is, the signifying frame which gives the symptoms their symbolic place and meaning. As soon as we enter the symbolic order, the past is always present in the form of historical tradition and the meaning of those traces is not given; it changes continually with the transformations of the signifier's network. Every historical rupture, every advent of a new master-signifier, changes retroactively the meaning of all tradition, restructures the narration of the past, makes it readable in another, new way.
>
> Thus, "things which mean nothing all of a sudden signify something *but in a quite different domain.*" (*Sublime Object* 55–56: my emphasis)

That *in a quite different domain* marks the multiplicity and autonomy of the different causal series involved, and the necessary breaking of any chain of causality across them. The symptom, as Freud describes it, is essentially *nachträglich,* supplementary. Freud is careful to argue that the symptom is not simply the eruption in adult life of an unresolved and never-quite-forgotten childhood trauma, for two reasons: on the one hand, such events can remain inactive and without consequence indefinitely, even for an entire lifetime; on the other, what analysis reveals of actual neuroses is that the set of libidinal experiences at their core "had no importance at all at the time they occurred but only acquired it regressively" (*Introductory Lectures* 409). What sets off the neurotic attack is a quite unrelated and contingent "precipitating cause" ("Notes" 75ff; *Introductory Lectures* 392, 408–409). The neurosis depends on what Freud will call the "complemental series" between two causally unrelated events: the infantile experience with its resultant fixation of libido, and the triggering adult experience (*Introductory Lectures* 392). Both of these are needed for the neurosis: without the latter, the former remains invisible, unproblematic; and without the former, the latter is merely transient and without lasting effect. The complemental series is constituted by a gap rather than a continuity: structurally, it depends on that unwarranted arrival of something from another domain altogether, the chance intersection of another causality altogether. It is in this sense that we should read the assertion that the construction of a symptom "is the substitute for something else that did not happen" (*Introductory Lectures* 320): the symptom does not stand for an event located somewhere on the same timeline as *either* of the components of the series, the infantile or the adult components. This is what allows Freud to say that the question of whether that infantile experience—the "primal scene"—is a fantasy or an actual experience which befell the child, "is not in fact a matter of very great importance" ("From the History" 238, 337).

This retrospective logic of the symptom is everywhere in *Ulysses* and *Finnegans Wake,* describing both their structure and Joyce's working procedures. It is a commonplace to say that *Ulysses* is a book to be reread rather than read: a first reading simply cannot pick up on all the small details which will find their echoes elsewhere in the book. This is what is behind the instability the book affords any narratological distinction between kernel and satellite: details which on a first and even many subsequent readings can only appear inconsequential will only take on meaning in retrospect, after the intervention of *another* series, quite independent of the first. One of the most famous and obvious cases of this is initiated by the word "Throwaway"—a word which, of course, one could only say is far from accidental were it not for the point that the accidental is just what is turned into a vast problem here. Having cadged a newspaper from Bloom so he can read the form guide, Bantam Lyons rushes off suddenly (*U* 5.526–42). We will only find out later what has happened. At Davey Byrne's in "Lestrygonians," Lyons announces he's just had a tip from Bloom, and is going to put five bob on it (*U* 8.1005–25). In "Wandering Rocks," Lenehan—who wasn't at Davey Byrne's earlier—tells M'Coy he has just "knocked against Bantam Lyons in there going to back a bloody horse someone gave him that hasn't an earthly" (*U* 10.517–19). In Barney Kiernan's pub, the Citizen's drinking partners are all put out because they had money on Lenehan's tip Sceptre, who was beaten by a "rank outsider," Throwaway (*U* 12.1218–28). Lenehan says Lyons told him he'd been tipped Throwaway by Bloom, "only I put him off it" (*U* 12.1554–57), and that "Boylan plunged two quid on my tip *Sceptre* for himself and a lady friend" (*U* 12.1222–23). Later on, in the cabman's shelter, Bloom will glance over the news of the win as he skims the late edition of the *Telegraph* (*U* 16.1242–44). Back at Eccles Street, the sight of torn-up betting tickets on the apron of the dresser will lead him to ponder the win and his retrospective prediction as he makes tea for Stephen (*U* 17.319–53). Molly will fill in the story of the tickets for us: Boylan was in a foul mood after he stepped out to buy the late edition, "tearing up the tickets and swearing blazes because he lost 20 quid he said he lost over that outsider that won and half he put on for me on account of Lenehan's tip cursing him to the lowest pits" (*U* 18.424–26). Only on reading back can we see what was happening in that first meeting: Lyons had taken Bloom's "I was going to throw it away" for the name of a horse. Two series meet, newspaper and horse, and it is the disjunction between the two which provides the motor of this complemental series. The series will, of course, divide again, and again, each time reaching back to rewrite what has already occurred. By "Lestrygonians," the second occurrence, there are already two *throwaways*: the horse, and now the Elijah leaflet Bloom has been given by a "sombre Y. M. C. A. young man" outside Graham Lemon's sweet shop (*U* 8.5–6), and which he will very soon toss into the Liffey. In "Wandering Rocks," we shall see some of the passage of a throwaway downstream,[12] and its crossing paths with the *Rosevean*, which Stephen had earlier glimpsed from Sandymount (*U* 3.503–505), and which carries Murphy, the sailor Bloom and Stephen will later meet in the cabman's shelter. So many of the well-known games and problems in *Ulysses* are built in this way, with an apparently innocuous detail taking on a retrospective and often highly ambiguous signification only after the intersection with another independent series: Breen's postcard, the figure of M'Intosh, the identity of Martha Clifford, Milly's absence in Mullingar, the movement of the furniture in the Bloom household during the day, Bloom's measurements, Molly's previous lovers.[13] Indeed, all of the final chapter works in this way, with Molly's unprecedented arrival in the text the occasion for a massive retrospective fleshing-out of the details of the Blooms' lives together. The accelerating process of rewriting which Joyce developed as the composition of *Ulysses* wore on makes such features into an increasingly important aspect of the text; with *Finnegans Wake* it will become the major structural principle.

The same sort of logic is also put into play in the Linati and Gilbert schemas, with their multiple and intersecting complemental series. That the two schemas are considerably different in their details only emphasizes the sense in which the choice of categories and their implementation are genuinely arbitrary, and the extent to which their meaning is generated by just this arbitrariness. Before they can be read as myth or archetype, strings which tug at Bloom, Stephen, and Molly from the very beginnings of human society, the Homeric columns have to be read as *symptom:* they intrude on that mundane Dublin, neither belonging to it nor deducible from it, but a frame whose very distance and arbitrariness generates a complex range of meanings. *Meanings,* plural, too: the Homeric columns are not the key to the single, real meaning of *Ulysses* underneath all its deceptive surfaces; they give us a proliferation of meanings whose relationships are problematic and asyndetic. Like the primal scene of psychoanalysis, myth comes from an absolute past, one which has never—or need never have—taken place as an event on a timeline; its explanatory power is that everything behaves as if it had. But the correspondences can only be read as myth because they are imposed *after* the event on the naturalistic events of this Dublin, from an absolute future which will never arrive in the narrative timeline of *Ulysses,* no matter how far we extend it.[14] The Homeric correspondences belong to the absolute past of myth only to the extent that they belong to an absolute future beyond the narrative's diegesis. Their model is first of all that of the other columns of the schemas, those Colors, Arts, Technes, and Organs. They function because they are arbitrary, not because they are buried deep in the necessities of human nature. There is no reason why two A.M. needs to be discussed in terms of skeletons, science, comets, and catechisms. It works the other way around: only by the imposition of such frameworks can the scattered data take on meaning. Or again, *meanings,* plural: what the schemas present us with is a number of such frameworks, all of them very elementary (thematic repetitions, generic patterns, narrative elements) and none with any guarantee of convergence: if the Technic of gigantism obviously reinforces the Homeric correspondences and the Art (politics) of "Cyclops," what are we to make of the linking of architecture and constables to Lestrygonian peristalsis? Rather than acting as archetypes—clusterings which under the apparent inconsequentialities of the surface would already be saturated and dense with meaning—the point of the Homeric correspondences and indeed of all of the categories of the schemas is that they are *empty.* A category such as Colors, for example, is not a compendium of mythic connotations; it is a set of differences which will come to mean all sorts of things depending on the other series with which they are put in contact, a moiré pattern of intersections and skew overlaps.

Oddly enough, this is exactly what we can see in Eliot's comments on *Ulysses* as mythopoeic. What Eliot is concerned with is not first of all the ways in which *Ulysses* brings age-old wisdom into the present, but the sheer novelty of what Joyce is doing. This "mythical method" is no longer a "narrative method," and perhaps *Ulysses* is no longer even a novel (which may be "a form which will no longer serve"). Though for Eliot this is undoubtedly mixed with questions of "a continuous parallel between contemporaneity and antiquity," Joyce's method "is simply a way of controlling, of ordering, of giving a shape and a significance to the immense panorama of futility and anarchy which is contemporary history" (*Selected Prose* 177). In this "giving a shape," we should hear the echo of the argument Eliot developed only a few years before, in "Tradition and the Individual Talent," with its famous statement that

> what happens when a new work of art is created is something that happens simultaneously to all the works of art which preceded it. The existing monuments form an ideal order among themselves, which is modified by the introduction of the new (the really new) work of art among them. . . . the past [is] altered by the present as much as the present is directed by the past. (*Selected Prose* 38–39)

The "ideal order" of these movements is not something which grows inevitably out of the internal qualities characterizing each work, for it is "modified by the introduction of the new": that is, by what is *not* reducible to what is already there. What modifies them is the *introduction* itself, the sheer facticity of it. The *event*, this irruption into the already-existing, is thus the very historicity of the work (and of art itself). It occurs as event, within time, and is even under certain conditions quite precisely locatable (as signature or dating); but to the extent that it is event and irruption it is not reducible to the linear unfolding of what is already there. Surprisingly, what Eliot is proposing comes close to Žižek's point of a historici*ty* whose difference from historici*sm* lies in the irreducible kernel of the event, in a sense quite foreign to narratology: the encounter, the contingent, the Real. And for all its making-possible of the historical, this kernel is itself unhistorical: it happens within history, but its sheer contingency is a residue irreducible to history. The kernel is the trauma that has not yet found its place.

Stephen and Mr. Deasy are in Mr. Deasy's study at the Dalkey school. Outside, the boys are playing hockey, and their noise can be heard through the window. Mark my words, says Mr. Deasy, England is in the hands of the Jews: they sinned against the light:

—Who has not? Stephen said.
—What do you mean, Mr Deasy asked.
    He came forward a pace and stood by the table. His underjaw fell sideways open uncertainly. Is this old wisdom? He waits to hear from me.
—History, Stephen said, is a nightmare from which I am trying to awake.

From the playfield the boys raised a shout. A whirring whistle: goal. What if that nightmare gave you a back kick?

—The ways of the Creator are not our ways, Mr Deasy said. All history moves towards one great goal, the manifestation of God.

Stephen jerked his thumb towards the window, saying:

—That is God.

Hooray! Ay! Whrrwhee!

—What? Mr Deasy asked.

—A shout in the street, Stephen answered, shrugging his shoulders.

Mr Deasy looked down and held for a while the wings of his nose tweaked between his fingers. Looking up again he set them free.

—I am happier than you are, he said. We have committed many errors and many sins. . . . Many errors, many failures but not the one sin. I am a struggler now at the end of my days. But I will fight for the right till the end.

For Ulster will fight

And Ulster will be right.

Stephen raised the sheets in his hand.

—Well, sir, he began. . . .

—I foresee, Mr Deasy said, that you will not remain here very long at this work. You were not born to be a teacher, I think. Perhaps I am wrong. (*U* 2.373–402)

There are two independent but interrelated series here: two games being played simultaneously.

On the one hand, hockey. Hockey, of course, is played according to a certain set of codified rules, but it is rule-governed in a crucially much looser sense than a Saussurean or structural model might suggest. For Saussure, a statement is treated as a syntagm which has been produced from a set of given elements according to systematic rules. The observable phenomenon, the statement, is only the product of a transphenomenal system, which is the true object of analysis. This system manifests itself only in its utterances, but it accounts for all utterances: know the system, and you know in advance all possible utterances. But the hockey game we have here is far looser—as indeed is actual speech, above and beyond the Saussurean system. Playing according to the rules still leaves everything yet to be decided, an infinite, opportunistic variety of actual play: that a move is legitimate says nothing at all about whether it can be a winning move, and under what circumstances. The cries and shouts of the boys chart out this juggling with the contingencies of circumstances: warnings, approbation, dismay, commentary; events and actions in their own right, all part of a tactical web of play whose boundaries are far from clear. The rules of the game provide the space of a certain dissension, where there is still much to be negotiated:

> He stood in the porch and watched the laggard hurry towards the scrappy field where *sharp voices were in strife*. They were sorted in teams and Mr Deasy came stepping over wisps of grass with gaitered feet. When he reached the schoolhouse *voices again contending* called to him. He turned his angry white moustache.
> —What is it now? he *cried* continually without listening.
> —Cochrane and Halliday are on the same side, sir, Stephen said. . . .
> And as he stepped fussily back across the field his old man's voice *cried sternly:*
> —What is the matter? What is it now?
> Their *sharp voices* cried about him on all sides. (*U* 2.184–96: emphases added)

Adjudicating the game is itself very like a game, a secondary game generated by the first, and like it involving negotiation and compromise with what is available. There is no simple outside to it, any more than there is to a story and the overbidding which both paralyzes it and sets it in motion.

And on the other hand—the second game—there is Stephen's conversation with Garrett Deasy. This game is somewhat less codified, a matter of playing things by ear. Deasy may be a sententious old fool and a bigot, but he pays Stephen's wages. Stephen is doing the difficult juggling act of marking out his disagreements from Deasy while evading direct opposition. His strategy seems to be one of throwing the older man off-balance, making him uncertain whether what he has just heard is opposition or not. And it works, to a point: Deasy, with that uncertain sag of the jaw, is always replying with a suspicious "What?" or "What do you mean?" Deasy too sees it as a game, an *agon* ("I like to break a lance with you, old as I am" [*U* 2.424–25]), but the two are not in any simple agreement about what the rules might be. In fact, the rules and who is to set them are two of the stakes in the struggle. Bested in one way, or at least left behind by Stephen's opacity, Deasy will attempt to change the terms of the game ("I am happier than you are"), or to give a reminder of his authority under an assertion of his perspicuity ("I foresee . . . that you will not remain here very long at this work"), or to get in the last word, even if incorrect and at the cost of running after the disappearing Stephen ("Ireland, they say, has the honor of being the only country which never persecuted the jews. Do you know that? No. And do you know why? . . . Because she never let them in" [*U* 2.437–42]).

These are not two different types of game. They are opposed to each other not as incompatible, but in a weaker and more important sense: simply, they are set opposite each other. The one encroaches on the other, makes demands on the time and the space reserved for the other: "What is the matter? What is it now?" cries the exasperated Mr. Deasy, without listening. Settling the hockey teams takes time away from the conversational sparring with the younger man. Juggling the demands of the two is itself a game, another game, whose strategies are not those of either of the games which have occasioned it. Games proliferate here: given one, there must also be the further game of adjudicating that; given two (and given one we now always have two), there is also the game of negotiating between them.

Two games, then, at least, and two series, each no doubt divided. They are independent: they do not share the same regularities, modes of play, aims, strategies; there is no ready commensurability between them.

Nevertheless, there is a window between them, and through that window, for all that incommensurability, some things nevertheless do come to pass from one to the other. Something produced in one game is cast adrift, transferred over to the other, to do something quite different. Cheers greeting a goal become a move in Stephen's game, his own attempt to score against Deasy. The goal of that second game is partly to determine who has the right to determine what will count as its goal, to determine just what a goal is. "All history," says Deasy, "moves towards one great goal, the manifestation of God." Deasy's history is convergent, unitary, teleological in its totality. Stephen's too moves towards goals, but plural rather than singular, centrifugal rather than centripetal, strategic rather than teleological: its model is the hockey game outside, where the contingent and the directed are locked together; not without order, but with an order which is always in the process of being seized; and not without totality, but with the added complication that whatever else they might be, totalities are also inevitably strategic interventions in the game, necessary claims one makes as a move. Stephen is affirming this complexity against the reassuring simplicity of Deasy's commonplaces: *Proverbs* 1:20–22, the very source of the figure he uses, has Wisdom decrying the lovers of simplicity ("Wisdom crieth without; she uttereth her voice in the streets . . . saying, How long, ye simple ones will ye love simplicity? and the scorners delight in their scorning, and fools hate knowledge?"). His very *taking* advantage of the hockey game as example is itself a precise example of the process: that it is there at hand *as* example is pure contingency.

And so all of a sudden, the shout comes to mean something else, in quite a different domain: not just an expression of jubilation at the score in a hockey game, but a statement about—of all things—the nature of God, and history, and the relationships both of these might have to chance. Of course, it can be this only because, after the event and in another game altogether, someone has taken advantage of the moment and made the graft; without that other game Stephen and Deasy are playing, the shout is a matter of hockey scores. But now the graft has been made, we can read in that shout, *as if it had been there all along,* an anasemic signature: nothing less than the name of God, signing agreement:

> Hooray! Ay! W*hrrwh*ee! (*U* 2:384)

First there is an event, which is at first of quite local significance at most and without consequences other than immediate; no internal logic perpetuates it far beyond its occurrence; left to the course of things, its faint ripples diminish, become imperceptible, die. Now there is a second event which is quite independent of the first, and which could in no way be predicted from it: it stands separated from the first by an interval of time, its causalities lie in a different series altogether. The effect of that second event is to leap across that interval and the difference of series, back through the window, and to endow the first event retrospectively with meaning. This is a meaning the first event would not otherwise have had, but the core of the paradox is that it is the meaning it *will have had already.* The temporality of this new series comes not from its first term, but from its second, in the light of which alone can the first even be recognized as first. What it produces is *what will have already been.* It everts that cry on the hockey field to produce, coiled up inside it, what will now, from this point on, already have been there all along, and in doing that it perhaps shows us—through another window, another collocation of events—that God we already know from elsewhere, "within or behind or beyond or above his handiwork, invisible, refined out of existence, indifferent, paring his fingernails" (*P* 233): the God of *symptom,* exactly.

And Garrett Deasy is edgy. Simply to play the game may be to play by Stephen's rules, whatever they are. To claim the convergence of history, after all, is to claim it as a move in a game (*see what you do with* that *one, young man!*): and the game, in all its divergent, serial temporality, is exactly what Stephen asserts against the single-mindedness of a master-plan:

history has goals, yes, it has many; here is one, outside the window. Deasy's every move may be an unwitting affirmation of Stephen's point: other windows open onto other series, and through them we can reach for Blake ("The harlot's cry . . ."), John's Gospel ("the true Light which lighteth every man that cometh into the world"), Tennyson ("one far-off divine event, / To which the whole creation moves") or Randolph Churchill ("For Ulster will be free. . ."), all of them grafted alike into the service of the argument in an endless strategic mobility which, by the same logic, Stephen will be free to cap in turn. And barely under the surface, cresting Stephen's consciousness, is last night's dream, which he has not yet remembered: another street, the street of harlots, *boul'Mich'* and Nighttown, the creamfruit smell of melons, and a red carpet.[15] What we have is not the inexorable progress towards one great goal, but a dense knot in which every instant sends out its prolepses, analepses, distant metalepses.

Hence Mr. Deasy's unease: Stephen's argument seems to be coiled up at the heart of his own, like a worm. It is as if Deasy too reads things in just the same way as Stephen, only inversely. He has just had Stephen read his letter to the *Evening Telegraph* on foot and mouth disease, and his certainty that he has the solution to the problem reveals itself from the beginning as somewhat threatened:

—[. . .] I am trying to work up influence with the department. Now I'm going to try publicity. I am surrounded by difficulties, by . . . intrigues by . . . backstairs influence by . . .
He raised his forefinger and beat the air oldly before his voice spoke.
—Mark my words, Mr Dedalus, he said. (*U* 2.341–45: first ellipsis mine)

Paranoia too has the retrospectivity of the symptom: Ah! Now *I see how it has been all along.* . . . What should be complete in the pure circle of Deasy's logic is forever emptied out, by something whose figure is ellipsis, hesitation, the wordless gesture marking precisely the words which cannot be formulated. If the circle fails to return on itself, this can only be because a nefarious agency prevents its completion, an agency which is simultaneously outside the completeness of the circle and yet, in order for it to have any effect at all on that closure, also uncannily within it. For Deasy, this is the place—simultaneously both nowhere and everywhere—of the Jew.

—Mark my words, Mr Dedalus, he said. England is in the hands of the jews. In all the highest places: her finance, her press. And they are the signs of a nation's decay. Wherever they gather they eat up the nation's vital strength. I have seen it coming these years. As sure as we are standing here the jew merchants are already at their work of destruction. Old England is dying. (*U* 2.345–51)

As those who "sinned against the light," the Jews are outside "the nation," and yet they are at its very center, "in the highest places" (finance and the press, money and the word: that which circulates), at the very heart of Empire: England, ruling Ireland, is itself ruled by "the jews." Because of this ambivalent position, they are "the signs of a nation's decay," a destructive self-consumption. "The jews" are both the end of commerce and commerce itself: the very sign of mobility and exchange ("wanderers on the earth to this day"), and the inward collapse of that exchange. Stephen underlines the unease of Deasy's position: "A merchant . . . is one who buys cheap and sells dear, jew or gentile, is he not?"; if the Jews "sinned against the light," who has not? Coiled up at the heart of where one has already always been, Deasy finds everywhere not the countersignature of the God of creation but the mark of a conspiracy which can maintain its closure only by becoming infinite. The cost of that "one great goal" of history is that it shatter itself to pieces, nefarious fragments which lurk wherever "chance" strikes meaning out of complemental series: "the jew" becomes the master-signifier that stitches together a vast economy of signs, the gravitational well which directs them in their movements. Stephen will take Deasy's imagined conspiracies and give them back to him, inverted: even the apparently random event bears a signature, but it is the name of God; and this God is not the demonized figure of conspiracy precisely because it is the assignation of meaning across contingent series and in retrospect, not in advance. God, this shout echoing across the empty space between series, is the very name for what dissolves the chains of such simple causalities.

The figure of the Jew comes before and after to frame the exchange about the ways of the Creator and the shout in the street. By the time Deasy makes his claim for the one great goal of history, its sententiousness will already have been undermined by its paranoid underside, a clear enough statement of which will end the exchange between the two men, and the chapter: Ireland, says Deasy, has never persecuted the Jews because she never let them in the first place (*U* 437–47), one of whom we are of course soon to meet. In Deasy's imaginary, the Jew is a figure of that space between series, a sort of universal connective capable of linking any apparently distant events, even if they seem to have no causal connection. The Jew has no legitimate place, but comes to occupy all of them, by subterfuge.

The Jew, then, is an excess. Lacanian terms are useful here: the Jew comes to stand for, or to marshal, what obdurately remains once the symbolic has done its work; a fragment of the real which always resists symbolization, and which seems to be everywhere because it is never in any one of the categories which might claim to contain it. The Jew fascinates Deasy because it is the figure of what is always left out of the equation and yet seems—and most puzzlingly, by virtue of its very exclusion—to account for the equation itself: the Jews sinned against the light, and thus work everywhere in the shadows. In its very instability, the Jew works as a suture: only because of those who are imagined to undermine it everywhere is it possible to sustain the fantasy of the unity of the social: unity is what the social *would have* if it were not for the Jew; which, turned around, is to say that the Jew is what *gives* the social that very unity, in the mode of that *would have*. As excess, "the Jew" is a figure which spills out over a number of levels of the text: characterological, obviously, in the figure of Bloom; political and social, in the world *Ulysses* depicts, where it is precisely a question of such unity and its outsides; but also everywhere in the very construction of the narrative.

Homer's Odysseus reaches home; in the past tense of narration, he has already reached home, before the narrative has begun. Reclaiming faithful wife, kingdom, and rightful heir, he completes a circle: his ten years' wandering the Aegean have been a mere interruption. But Joyce's Ulysses is a Jew: the return home is yet to come, a projection into the future, like Agendath Netaim[16] or the second coming of Elijah, and with it the affections of Penelope and defeat of the suitors. The circle is still open, suspended. *Ulysses* re-cites the *Odyssey* into difference from itself, takes it elsewhere, puts in another (con)text. Jewgreek may be greekjew, as Lynch's cap suggests later in "Circe," but the very copula and inversion separates even as it is asserted that "Extremes meet" (*U* 15.2097–98). And just how *are* we to read that meeting which is resolutely *not* a union between jew Bloom and greek Dedalus, but a complex crossing of paths in two irreducibly different journeys? Already it is a matter of translation, where Odysseus ends up somewhere other than at home. Analogy, even an analogy of return itself, must—in order to *be* analogy—be incomplete, describe a circle which never *quite* returns on itself. The condition of homecoming is diaspora, and Odysseus is Greek only because he is first a Jew, only Odysseus because he is already Ulysses.

At the heart of History, then, there is something which is not reducible to history and yet is its very motor. The one great goal Deasy imagines depends for its very possibility on the utterly contingent "introduction of the new (the really new)" as Eliot has it, from which such a goal can only always appear "a retrospective arrangement."[17] The kernel of historicality is not itself historical. If there were a principle of continuity and homogeneity at the heart of history, it would no longer be history but the tautology of ironclad law, determined from the beginning. For history, minimally, there is *dis*continuity. Two series meet. Even if those series should be lawbound and determined, the contingency of their meeting guarantees that what results will not be entirely predictable from either. Something new ("really new") has occurred. At the heart of historicality is that empty window through which a shout comes, and in which the "time of the now"—in Benjamin's memorable phrase from the "Theses on the Philosophy of History"—"is shot through with chips of Messianic time" (255), like the unpronounceable letters of a God's name.

The genuine historical materialist, says Benjamin, will look for these Messianic chips of discontinuity in the apparently continuous. This involves thinking

> not only the flow of thoughts, but their *arrest* as well. Where thinking suddenly stops in a configuration pregnant with tensions, it gives that configuration a *shock* by which it crystallizes into a monad. A historical materialist approaches a historical subject only where he encounters it as a monad. In this structure he recognizes the sign of a Messianic cessation of happening, or, put differently, a revolutionary chance in the fight for the oppressed past. (254: my emphases)

"You see I use the word *arrest*," Stephen says to Lynch in the *Portrait* (*P* 222), describing the proper aesthetic emotions of pity and terror in an argument we shall examine further in chapter 4. This *arrest* opens up the possibility of a radical refusal, that "revolutionary chance in the fight for the oppressed past." Benjamin's choice of words seems at first peculiar: a fight for the oppressed *past*, rather than for a future without oppression? But the logic of the Messianic moment is precisely the *Nachträglichkeit* of the "retrospective arrangement": it produces a new past, new possibilities for the past, new and non-homogeneous narratives of the past. History is not a steady accumulation filling an essentially empty time; the historical moment is above all an arrest opening out into a number of quite irreducible and specific processes and levels, all of which may conceivably operate according to quite different regimes and temporalities. What this "historical materialism" reveals is not the representative and the unitary, but heterogeneity and struggle. In place of that one great goal towards which all things move, there are gaps, and they involve more than disagreement over a particular question, a *yes* versus a *no:* disagreement over what the very question is or should have been all along. Stephen is not just denying that history has a goal, or Deasy's goal, he is trying to throw Deasy off-balance, to shift the very ground of the contest under him. What the *Portrait, Ulysses,* and the *Wake* develop is an elaborate and novel thinking-through of that arrest of the Messianic within history, that kernel of history itself across several dimensions: the broader history of a nation, the "mysterious birth of the soul," a career (or at very least, two).

For Benjamin, that arrest is also a *shock.* The word has great importance in his thought: *shock* is the threatening but also salutary arrival of and improvisation on the new—the affect, we might say, attendant on Eliot's apparently affectless "introduction of the new (the really new) work of art." It is a term Benjamin makes much of in "The Work of Art in the Age of Mechanical Reproduction" and in particular "On Some Motifs in Baudelaire," where he derives it specifically from the experience of the metaphorical animalcule of Freud's *Beyond the Pleasure Principle* (297ff), which aims to remain in a state of equilibrium by minimizing the effects of external disturbance. That is, *shock* is the point at which the homeostatic model of the earlier Freudian metapsychology begins to break down, and the two principles Freud has hitherto largely seen as synonymous—pleasure principle and constancy principle—begin to drift apart. Shock forces the animalcule into a new and fortuitous state, no longer the stasis of minimal excitation, but a sort of open and indefinitely extensible crisis, maintained in strategic imbalance. What this arrest or shock opens up within the now is Messianic in the sense that it comes from an absolute outside, which is in no way foreseeable from within the series, either series, because it comes from the contingencies of their meeting. And this idea of a *beyond* of the pleasure principle does for Freud's thought exactly what shock does for the organism: pushes it into fertile crisis.

The novelty of Joyce's work is—among other things, as one always has to say—in the rigor with which it investigates the logic of this arrest, indeed turns it into a structural principle of an unprecedented sort through its deliberate and extraordinary multiplication of it. Here we can see the considerable distance which after all separates Joyce from Eliot. *The*

Wasteland looks forward, hope beyond hope, to a final payment of the debt: the moment of rain which will bring an end to the agonized arrest, the full stop to a history which is already over. True, it can scarcely believe this will ever eventuate, but it sees no other possible way out of the impasse—hence the intensity of its abjection. *Ulysses,* though, responds to the debt by proliferating it, borrowing against it, injecting it everywhere, into every moment, every action that it can. This is one of the functions of the schemas, as we have seen, and of Joyce's accelerating rewriting of earlier chapters to sow the proleptic seeds of those "retrospective arrangements" throughout them. Time becomes elaborately serial in its ramifications, with the moment scattered out into a myriad of other points and other times. If for the Eliot of *The Wasteland,* the nightmare is the arrest in which everything is open and nothing secured, then this may be just what Stephen is so fervently hoping to escape *into;* the nightmare *from* which he is trying to escape is the "one great plan" of a Deasy-directed history. From the rupture of arrest, other times and other possibilities open out. Or perhaps simply possibility itself.

This Messianic time is everywhere in *Ulysses.* It achieves its moment not in the long arcs of narrative symmetry and resolution, or promises of a New Bloomusalem (or even the infinitely more modest Bloom Cottage), or the promise of friendship and understanding between young man and older, Jew and apostate, aesthete and pragmatist, egoist and Samaritan (all those familiar moral couplings the book offers and then shrugs off), but in the gaps between series without common measure, so that what arises there has the nature of a problem rather than an answer, a diaspora rather than a homecoming. It works against narrative and its resolutions, even at the apparent moment of resolution itself. When the meeting towards which the entire novel has been heading eventuates, what we find is not the bridging of the differences between Bloom and Stephen (presumably to the enrichment of both, in a fond rewriting of *Ulysses* as fantasy), but their restatement and insistence. Perhaps even their exacerbation: repaying his host's generosity, Stephen sings an anti-Semitic song. Whatever his intentions in the matter, though, its main effect on Bloom is not offense but the triggering of a chain of thought about Milly, that other "Jew's daughter" (*U* 17.829ff). And they part, to one of the many extraordinary stylistic effects of "Ithaca":

How did they take leave, one of the other, in separation?
Standing perpendicular at the same door and on different sides of its

base, the lines of their valedictory arms, meeting at any point and forming any angle less than the sum of two right angles.

What sound accompanied the union of their tangent, the disunion of their (respectively) centrifugal and centripetal hands?
The sound of the peal of the hour of the night by the chime of the bells in the church of Saint George.

What echoes of that sound were by both and each heard?

By Stephen:
Liliata rutilantium. Turma circumdet.
Iubilantium te virginum. Chorus excipiat.

By Bloom:
Heigho, heigho,
Heigho, heigho.

(*U* 17.1220–34)

A symmetry: in the second-last chapter of the book, just as he was in its second, Stephen is sparring covertly with an older man, not letting down his guard completely, refusing that role of son even as the Homeric correspondences are suggesting he is playing it most. Again, two players of a game, or perhaps two different games, each playing to different rules or to different ends. And again, there is an opening between them, a doorway this time, through which various things, including a cat, can pass. A strict geometry: the two men standing perpendicular; between them, at right angles to the height of both, the base and sill of the door; and crossing that, at right angles to both men and doorbase, their hands extend to meet—somewhere just over that line which divides inside and out, Bloom's home and homeless Stephen, jewgreek and greekjew—in a handshake, emblem of all the disjunct, divergent syntheses of this vast book, a union in disunion: hands tangential, touching, but already moving in opposite directions, away from one another. And again, just as it did in the earlier chapter, a quite fortuitous and unconnected sound comes through that opening across which they are poised. St. George peals the hour, the bells sound in the text, stitching together with their very contingency these two different games.

And Stephen and Bloom each hear something different in the sound. For Stephen, it carries the words of the Prayer for the Dying, and with them the still-unresolved guilt over his mother's death; for Bloom, it is simply the song of its rhythm, like a nursery rhyme. What marks this strange union in disunion is not some communicated content which passes between them, for their words have all been subtly at cross purposes, like all those lines of the upright bodies, the doorframe and the clasped hands, all right angles, skew and never meeting. What unites them, if it is that, is something tangential and contingent, which by nothing more than fortuity crosses both their orbits.

We could follow this throughout "Eumaeus" and "Ithaca" as, for a couple of hours, each is a mirror to reflect the other's fantasy of himself, and then, just as willingly, everything is dissolved. Ever since the cabman's shelter, Bloom has been bubbling with ideas about what the meeting could lead to: Stephen has a good voice, Molly is a singer, Stephen knows Italian and can teach Molly the correct pronunciations, the Blooms have a spare room, they could even "inaugurate a series of static, semistatic and peripatetic intellectual dialogues" (U 17.964–65)—the New Bloomusalem meets the New Athens. In turn, Bloom willingly acts as audience for Stephen, confirming him as "professor and author," as he will later describe him to Molly (U 17.2270). Stephen, of course, has no intention of taking up any of Bloom's plans, and even the offer of a room for the night is declined "promptly, inexplicably, with amicability, gratefully" (U 17.955). Not even Bloom, perhaps, really believes they are any more than fond dreams: if there could have been a bed for the night at Eccles Street, there doesn't seem any particular place for Stephen in Bloom Cottage, that long-held fantasy reviewed once again before the fantasist goes upstairs to bed and Molly (U 17.1497ff)—indeed, there's barely room for Molly (U 17.1568–69, 1614). The stylistic balance and answer of the extraordinary phrases is forever turning what is happening between Bloom and Stephen into a hall of mirrors and the dizzying reflection of the abyssal space between and above them:

> What, reduced to their simplest reciprocal form, were Bloom's thoughts about Stephen's thoughts about Bloom and about Stephen's thoughts about Bloom's thoughts about Stephen?
>
> He thought that he thought that he was a jew whereas he knew that he knew that he knew that he was not. (U 17.527–31)

Fragments of ancient Irish verse call forth fragments of Hebrew: "*suil, suil, suil arun*"; "*kifeloch, harimon rakatejch m'baad l'zamatejch*" (U 17.727–29). The Irish gee, eh, dee, em call forth Hebrew ghimel, aleph, daleth, and "a substituted qoph" (has Bloom forgotten?) on "the penultimate blank page" of that copy of *Sweets of Sin,* discreetly laid cover down (*U* 17.731–40). Stephen hears "in a profound ancient male unfamiliar melody the accumulation of the past"; Bloom sees "in a quick young male familiar form the predestination of a future" (*U* 17.776–80). In their "quasisimultaneous volitional quasisensations of concealed identities," Stephen sees in Bloom the "traditional figure of hypostasis," Christ, while Bloom sees in Stephen the "traditional accent of the ecstasy of catastrophe" (*U* 17.781–86): not, in either case, a true self under the surface presented to the world, but for one, another metempsychosis, and for the other, the willed arrest of refusal.

Everywhere in this call and response things are skew, tangential. Bloom tells Stephen what to his mind constitutes a *good* advertisement, and cites one of his own:

What example did he adduce to induce Stephen to deduce that originality, though producing its own reward, does not invariably conduce to success?

His own ideated and rejected project of an illuminated showcart, drawn by a beast of burden, in which two smartly dressed girls were to be seated engaged in writing. (*U* 17.606–10)

But Stephen is not induced to deduce that at all, or at least give any sign of it, or make any comment on its success. Instead, he produces a story of his own, tenuously linked to what Bloom has just said by nothing more than the circumstance of a woman writing. A performance by an advertising man; now, a performance by a writer:

What suggested scene was then constructed by Stephen?

Solitary hotel in mountain pass. Autumn. Twilight. Fire lit. In dark corner young man seated. Young woman enters. Restless. Solitary. She sits. She goes to window. She stands. She sits. Twilight. She thinks. On solitary hotel paper she writes. She thinks. She writes. She sighs. Wheels and hoofs. She hurries out. He comes from his dark corner. He seizes solitary paper. He holds it towards fire. Twilight. He reads. Solitary.

What?

In sloping, upright and backhands: Queen's Hotel, Queen's Hotel, Queen's Hotel, Queen's Ho . . . (*U* 17.611–20)

In its deflection of the words of another, placing them in a new context and making them serve another desire, the story plays out in miniature exactly the processes of this exchange between Bloom and Stephen. The letter is all but without content: all it does is repeat the name on the letterhead, over and over, but in that becomes something like the pure token of an exchange. What it signifies is its own bare exchangeability: that some time in the future, in another series altogether, it may be received and read by another, someone unknown and unforeseeable, who will make of it something its writer could neither know nor foresee. And in turn, in the exchange between Bloom and Stephen this story immediately opens out into yet another series, one which Stephen presumably does not know about: Bloom's father's death:

What suggested scene was then reconstructed by Bloom?

The Queen's Hotel, Ennis, county Clare, where Rudolph Bloom (Rudolf Virag) died on the evening of the 27 June 1886, at some hour unstated, in consequence of an overdose of monkshood (aconite) selfadministered in the form of a neuralgic liniment composed of 2 parts of aconite liniment to 1 of chloroform liniment (purchased by him at 10.20 a.m. on the morning of 27 June 1886 at the medical hall of Francis Dennehy, 17 Church street, Ennis) after having, though not in consequence of having, purchased at 3.15 p.m. on the afternoon of 27 June 1886 a new boater straw hat, extra smart (after having, though not in consequence of having, purchased at the hour and in the place aforesaid, the toxin aforesaid), at the general drapery store of James Cullen, 4 Main street, Ennis. (*U* 17.621–32)

And even here, there is a collision of independent series, whose relationship is worrying in its apparent arbitrariness: what—say the repetitions of that "after having, though not in consequence of having"—*does* link hat and poison? Stephen goes on to recite, for the second time that day, *A Pisgah Sight of Palestine* or *The Parable of the Plums;* Bloom thinks of "certain possibilities of financial, social, personal and sexual success" which might come from making a collection of stories like that for the edification of junior grade students (which shows how little he's paying attention to what Stephen's actually *saying* in that obliquely scatological story), or from offering them to a magazine like *Titbits* (ditto), or from making them available for oral telling during long summer evenings (sigh) . . . (*U* 17.639–54).

This is a union which is all disunion, burgeoning and multiplying series beyond foresight, all tangents and switches of emphases which send the apparently centripetal zooming off again, like the orbits of the Comets Gilbert gives as the Symbol for "Ithaca." The comet—Ball's *Story of the Heavens*, or the *Handbook of Astronomy*, both on Bloom's bookshelves, will tell him this—has two possible orbits. One is elliptical, an elongated version of the orbits of the planets which eventually brings the comet back, even though it may be only after many years. The other is parabolic, where the second focus of the ellipse flees to infinity, the curve opens up, and the comet never returns.[18] The asyndetic promise: return or singularity, and the edge between them, on which Bloom's coin is still traveling:

> once in the summer of 1898 he (Bloom) had marked a florin (2/-) with three notches on the milled edge and tendered it in payment of an account due to and received by J. and T. Davy, family grocers, 1 Charlemont Mall, Grand Canal, for circulation on the waters of civic finance, for possible, circuitous or direct, return. . . .
>
> Had Bloom's coin returned?
>
> Never. (*U* 17.980–88)

In that gap, we find the possibility of a history which can now go somewhere else; in that disunion of hands, the glimmer of the paradox which underlies friendship, whether or not Bloom or Stephen are to meet again.[19] As the two men go out into the garden, a "celestial sign [is] by both simultaneously observed": "A star precipitated with great apparent velocity across the firmament from Vega in the Lyre above the zenith beyond the stargroup of the Tress of Berenice towards the zodiacal sign of Leo" (*U* 17.1210–13).

The refrains the bells bring to mind—the *Liliata rutilantium* and *Heigho! Heigho!*—have been recurring minor motifs during the day.[20] In particular, they are used to sign off the first chapter given to each character. Bloom hears the bells as he sits on the jakes at the end of "Calypso":

> A creak and a dark whirr in the air high up. The bells of George's church. They tolled the hour: loud dark iron.
>
> *Heigho! Heigho!*
> *Heigho! Heigho!*
>
> Quarter to. There again: the overtone following through the air. A third.
>
> Poor Dignam! (*U* 4.544–51)

—and Stephen, leaving the swimmers at the end of "Telemachus," is reminded again of his mother:

> He walked along the upwardcurving path.
>
> *Liliata rutilantium.*
> *Turma circumdet.*
> *Iubilantium te virginum.*
>
> The priest's grey nimbus in a niche where he dressed discreetly. I will not sleep here tonight. Home also I cannot go. (*U* 1.735–40)

Stephen may not be hearing church bells, as Bloom is. They are nowhere on the surface of the text, and we can guess that Stephen's mother has been much in his mind in this chapter anyway, though she has not been overtly mentioned since the opening scene on the top of the tower. Nevertheless, the suddenness with which those thoughts return may suggest some external stimulus has sparked them off. Whatever the case, as "Telemachus" and "Calypso" are parallel in time, these two events are approximately simultaneous, each at the end of its chapter and its hour. And as if to underline this, there is at least one other shared event in both chapters:

> A cloud began to cover the sun slowly, wholly, shadowing the bay in deeper green. It lay beneath him, a bowl of bitter waters. Fergus' song: I sang it alone in the house, holding down the long dark chords. Her door was open: she wanted to hear my music. Silent with awe and pity I went to her bedside. She was crying in her wretched bed, For those words, Stephen: love's bitter mystery. (*U* 1.248–53)

> A cloud began to cover the sun slowly, wholly. Grey. Far.
> No, not like that. A barren land, bare waste. Vulcanic lake, the dead sea: no fish, weedless, sunk deep in the earth. (*U* 4.218–20)

In each case, this cloud brings up thoughts of death, and for Stephen again the death of his mother. But even though this might be the same cloud for both, the distance the cloud has to cover between Sandycove and Eccles Street means it is not quite the same instant of time. (Something similar has happened with the throwaway announcing the coming of Elijah, against which various of the events of "Wandering Rocks" have been juxtaposed.) Even if Stephen is hearing bells pealing the quarter-hour, they are not the bells Bloom hears some seven or eight miles away on the other side of the city. But they do not have to be; a handshake some fifteen or sixteen hours and several hundred pages into the future will realign them.

What is happening here—what the shooting star in Vega does, and what all those tangential, glancing swerves of the conversation do, and the bells which counterpoint the handshake, and the cloud and the viceregal carriage, and that shout in the street or from the hockey field—is a set of *triangulations,* which immerse everything in a complex and sometimes highly unstable series of differences. What brings two disparate things together is not some internal and necessary identity of essence, but the external and fortuitous intervention of a third disparate thing, in a trajectory across them. This is not the unity given by the gaze of a character, even of God (or his stand-in, that narratological catachresis the "omniscient narrator"); what stitches things together in the last section of "Wandering Rocks" is not William Humble, Earl of Dudley, who knows nothing of the individuals he passes, but the mere passage of the carriage. The interpolations which layer the various sections one into another come from no one; they are performed by style itself, in the work of the words.[21] This is one of the things that extraordinary catechistic style of "Ithaca" emphasizes, in the sheer impossibility of those indefatigable sentences which painstakingly and patiently elicit data from what seems an infinite store, coming from and belonging nowhere, uninhabitable and unspeakable. Before it happens in the streets, or in the weather or a doorway, that triangulation happens in language. It is this to which we must now turn.

3

In the Language Machine

The *arrest* that increasingly comes to structure Joyce's writing sends any point elsewhere. Under it, the moment opens into a series of other moments, other events, scattered across the surface of the text. As we have seen, these are not narrative elements which could be taken out of their narrated order and reconstituted into the logical and chronological sequence of a story, but repetitions across a distance, frequently refusing to come together into narrative sequence. The event which is the arrest which opens them up does not exist entirely within the horizon of meaning: it *is* that horizon, and provides the very possibility of meaning. In this arrest, there is always something of the irruption of a non-sense.

The history Garrett Deasy sees as moving towards one great goal is replete with an already communicable and intelligible meaning—so much so that it has already in effect been communicated to him before the event and is now kept safe in his repertoire of Polonianisms. There are no surprises in Deasy history. To this stifling (and as Deasy shows, paranoid) overabundance of meaning, Stephen's response is the unforeseeable, the accidental, a noise: something which just happened to have been there, but could just as well not have been. That "shout in the street" communicates nothing. What it does is bind phatically, or unbind, bringing together or separating as the case may be. On the hockey field outside the window, the shout is one team's jubilation at a goal, and the other team's defeat. It does not matter that only one team might actually be producing the noise: the phatic is a demarcation, and thus hangs somewhere in the space *between* teams: here, the victors; there, the losers.

In this sense the shout is a quite impersonal utterance: these players are there producing it only because they are part of a situation which goes beyond them as individual persons, but which they are affirming at every stage. Within this situation, a number of games are simultaneously at play: hockey, obviously, but also things like the management of the school day, or the ways in which school authority works, and cutting across all of these the complex broader social interactions in which game and school take part. The hockey game occurs in a scheduled break in the school day; Cyril Sargeant has to write out his sums again before going out to play; Mr. Deasy the headmaster has told him to do it, and to check the results with Mr. Dedalus, the deputized junior and part-time teacher; there often seems to be trouble when Cochrane and Halliday are on the same side; Mr. Deasy is Stephen's employer. The hockey game whose sounds float in through the open window will be embedded in yet another situation and another game, the tacit sparring between the two men. At the heart of this shout of jubilation, there is a complex and—in the sense that it does not stem simply from the desires, intentions, or actions of the personages involved, but rather provides the horizon against which they desire, will, and act—impersonal machinery of the event. We shall find this everywhere in Joyce, even—or particularly—in that apparently most single-mindedly personalizing of all texts, the *Portrait*.

So here is the young Stephen, very young, at the first moment we see him, in the very beginning of the book which is his portrait. And right at what would seem to be the first flickerings of that consciousness we will think of as Stephen's own, there is no Stephen. Instead, there is a moocow, and then there is a nicens little boy named baby tuckoo. In the very next sentences, of course, we will find out what we have no doubt expected: he, Stephen, was baby tuckoo, and his father told him that story. Nevertheless: before there is Stephen, the child who is listening and taking this in, there is baby tuckoo, a Stephen-in-a-story: a place prepared for him which, as the lack of capitals suggests, is not even yet *quite* a name, just a generic noun and a noise of endearment.

What's more, the iterative mode of the first section suggests that this is not just a singular occasion but one of a repeated series, like singing the song or the change from warm to cold when you wet the bed. These moocows and baby tuckoos have been going on for a while, from before there is a sense of a Stephen there to register them as *his* and baby tuckoo as *him*. The usual conventions of children's tales would suggest that this is not even first of all baby tuckoo's story, but the moocow's: *Once upon a time there was a moocow,* rather than *Once upon a time there was a nicens little boy.* Only later, some little time after it has all begun, will the moocow meet baby tuckoo. Before there is a Stephen, he is ever so slightly displaced from the center of what the *Portrait* calls "his story," just as in a quite different fashion he will be displaced from the absolute center of the novel by its third-person narration. The tale begins as someone else's, and only becomes his: like the moocow, it goes down the road apace before meeting baby tuckoo. The opening of this story is about how baby tuckoo—like Stephen—is a late arrival onto the scene of a story which started without him.

It is not only his stories which work like this. From the beginning, the child is surrounded by a clamor of utterances from elsewhere: nursery rhymes, songs, homilies, dance, and the rhythms of clapping. These already carry with them so many of the relationships into which he will gradually come to know himself as having already been: family and its degrees of relation, age groupings, sexual difference—even, in the case of Dante's two brushes, politics. At first, all these wash over the child, but they constantly offer him places prepared for him to occupy, some of them even conflicting and contradictory. Stephen is to find himself already elsewhere, scattered out across other utterances, the utterances of others, incessantly triangulated. The road the moocow comes down is the one on which Betty Byrne sells sweets. His world takes shape in and through these triangulations.

These utterances make demands of him, demands that he take up these utterances as his own: *you are baby tuckoo; sing, Stephen, sing!; dance, clap; apologize, apologize.* This does not yet necessarily have anything to do with processes of understanding a content, only with repetition: say these sounds, do this action. In this, the question-and-answer form of "Ithaca" actually appears far stranger to a present-day audience than it did to Joyce's contemporaries, for whom catechistics, both religious and secular, would have been some of the earliest forms of learning. The ability to repeat required answers was part of early childhood training in the middle-class home, involving as discipline the memorization of material whose content the child could not yet have comprehended. The song about the roses "was his song" not because he has invented it, or even understands it, but because it is given to him to repeat. His first hesitant and altered repetitions confirm the receipt of what has already been given to him. The very imperfection of the repetition—the childish lisp, the as-yet-undeveloped fine-motor controls, the basic knowledge of the shape of a sentence coupled with the lack of comprehension of its content—acts as a countersignature: *yes, this is my song.* He is baby tuckoo, he is the little green place on which that impossible, cobbled-together green rose blossoms out of others' words, demands, sounds, rhythms. Before it is a matter of a mind brought into contact with the world for the first time, the child Stephen is an index of refraction of what passes over and around and through him, addressing him, calling on him, calling him into being. In the opening pages of the *Portrait*, we catch a glimpse of what the older Stephen, at the other end of the book, will characterize as the "slow and dark birth" of the soul (*P* 220), and what Fairhall will call the beginning of his "growing into history" (112).

Before they are the bearers of any content, these words and demands which wash over Stephen are events. Something happens. Never quite for the first time, always again, as the imperfect tense of the narration suggests: *he was, already, baby tuckoo; he sang that song, again; he danced, as he would.* The event is already serial, rhythmic like the refrain of *tralala*s he sings, or the clapping of hands, or the moocow which regularly comes down the road at bedtime, or the pattern of demand and response. Stephen has done something naughty and is hiding under the table, and his response is to turn his mother's demand and Dante's threat into a jingle: to pick out the pure form of demand and response from the exchange which is happening over his head, to hold it up as an object and turn it round, listening to the phrases answering each other:

> *Pull out his eyes,*
> *Apologise,*
> *Apologise,*
> *Pull out his eyes.*

> *Apologise,*
> *Pull out his eyes,*
> *Pull out his eyes,*
> *Apologise. (P 4)*

Here at the end of the first section of *Portrait*, in the child's fascinated concentration on the accident of the signifier and its repetitions in the event, we have an adumbration of Stephen as the artist-in-the-making promised by that generic title: the artist *as* early promise. As we shall see in the next chapter, this serial, rhythmic elaboration of the word-event will provide a massive underpinning for the entire novel.

And rhythm, of course, sets up difference. The stress, and the silence; the mark, and the background which, only now there is a mark, can be seen to surround it. Across these rhythms, Stephen is learning all sorts of differentiations, in spreading ripples. Wet the bed: first, it is warm; then it is cold. A bed without the oilsheet: a bed with the oilsheet. What marks the difference of the oilsheet is also its smell, which is *queer*. Other smells are *nice*, like that nicens baby tuckoo, or the nice smell of his mother. Within *nice,* there are differences, arranged by mores and lesses: his mother smells nicer than his father. There are other mothers-and-fathers: the Vances in number seven have a different mother and father. There are pairs who are not mother-and-father, like Uncle Charles and Dante, who are older than his mother and father, who in turn are older than their nicens little boy. The differences set up roles which in their very multiplicity can be separated from the given persons who fill them, reassigned: someday Stephen will grow up and marry Eileen from down the road, and the two will themselves become mother-and-father. And beyond family and neighborhood, other wider differences make themselves felt, played out as rhythm. This brush, that brush: the maroon brush and the green, Davitt and Parnell: the green of that rose is already embedded in a network of correspondences which Stephen will not comprehend for years yet. Even causalities are tapped out as rhythm: wet the bed, then warm, then cold; bring a tissue, have a cachou; apologize, pull out his eyes.

This concern with rhythm and the presignificative differentiations in tonalities and sound-colors is not simply discarded as the child begins to take on a command of language and meaning. It informs the *Portrait* in all sorts of ways. We could follow the workings of this seriality throughout the *Portrait;* as I shall argue in chapter 4, it structures Stephen's aesthetics and the functions they have in the novel. At school, Stephen will find that there are "nice sentences" in Doctor Cornwell's Spelling Book, which, though they are "only sentences to learn the spelling from" are "like poetry," with something of the fascination the refrains and songs afforded the younger Stephen:

> *Wolsey died in Leicester Abbey*
> *Where the abbots buried him.*
> *Canker is a disease of plants,*
> *Cancer one of animals.* (P 6–7)

Nice is the tonality of this pleasure where the sense is led by the differentiations of rhythm: trochaic scansion, or the difference between related words (Abbey/abbot), or even just between two letters (k/c): "It would be nice to lie on the hearthrug before the fire, leaning his head upon his hands, and think on those sentences" (*P* 7). Sitting in the train on the way home from Clongowes, he hears the guards locking the doors of the carriages: "they had silvery whistles and their keys made a quick music: click, click: click, click" (*P* 18), a sound which quickly merges with the sound of the wheels over the rails, the racing telegraph poles ("passing, passing") and the movement of the train itself ("on and on"), and even the larger alternation of term and holidays, in a festooning of rhythmic permutations which only eventually reveal the figure of the boy:

There were colored lanterns in the hall of his father's house and ropes of green branches. There were holly and ivy round the pierglass and holly and ivy, green and red, twined round the chandeliers. There were red holly and green ivy round the old portraits on the walls. Holly and ivy for him and for Christmas. (*P* 18)

(That ivy will return much later in the book, again connected to the rhythm of Stephen's travel [*P* 193]. We shall return to it in chapter 4.)

Words fascinate Stephen beyond or prior to their signification, charged with an affect which is always somewhat ambiguous and slightly unsettling:

and when the rector had stooped down to give him the holy communion he had smelt a faint winy smell off the rector's breath after the wine of the mass. The word was beautiful: wine. It made you think of dark purple because the grapes were dark purple and grew in Greece outside houses like white temples. But the faint smell of the rector's breath had made him feel a sick feeling on the morning of his first communion. (47)

Again, as with the boy's fascination in "The Sisters," it is the *word* which was beautiful. These are, after all, highly bookish grapes Stephen is invoking, grown in the soil of Doctor Cornwell's primer: they are commonplaces, like the snatch of wisdom immediately following, that the day of your first communion is the happiest day of your life. And just as with the narrator of "The Sisters," the fascination is accompanied by an inseparable queasiness, associated again with the body of a priest. In the *Portrait,* the sense of sin and unease is also linked to the knowledge of an earlier theft of altar wine by boys who were later found out by the smell of it on their breaths. Smell, smoke, grains, a film of moisture: an attenuated tangibility, everywhere and nowhere and all the more ineradicable for that, carrying with it both desire and loathing: the very images which will fill to the brim the adolescent Stephen's villanelle. Before it begins to signify—and even in the absence of signification—rhythm produces a series of singularities charged with affect.

And at the heart of this affect, these singularities in their repetition, there is something deeply impersonal. That "once upon a time" plunges us into the generic, the anonymous, the already-read. There are no quotation marks to offset this anonymity by giving it a situation, in which someone is telling a story to someone else at a particular time in a particular place; not even Joyce's habitual *tirez*. The narrative floats. In its generic anonymity, it is not even really first of all Stephen's father's story: Stephen's father is the way something already told reaches a Stephen who does not quite yet exist. And the story itself is not so much a communicable content as a *frame* for that Stephen-to-be to occupy, an invocation calling on him to respond. What it provides is not origins and destinations so much as a series of mobile and essentially empty positions of address, available to be occupied: an addresser, a role which is not to be confused with Stephen's father, who plays many roles (Stephen will later enumerate some of them for Cranly: "A medical student, an oarsman, a tenor, an amateur actor, a shouting politician, a small landlord, a small investor, a drinker, a good fellow, a storyteller, somebody's secretary, something in a distillery, a taxgatherer, a bankrupt and at present a praiser of his own past" [*P* 262]) but is here playing that of teller of a children's story; and an addressee, the role of listener. Already, here at the very opening of the story, in its address and the response it demands from a subject which is not yet quite there but is formed as subject in the response, it brings with it a complex series of issues of framing: heritage, tradition, legacy, paternity, origins and beginnings, publication, commentary, and elaboration: all of these things which will so trouble the older Stephen are there, implicit in the very procedures of the *Portrait,* from the beginning.[1]

The arrest is an event. Before that shout which comes through the schoolroom window or those utterances which bathe the infant Stephen have any content—or even in the absence of their having any paraphrasable content—what is important is the simple fact of their occurrence. Something happens, in its arrival something marks itself off. A modest epiphany: the empty *this moment, now.*

In this, we have something quite different from communication. Communications models use as their yardstick the presumed integrity of a communicable, paraphrasable, translatable content; anything which alters this can only be a leak in the pipes, a falling-away towards the meaningless. And yet, as such models readily admit, this full communication remains unattainable. What *does* occur in the world—the vagaries, intrusions, and divagations of the event—is treated as a set of secondary misadventures which befall meaning, rather than as anything constitutive of meaning; what *never* occurs becomes the fixed framework and ideal measure of all. But the shout in the street, the Joycean arrest, is not a lack or degradation of meaning: its very figure in Joyce is the epiphany, the sudden and uncalled-for access of an unforeseen meaning which has nothing to do with a communicated content, everything to do with that empty but indefinitely proliferating *now*. The arrest arrives from somewhere outside, and its non-sense opens the question of the frameworks within which meaning can occur. That is, it does not simply and smoothly provide another (presumably wider) framework which can incorporate both the former framework and the new intrusion into it, but makes framework itself into a question. The event *happens* before it communicates.

This is the sting in Denis Breen's postcard in *Ulysses*. What its content signifies remains one of those puzzles the book delights in. Indeed, what exactly is written on it is not altogether clear, let alone what that might signify. Bloom has met Josie Breen, and tactfully asked after her obsessional husband:

> She took a folded postcard from her handbag.
> —Read that, she said. He got it this morning.
> —What is it, Mr Bloom asked, taking the card. U.P.?
> —U.p: up, she said. Someone taking a rise out of him. It's a great shame for them whoever he is. (*U* 8.255–59)

A puzzling message—but what *is* it? Just what *is* written on the card? Joyce will often indicate direct citation-within-citation by italics (as he does, for example, when Joe Hynes reads out aloud H. Rumbold's letter to the High Sheriff of Dublin in "Cyclops" (*U* 12.415–31), complete with such writerly features as indented salutation and closing, misspellings and a lowercase *i* for the first-person pronoun). But there are no italics here. As Shari Benstock says of the interpolated letters of *Ulysses* in general, "the Joyce who abjured the use of quotation marks to set off speech, precisely *because* quotation marks set off quoted speech, [thereby produces] an amalgam of speech and narration that is difficult, if not impossible at certain junctures, to untangle" ("The Printed Letters in *Ulysses*" 424); among the "messes of mottage" which surround Shem in the "inspissated grime of his glaucous den" in *Finnegans Wake,* we find "quashed quotatoes" (*FW* 183.22–23, 179.25–26). The absence of markers suggests, without necessitating, that Bloom's "U.P.?" and Josie Breen's "U.p: up" may be more their perceptions or constructions of the postcard than faithful transcriptions. Bloom's "U.P.?" may belong either to his interior monologue or to his speech: either Bloom is mentally registering what is in front of him, or he is reading it aloud. In either case, there are two ways to read that question mark. The most obvious way is to take it as Bloom's, marking his puzzlement. But it is also possible that Bloom sees a question mark on the postcard, which would then be addressing a cryptic question to Breen, the punning "U." turning it into an invitation of just the sort we have been discussing: *U.P.? Is this you? Here's a role for you: are you going to take it up?*

Mrs. Breen's response, "U.p: up," opens up further possibilities. First of all, it may suggest that what the card *actually* says is "U.p: up": that is, she is correcting or completing Bloom's statement, or, if his reading of it was silent after all, simply saying what the card will let him confirm. This is the way the card's contents are referred to later in the text, by Bloom some lines later (*U* 8.274), by Alf Bergan and J. J. O'Molloy in "Cyclops" (*U* 12.1031, 1044), again by Alf Bergan in "Circe" (*U* 15.485), and finally by Molly in "Penelope" (*U* 18.2299—without the punctuation, of course). This is also the way in which the card is most frequently read in the critical literature: as if it says "U.p: up," which is the message to be deciphered. But in that case, Bloom's "U.P.?" is slightly puzzling: whether it's what he sees on the page or what he reads aloud, why would he miss the "up"? The second possibility is that the card actually just says "U.P.," as Bloom saw or read, and the "up" is the gloss everyone makes of it (glossing *over* the punctuation). This works somewhat better on the realistic level of the narrative, but still of course says nothing about the meaning.

The Gabler text, which I have been following here, reveals another layer of complications. According to it, where Bloom reads "U.P.," Josie Breen's response demotes the P to lowercase, and does away with the full stop that marks it as an abbreviation: "U.p: up." Her version of it is the one the text will follow from now on (except of course in "Penelope," where all punctuation marks will vanish): even Bloom will use it in his later reference. The 1922 Shakespeare and Company edition, on the other hand, has Mrs. Breen replying with the capital and the full stop, "U.P.: up" (*U:S&Co* 151), and Alf Bergan and J. J. O'Molloy using lowercase and full stop but now omitting the colon: "U.p. up" (*U:S&Co* 307), while in "Circe" Bergan will have it "U.p: Up" (*U:S&Co* 424) and in "Penelope" the lack of spacing reduces it simply to a repeated word "up up" (*U:S&Co* 696). The 1960 Bodley Head edition keeps these, though it has Bergan in Nighttown saying "U.p.: Up" (*U: BH* 575), now *with* the full stop.

In short, every version of the text gives at least four slightly different possible versions of what is on the card. Even though we appear to be reading over Bloom's shoulder when he glances at it, we do not really know what is there. And this is before we have even gotten to the question of what "U.P." or "U.P.?" or "U.p" or "U.p: up" or "U.P.: up" might signify once we had established which, if any, it might be. Something is blocked here: we do not have to assume a determinable content which would have passed from its unknown writer to a Breen who would recognize it. It works simply by *address:* from nobody and everybody, *You,* it says: *Breen.* Indeed, the joke might be precisely that anything cryptic on an anonymous and yet semi-public postcard is bound to drive the increasingly demented Breen into a frenzy of interpretation. Breen's claim that it is libelous becomes quite true after the event, in a self-fulfilling, performative sense: it drives him to precisely the sort of actions that lead others to think of him just what he seems to have thought the card was originally saying. There is no misreading this card, it seems. What is important is not the hidden and authentic heart of the message, but the more or less external effect the postcard has: circulated, received, acted on, arriving before any signification. Breen has even dreamt it, before the event:

—Woke me up in the night, she said. Dream he had, a nightmare.
Indiges.
—Said the ace of spades was walking up the stairs.
—The ace of spades! Mr Bloom said.
She took a folded postcard from her handbag.
—Read that, she said. He got it this morning. (*U* 8.251–56)

Before the ace of spades signifies anything, it is an arrival: inside the very house, an enigma is walking up the stairs to deliver itself to the sleeping, powerless Breen. You can hear the tread and already feel the consequences of it, as it disturbs not only his sleep and then the waking day to follow, but those of his wife and family. The ripples spread outwards, and we catch glimpses of them in their passage and their interference with other ripples: topic of gossip in the pub, part of a guilty fantasy in Nighttown, Molly's latenight thoughts.

Around the postcard, a number of tenuous, unsubstantiated, even unsubstantiable webs of signification will be spun. But the postcard itself is irreducible to signification: it is a thing, a mute object whose writing we cannot quite make out and do not even need to, and which is already marked by its passage through a number of hands before it now gets refolded and put back into that "untidy bag" of Josie Breen's (*U* 8.266), where it will continue to jostle with all sorts of other things. We keep running across a host of little objects circulating their way through *Ulysses:* personal effects like a bar of lemon soap, a hat, a pair of glasses, even fat pears and ripe shamefaced peaches blushing their way to Eccles Street

(*U* 10.305–23), or a condom which stays modestly in a pocketbook (*U* 13.877); and messages, letters, scraps of paper whose message may remain unread or irrelevant but which describe their own insistent trajectories throughout the book: that crumpled throwaway Bloom tosses into the Liffey to bob downstream, or the more modest trajectory of the Martha Clifford letter as it moves from Bloom's pocket to his newspaper to his pocket to his hat, or another postcard which this time has "no message evidently" (*U* 16.490); a letter on foot-and-mouth disease with some of the blank paper at the end of the page torn off to make way for a poem (*U* 3.405, 7.519), the sandwichboarded letters of H.E.L.Y.S. trudging their way in single file around Dublin, or the glimpse of a "strip of torn envelope [peeping] from under the dimpled pillow" which Molly will discreetly withdraw from further circulation (*U* 4.308). In particular, the chapter in which Bloom reads the Breen postcard is full of them: "Lestrygonians," where the schemas' Scene (The Lunch), Organ (Esophagus) and Technic (Peristaltic) are forever playing off the processes of meaning and digestion: meaning as digestion.

Or rather, meaning as *in*digestion: "Indiges," thinks Bloom, in ready explanation of Breen's only partly digestible dream of the ace of spades, and prompted no doubt by the rumblings of his own stomach. What "Lestrygonians" emphasizes is the ways in which all these objects are residual: leftovers from something else, negligible in content, or worse, dejecta, excreta. If signification is a matter of appropriation and assimilation into systematicity, then meaning, in as much as it has to do with the event, is always confronted with the unassimilated and the nonfunctional, the purely circumstantial. Right at the very beginning of the chapter, those sweets Bloom sees a Christian brother buying may be bad for his boys' tummies (*U* 8.1–3). At the door of the Burton restaurant, Bloom's gorge rises at the sight of the customers "wolfing gobfuls of sloppy food" (*U* 8.655). In a lane, "a ravenous terrier choked up a sick knuckly cud on the cobblestones and lapped it with new zest" (*U* 8.1031–32). Even the seagulls cannot swallow "Elijah thirtytwo feet per sec is com" (*U* 8.57–58). Meaning operates on the edges of systematicity, on the uncertainties between inside and outside. This is why in "Lestrygonians" it is shadowed everywhere by physical disgust: the subject is not so much expressed *by* the event of meaning as expressed *from* it, like an exudate. (As we shall see in chapter 4, this is already something the *Portrait* has explored.) Objects come across all sorts of signifying systems and temporarily take on all sorts of possible meanings from them, but they are fully absorbed into none of them and pass through all: the scrap of paper bobs its way downstream, reappearing in all sorts of contexts in the stream of the narrative. These objects slip in and out of signification according to the contingencies of their conjunctions: here, coming upstream to meet Elijah, is the three-masted schooner *Rosevean* from Bridgewater with bricks (*U* 10.1008–1009) which Stephen earlier saw from the beach at Sandymount (*U* 3.503–505). They have a tenuous hold on signification: we cannot even simply say they *have* signification, for they *arrive into* such a system, which invests them with signification only in retrospect: the *Rosevean* will only later become the ship which has already carried the sailor Murphy into Dublin. These are the objects which triangulate, in their very fortuity. What they mean is not the content they bring with them, but what they will enable in that triangulation.

Such an object plays a game of hide-and-seek with signification. More radically, it functions asyndetically, through the constitutive ambiguity of its signification. It does not offer us a face behind which a truth is already patiently waiting to be read, but a tenuous promise which balances between signification and brute (and mute) facticity. The logic of these objects is not that of the object of knowledge: we cannot understand what these letters are doing in terms of a model of communication, say, or the throwaway as an example of advertising or persuasion; we have to take them as event, in their absolute singularity and contingency, for that is exactly what makes them able to link disparates in this way, to countersign across series. To take them as manifestations of a wider underlying meaning would be to risk reading them as Breen does, lending them a speech which can only be paranoid. But even in "Circe," where everything gains a voice, what we have is not that dream of medieval exegesis, the great seamless book of the world, but a vast clamor of scattered and overlapping voices. When Stephen muses on those "signatures of all things I am here to read" in "Proteus" (*U* 3.2), he is marking the same distance from this as the shout in the street marked from Mr. Deasy's great purpose to which all things move.

The object is legible in the very tenuousness of its legibility, and in the *dis*continuity of objects which set off irreducibly from one another. To read a new object is always to bring in the possibility of other contingent and unforeseen ways of reading what one has already read, or what one already knows. We come back to those enigmas and puzzles which are keeping us dutifully busy: what Joyce is describing in that boast is not only the Joycean text, but *the Joycean object*. Joyce *treats language itself as*

object in just this sense, forever pulverizing it into *pre*significative elements which combine in serial and contingent ways. When Bloom takes
the throwaway from that somber young man outside Lemon's sweetshop,
he is momentarily startled:

> Heart to heart talks.
> Bloo . . . Me? No.
> Blood of the Lamb. (*U* 8.7–9)

For an instant, it is as if he is being addressed personally by the pamphlet.
Due to an accident of orthography, something which is not even quite a
word but just a sequence of letters, that partial object *Bloo*, rapidly
traverses two different series. One of them, connected with the religious,
has already occurred in "Lotus Eaters" and "Hades," and in a more secular form in the Agendath Netaim advertisement Bloom picked up at the
pork butcher's that morning (*U* 4.154–63, 191–99); it will be expanded
vastly in the eschatological and apocalyptic fantasies of "Circe." The
other series is on the name, and is itself already multiple: at various other
parts of the text it will yield the sequence Bloom—Virag—Henry
Flower—flowers—flows—Molly—. . . , or the signature to a poem (*U*
17.401), anagrams and an acrostic (*U* 17.404–16), its musical decomposition throughout "Sirens" ("A husky fifenote blew. / Blew. Blue Bloom is
on the"; "Jingle. Bloo. / Boomed crashing chords" [*U* 11.5–6, 19–20]), or
the L. Boom of the *Telegraph*'s report on the funeral (*U* 16.1260).[2] The
word is something to be taken apart and recombined, given new and
sometimes quite unexpected meanings as it migrates—like everything else
in this wheeling, ambulatory, fidgety Dublin where everybody and everything is coming down a road—across or through all sorts of other series
and systems of significations. The wanderings of *Ulysses:* a metempsychosis of the word as object, even of the word *metempsychosis* itself,
which in Bloom's mind readily becomes confused with *metamorphosis* to
give us a string of Ovidian references, and in Molly's version of which
("met him pike hoses" [*U* 8.112, 13.1281–82, 17.686]) we can see loom-
ing dimly a meeting at four, the shape of Boylan and those new tan shoes,
and even those frillies on which the heroine of *Sweets of Sin* will spend her
husband's dollar bills, all for Raoul (*U* 13.1280–81). . . . The word—or
rather the letter, for it does not even yet have to be a word—is itself event,
a window through which a shout comes, as an interpolation or possible
triangulation from another system entirely. What "Wandering Rocks"
suggests with the trajectories and intersections of its characters, the next

chapter, "Sirens," as its overture insists, will perform on the level of the phrase, the word, the melody, the sound.

The word as event. In Joyce, utterance is not to be assimilated to the sentence (a regularity generated by a prior system of rules), or to the proposition (the transmissibility of an essentially paraphrasable content). Those doubtless lay their claim in all sorts of ways, but only—quite literally—after the event: the condition of their possibility is the very simple one that, before anything else, utterance must *happen*. In this respect, like the Foucault of *The Archaeology of Knowledge*, the Joycean text is fascinated with the positivity and contingency of the utterance-event, and the stochastic rather than systemic logic of this contingency: the ways in which utterances cluster, spread, and are delimited; their points of diffraction, connection, and differentiation; the ways in which they form practices which are never entirely separable from other non-discursive practices; their existence within and against certain multiple relations of power; and—to stop there—the positions of enunciation they open.

To characterize the utterance in Joyce as *discourse* in this sense is to emphasize what we have already seen: that the utterance does not first of all express or belong to a subject, but that subjects arise within discourse, marked out by and in utterance. But there are of course other quite different senses in which that term *discourse* is used, some of them much more likely in talk about Joyce. The term has at least two broad senses in narratology, and one of these includes as a particular case one of the richest and most frequently invoked concepts in Joyce criticism, *free indirect discourse*. This broad use of *discourse* has little at all to do with Foucault's; it comes largely from Emile Benveniste, for whom *discourse* is a type of utterance bearing traces of the enunciative situation in which it is made, such as deictic shifters and certain marked roles of addresser and addressee (Benveniste 67–68, 110; Prince 21). Of course, Foucault and narratology are not talking of the same thing when they use the same word. But that difference is precisely what Foucault's sense of the word describes: *discourse* is *itself* a word-object which has been taken up and used in a number of different series, each with its own specific histories and conditions of use, its own economies of signification and domains of application. The Foucauldian warning is altogether appropriate: rather than see the word as only the marker of the continuities of a concept which underpins and guarantees it, we should think of it as discontinuous, with its own multiple specificities and materialities (Foucault, *Archaeology* 8–11, "The Order of Discourse" 67–69). And as we have seen, the Joycean

text too is on every level all about what happens when causally autonomous series intersect. It works, in particular, on the edges between these
two series within the word *discourse,* where each countersigns the other.
Joyce's writing is always concerned with both of these: with the whirl of
utterances which pass over and through and around us, and at the same
time with the ways in which, within this blizzard of events, something like
a subject is tenuously marked off, pointed to from elsewhere.

For classical and structural narratologies, free indirect discourse is usually characterized by two broad features: the manifestation of some of the
characteristic features of a speaker's enunciation, and at the same time an
absence of the tags which might formally demarcate that enunciation from
another in which it is embedded, such as quotation marks, verbal formu-
lae such as *she said,* grammatical changes of tense or person (Prince 34–
35). Two series collide. Since Kenner's *Joyce's Voices,* the *Portrait* has
provided what is almost the canonic Joycean example of free indirect discourse. When Uncle Charles repairs to the outhouse, that *repairs* is not the
lapse in authorial sensibility Wyndham Lewis gladly took it for, but the
way Uncle Charles himself would describe it if asked. Kenner memorably
describes this as having words "in such delicate equilibrium, like components of a sensitive piece of apparatus, that they detect the gravitational
field of the nearest person." A word which Uncle Charles "need not even
utter is there like a gnat in the air beside him, for us to perceive in the same
field of attention in which we note how 'scrupulously' he brushes his hat."
Kenner's phrasing of the Uncle Charles Principle is that *the narrative
idiom need not be the narrator's* (Kenner, *Voices* 16, 17, 18). In the flickering triangulation performed by that gnat of a word, there is an Uncle
Charles.

Or almost, for in its formulation all of this clearly seems to depend on
certain psychologizing and personalizing assumptions about what characters and narrators are, and their relationships to each other as the sources
of various enunciations. *We know that this phrase belongs to this character because it is just the sort of thing that character would say.* We know
the character before the phrase arrives, and in the light of that prior
knowledge we can then judge the phrase according to its plausibility. Even
if it should effect some sort of reversal in the character (the trusted helper
becomes the treacherous opponent, the overlooked confidante becomes
true lover), the phrase can tell us only what we already know, even if that
should be in retrospect.

One response to this would be that it is nothing more than circular
reasoning, something like those schoolroom exercises in literary apprecia-

tion which give us an unseen poem, ask us to read the author's intentions from it, and then judge whether it really achieves those intentions. It is to get things the wrong way round: what we are given is not characters but words, among whose effects we can include those of "character." "Character" is something we have to explain in terms of words, not vice versa. All of which is true enough, but as an answer it risks moving altogether too fast, and thus missing what is going on here. A clue might be in that very reversal, *That's just the sort of thing this character* would *say:* what the hasty answer passes over is the quite obvious point that nobody is in fact taken in by this supposed priority of character. "Everybody knows" these are just fictional characters. To talk of what a character *would* say or *might* say is not at all inconsistent with knowing full well that characters are produced as effects of the text, in the mode of an "as if." If we stop here, we would appear to have something close to the classic disavowal that is fetishism—*I know that this is not the case, but nevertheless I will behave as if it were*—and indeed there would be much to make of this in *Ulysses* in particular, in both the Freudian and Marxist senses of the fetish.[3] But it goes further: what if we were to take this "as if" seriously, as the suggestion that character is *produced as* something *already there*? What is character in *every* sense but a typology—an impression, a memory, the already-written through which alone the book is readable? *Repairing* to the outhouse is an Uncle Charles phrase not because we already know the soul of a man who exists only as a few dozen words in a novel, but because we "know the type," this loose literary-familial-psychological category which functions as a cultural reference point for the text.

Kenner puts his finger on this exactly in speaking about the apparently much clearer contrast between what belongs to "character" and what to "narrator" which is afforded by the passages of what we shall continue to call interior monologue:

> an odd conclusion emerges: that the domain of the interior monologue is actually external. It is the idiom of the perpetual outsider. "Be a warm day I fancy. Specially in these black clothes feel it more. Black conducts, reflects (refracts is it?) the heat" [*U* 4.78–80]. Bloom is outside his theme, fumbling for its knob: the word he can't think of is "absorbs." (Kenner, *Voices* 32–33)

Bloom inhabits vast swathes of his own utterances as a visitor,[4] an outsider looking in on that imagined realm of the felicity of the one who would be their master. This is, after all, part of the attraction Stephen has for him.

That Bloom should be a Jew, a professional traveler, an autodidact, a cuckold, and the child of an immigrant—all of these are easily recognized tropes of displacement from a center, and all of them are multiple refractions of, or refracted in, a basic relationship to discourse: Bloom's utterances, the discourses on which he draws and within which he moves, are not his own. Or rather, Bloom's words are their own in just the sense in which the story of the moocow coming down along the road is Stephen's story. They neither begin nor end with him, but traverse him and offer a tentative, unstable, and ultimately empty position, all without even necessarily impinging on his understanding. With "absorbs," he reaches for a word he cannot quite find at the moment, lost as it is in a thicket of similar words which in this light are not quite as distinct as he knows they could be. *Metempsychosis* runs into *metamorphosis,* and *parallel* is the metamorphosis of *parallax,* from that "[f]ascinating little book . . . of sir Robert Ball's" (*U* 8.110–13), *The Story of the Heavens,* on the bookshelf at home in Eccles Street (*U* 17.1373). In this externality, Bloom is always elsewhere than where he is: not as the lack of a substantiality he should have, so much as a perpetual overbidding of any and all positions he might come to occupy.

But this externality of discourse does not belong to Bloom alone. While with Bloom it leads to some of the most comic passages of *Ulysses,* in itself it never functions simply as a satiric (or conversely approving: we recall Iser's point about the externality of all those Homeric correspondences) marker of Bloom's relative lack of education, his distance from Stephen's intellectualizing and aestheticizing, his pragmatism or common sense. Externality is just as much a feature of Stephen's utterance, whose monologue is characterized by its voracious and rapid rhythm of borrowings from scholasticism, philosophy, theology, and literature. Almost every sentence in "Proteus" ransacks the cultural archive Stephen has at his disposal: if it happens to be a more rarefied and scholarly typology than the ones Bloom tends to draw on, and if its effects are not as broadly comic, the processes at work are not essentially different. Stephen inhabits a number of discourses as one who feels the need to assert his mastery of them before others and himself, but always marks himself off as in excess of these and not confined by them. If the lamp of Aristotle or Aquinas should prove faulty, he tells the *Portrait*'s dean of studies, he will fix it or get another (*P* 202); when pressed in the library, he is prompt to declare he does not believe his own theories about Shakespeare (*U* 9.1065–67). What he is doing with this archive, this typology of the remembered, is not faithful and intact transmission, but countersignature deflecting it to other uses. And given that the effects of such a performance are not calculable, we should not be too hasty even to call these *his own* uses. Or even, for that matter, Joyce's: "My head," he wrote to Harriet Weaver, "is full of pebbles and rubbish and broken matches and lots of glass picked up 'most everywhere'" (*L1* 167).

That the domain of the interior monologue is external is not a mark of its artifice, or its fall from a genuine and inevitably lost interiority. In that externality, we see again why Joyce so insistently maintained a distance from and rivalry towards Freud's work: though it comes from different sources and proliferates in other series, with the interior monologue we find again that radical exteriority which, for Freud, lies at the heart of the psyche itself, that *Kern unseres Wesen* which is forever its internal foreign territory (*New Introductory Lectures* 88). Lacan pithily characterizes this as *extimacy*, that "intimate exteriority" (*Ethics* 139) which is "in you more than you" (*Four Fundamentals* 263). *I think where I am not, therefore I am where I do not think* is one of Lacan's many ways of rendering Freud's *Wo Es war soll Ich werden* (Lacan, *Écrits* 166; Freud, *New Introductory Lectures* 112). And here, suggests Žižek,

we have one of the possible definitions of the unconscious: *the form of thought whose ontological status is not that of thought,* that is to say, the form of thought external to the thought itself—in short, some Other Scene external to the thought whereby the form of the thought is already articulated in advance. The symbolic order is precisely such a formal order which supplements and/or disrupts the dual relationship of "external" factual reality and "internal" subjective experience. (*Sublime Object* 19)

I am always to one side of where I am: in the words of others, in the signs and noises on either side of me as I walk down the street, in the common sense on which I act or the bits and pieces of Aquinas and Aristotle from which I try to formulate a new aesthetic or the detritus of the day which settles everywhere: *four o'clock, agenbite of inwit, Dearest Papli, the cracked lookingglass of a servant, For him! For Raoul!, Rose of Castile, Honoured sir i beg to offer my services, IN THE HEART OF THE HIBERNIAN METROPOLIS* . . . It is strangely enough even when Stephen is at his most concentratedly allusive, in "Proteus," that we can approach closest to him and feel most for him. The arch displays of erudition to no one in particular, the labored jocularity about phone calls to Edenville, the rapid switches from Aristotle to kabbala to Lessing and Boehme to the *Vaticinia Pontificum:* place these against the recurrent memory of his mother's deathbed and they all suddenly invert themselves to suggest that the performance is a way—and never more than a briefly successful one— of keeping at bay the unbearable guilt and loss he feels and which still, almost a year after her death, keeps him from even really beginning the process of mourning.[5] What the externality of interior monologue reveals is not just a matter of the limits of a literary technique of representation, behind which some very familiar psychologistic ideas of character could again recede into a comfortable interiority, but the debt of extimacy which is constitutive of the subject itself. And this lets us approach a related figure common to nearly all forms of narratology, highly problematic in general but never more so than in Joyce's writing: the figure of the *narrator*.

The narrator is usually conceived on an analogy with character, as Kenner's phrasing of the Uncle Charles Principle makes clear: *the narrative idiom need not be the narrator's.* And again, what this amounts to is, *We know that this phrase belongs to this narrator because it is just the sort of thing such a narrator would say:* it is, in short, in character. Effects of character come about when a series of repeated proper names or pronouns provide the point of condensation for a psychologistic typology. Something similar happens with the personalized narrator, except the point of condensation here lies not in the names but in the text's *deictics:* those marks of a perhaps quite fictive situation of enunciation which would— now once again in Benveniste's sense of the term—designate the text as *discourse.* We can make the distinction in a nutshell with Jakobson's well-known model of language-functions (350–52): effects of character are clustered around certain of a text's *referential* functions (those nouns and pronouns which seem to objectify and point confidently outwards to a positivistic knowledge of real, objectified "human character"), whereas effects of narrator come about through the functions of *address*—the emotive, the conative, and the phatic.

The innovation of interior monologue is not that it provides the most accurate microscope yet on the human object, but that it *de*-objectifies— and precisely because the subject of the interior monologue is external to itself, at the mobile, overdetermined but never entirely determinate, proliferating intersection of series. Something very similar happens with the effect of narrative voice in Joyce, which also becomes multiple and serial and no longer gives the impression of being the expression of a single or consistent source: free indirect discourse, in other words. In this sense, *free indirect discourse is to narrator what interior monologue is to character.* And in this respect, the innovation of *Ulysses* is not so much interior monologue (which in Dujardin remains realist and psychological), as *the realization of the complementarity of free indirect discourse and interior monologue*. As *Ulysses* progresses, this realization will disrupt so many of the pairings on which narratology has classically depended: internal and external, certainly, and with them narrating and narrated, *fabula* and *sjuzhet*, *histoire* and *discours*, diegetic telling and mimetic showing, kernel and satellite, closure and openness, figure and ground . . . To borrow Žižek's formulation, interior monologue opens that "form of the subject whose ontological status is not that of the subject," but exploded out into that busy, commonplace Other Scene which has been there all along, and which free indirect discourse makes strictly irrecuperable to any psychology, including any narrator's.

By and large, narratology has been content to discuss interior monologue and free indirect discourse in terms of that psychologizing "as if," and so has often been unable to cope with the radicality of Joyce's use of them. Rather than a principle of continuity, *narration* tends in general to be a negative category, a list-like remainder comprising everything left over after the various forms of citation—direct speech and interior monologue—have been marked off and identified. As a result, it may include a large number of actually quite disparate processes, including unstable forms such as free indirect discourse which always threaten to disrupt that distinction. One way of giving all these disparate features an apparent unity is of course to attribute the narration to a personalized Narrator, who is not one of the characters but is inevitably seen in terms which are at least covertly characterological—*point of view, focalization, voice*.[6] The potential divergences between dialogue and interior monologue, for example, can be seen as demonstrating the clash between what a person says and means, public and private, outward personality and real person. Divergences between narration and dialogue or interior monologue measure with irony the gap between the self-deception of the character and the genuine knowledge of the Narrator, who sees through all points of view, and harmonizes all other voices as citations within its own, and thus guarantees the unity and coherence of the text as it works towards its one great goal.

It is common to see the first six chapters of *Ulysses* in this way, as made up of three broad but easily distinguished tonalities: interior monologue, direct speech, and a framing narration.[7] First we get three chapters which introduce us to Stephen and the characteristic patterns of his reported speech and interior monologue; then we get three which backtrack and tell us what Bloom has been doing all this while, and give us the chance to become familiar with his quite different styles of speech and interior monologue. By the time both Bloom and Stephen are out in the streets, crossing each other's paths and working their way towards what they do not yet know will be their meeting at the end of the day, we are able to distinguish the stylistic features associated with each, and have been given a firm ground bass on which later chapters will be able to make increasingly elaborate stylistic variations. And the first of these occurs immediately after those two sets of three chapters, in the first chapter Stephen and Bloom share, though its comedy of opening and closing doors means that they are forever just missing being on stage together. Something new enters through those doors: "Aeolus" is punctuated by headings which resemble the headlines of a newspaper. This poses a problem for any assumption of a psychologistic Narrator: the headlines are quite definitely not the sort of thing the narrator of the previous chapters might say. Indeed, they are not the sort of thing anyone would *say*: they belong to writing rather than speech, and what's more to a form of writing, journalistic subediting, which is generally quite anonymous and relies much more on generic convention than on any form of individual attribution—no less so when the headlines of "Aeolus" are increasingly idiosyncratic versions of the form.

One very frequent way of trying to get around this, starting with Hayman and since taken up by others,[8] is to divide the narrative function among *two* personages: the Narrator is now joined by an Arranger, who adds increasingly odd and flippant comments which seem to go quite unnoticed by the Narrator. If the Narrator started off as an attempt to unite a number of disparate features under the one hypothesis, it now shows itself in turn incapable of accounting for all such features, and is forced into a multiplication, a new pseudo-Narrator for each feature the first was unable to explain. What is reintroduced at a second remove is the very proliferation the original hypothesis was intended to unify. And this time, once the proliferation starts, there is no stopping it. Out of all the discursive features which distinguish "Aeolus" from the chapters before it, the headlines are only the most obvious to the glance. For both the Gilbert and Linati schemas, the windy Art of "Aeolus" is Rhetoric, and the chapter displays "practically every rhetorical figure outlined by Quintillian and the classical rhetoricians" (Gifford 635). These figures do not simply affect the narration, they fill the dialogue and interior monologues as well, and thus blur the apparent distinctness of Narrator from both of these. Should we not therefore insist that there is a Rhetorician at work here as well, pulling the strings of characters, Narrator and Arranger alike? Virtually every chapter offers its variations. Surely we could make a case for the existence of a Choreographer in "Scylla and Charybdis," who would be responsible for the "step a sinkapace forward on neatsleather creaking and a step backward a sinkapace on the solemn floor" and the "Swiftly rectly creaking rectly rectly he was rectly gone" (*U* 9.5–6, 969), movements which are simultaneously literal descriptions of what characters are doing, figures of the ebb and flow of conversation and the dialectic of argument, and, in their own chiasmic inversions and onomatopoeic effects, direct performances of what they say; they are also quite unmissably different, in every respect from sheer typography up to effect, from anything attributed to an Arranger in "Aeolus." And the same could be said for virtually any chapter, to all of which the Gilbert and Linati schemas assign a different Technic. We would need an Interpolator in "Wandering Rocks," an Exaggerator in "Cyclops," a Pasticheur in "Oxen of the Sun," and paired Catechist and Catechumen for "Ithaca," at very least. In each case, the economy of narration is quite different: does this suggest that finding a common Narrator across a number of chapters can be done only at the cost of ignoring the differences—of not reading closely enough? The narratorial differences among the first six chapters are certainly much smaller than those between any consecutive two of the later chapters, but they are there and significant. "Telemachus," for example, uses adverbial modifiers of its speech tags with a frequency not matched in any other chapter (Kenner, *Joyce's Voices* 9–70; Lawrence 45): "he said sternly," "he cried briskly," "he said gaily," "Stephen said quietly," "he said frankly," "he cried thickly," "Stephen said gloomily." Does it actually tell us anything if we attribute this to a Speech-Tag Adverbialist? The hypothesis of a personalized Narrator can be sustained only at the cost of a potentially endless multiplication of entities, epicycle upon epicycle, as asyndetic as anything they were meant to explain. As Kenner points out elsewhere, the modernist and in particular the Joycean text is one in which "no uttering voice need be specified, nor unified. (Who asks, who answers in grave polysyllables, the questions in the seventeenth section of *Ulysses*?)" (*Homemade World* xiii). To personalize narration as the work of a Narrator is not to give an explanation, but simply to ask the wrong questions of narrative.

So we could strengthen the Uncle Charles Principle, at least initially, into something like what Foucault (speaking of that non-narratological sense of the word *discourse*) calls a principle of exteriority: *the narrative idiom can no more be a Narrator's than a character's can be just the character's*. The instability and complexity of *Ulysses'* use of free indirect discourse goes well beyond what one can achieve by *adding* to the backstage crew of discrete and distinguishable Narrators, Arrangers, Choreographers, and Catechists, each with their own task to perform and their own audible voice or legible signature. Narrators and their colleagues are effects, not sources; they explain nothing. At most, they are a matter of subtraction: a ghostly residue, the tenuous and momentary effect of something crystallizing out of the solution only to dissolve back into it at the next moment.

We need to look at the complexity of this in a particular case. Let us take one of Kenner's examples, the chapter of *Ulysses* which almost dutifully falls into two asymmetric but roughly equal halves, the first of which is dominated by free indirect discourse and the second by interior monologue.

"What is the first half of 'Nausicaa,'" asks Kenner very shortly after postulating the Uncle Charles Principle, "but Gerty MacDowell's very self and voice, caught up into the narrative machinery?" (*Joyce's Voices* 17). Clearly, the first half of the chapter invites us to think of it as Gerty's: in narratological terms, it is internally focalized, for example. Just as clearly, though, the third-person pastiche of romance novels and serials from women's magazines of the day says this is also *not* simply Gerty's. One of the most common critical reactions to this *non*-originality is to read it in moral and inevitably condemnatory terms: as Gerty's self-portrait, but one which unwittingly reveals itself and her as *un*original. This Gerty is in thrall to an enervated and enervating mass culture which has infiltrated itself into her very being, so that she is incapable of reacting to anything except through cliché and stereotype. The most notorious example of this is undoubtedly Q. D. Leavis's condemnation in *Fiction and the Reading Public*:

> for Gerty MacDowell every situation has a prescribed attitude provided by memories of slightly similar situations in cheap fiction, she thinks in terms of clichés drawn from the same source, and is completely out of touch with reality. Such a life is not only crude, impoverished, and narrow, it is dangerous. And it is typical of the level at which the emotional life of the generality is now conducted. (245)

Chris Baldick's reaction is to the point:

> Such a method of making confident sociological statements about the attitudes of the "generality" upon purely literary evidence is itself crude, narrow, and dangerous. . . . And it is surely remarkable

that Leavis should pronounce upon the inner thoughts of millions on the sole basis of—slightly similar situations in expensive fiction. (183)

Or to *a* point, for like Leavis, Baldick has no problems in attributing this first half of the chapter to Gerty; the only difference is that he affords this Gerty and her tastes sympathy rather than scorn. But what if this section is *not* simply Gerty—or not even Gerty *and* the discourses on which she draws? What if this figure of Gerty is something which arises only through a much more complex triangulation? Indeed, as the narrative will very quickly ask, who *is* Gerty? (*U* 13.78).

We shall not meet her immediately. Instead, we find once more a window:

> The summer evening had begun to fold the world in its mysterious embrace. Far away in the west the sun was setting and the last glow of all too fleeting day lingered lovingly on sea and strand, on the proud promontory of dear old Howth guarding as ever the waters of the bay and, last but not least, on the quiet church whence there streamed forth at times upon the stillness the voice of prayer to her who is in her pure radiance a beacon ever to the stormtossed heart of man, Mary, star of the sea. (*U* 13.1–8)

Inside the church, a men's temperance retreat is in progress. Outside the church, this summer evening is lifted straight from—well, the chapter will name some of them: the Princess Novelette's Woman Beautiful page, and the *Lady's Pictorial,* and *Pearson's Weekly,* and *The Lamplighter* by Miss Cummins, author of *Mabel Vaughan* and other tales (*U* 13.110, 151, 291–92, 633–35); there are others.[9] Between the two, a window through which a noise comes (again carrying the divine name as its signature), to be taken up by what is on the other side and made to serve another purpose: the point is not temperance or the church, but *what a lovely setting this is for a romance.* . . . Some sort of game is under way, like that between Stephen and Mr. Deasy—not, this time, between two individuals, but *within discourses themselves.* One site is reworked in the discourse of another. Before Gerty has even been introduced, and before the chapter leads us to associate her with what is happening here, we have a discursive frame which is already impersonal in its very familiarity, without need of Gerty to activate or guarantee it, and which is already busy folding everything into the embrace of that summer evening of romance.

Much of the comedy of this first half of the chapter will be in the apparent intrusions into this diction, and the ways in which they are folded back into its embrace: "[Gerty's] figure was slight and graceful, inclining even to fragility but those iron jelloids she had been taking of late had done her a world of good much better than the Widow Welch's female pills and she was much better of those discharges she used to get and that tired feeling" (*U* 13.83–87). It is easy to read this as satire on the romance fiction for which physical fragility is mainly moral and sentimental, and in which vaginal discharges simply do not exist. Satire would bring back what has been repressed, and force the one repressing it to face up to it. Salutary and bracing, it strengthens and does a world of good, just like iron jelloids. (If this *is* satire, do we not at least have to take into account this odd and oblique doubling, in which one of the apparent targets of the satire is precisely the very stance of satire?) But to what extent *are* these more mundane concerns simply intrusions into the romance, repressions it is forced to face? Those brand names ("iron jelloids," "Widow Welch's female pills"), the reassuring familiarity of that "world of good," the demonstrative of "*that* tired feeling" which offers it as a shared experience—all of this may not seem to be romance as such, but it is certainly what is right *next to* romance there on the pages of the *Lady's Pictorial* and *Pearson's Weekly*. The copy of the *Evening Telegraph* Bloom reads later that day is full of it: Vita-Leo ointment ("a certain cure for the worst sores or ulcers"; "Don't swallow drugs"), Beecham's Pills ("They rid the system of impurities, improve the digestion, banish headache and give positive relief in all cases of Biliousness, Constipation, Indigestion and Disordered Liver"), Cuticura ("Eczema. The World's Greatest Skin Humour. Affects Every Age and Condition. The Only Sure Cure is Cuticura"), Clarke's Blood Mixture ("This Famous Medicine will cleanse the blood from all impurities from whatever cause arising. A safe remedy for Eczema, Rheumatism, Gout, Bad Legs, Scrofula, Blood Poison, Sores of all kinds, Boils, Eruptions, Ulcers, Glandular etc. Of all Chemists, Stores, etc. Thousands of unsolicited Testimonials. Forty years' success. Beware of worthless imitations and substitutes").[10] None of this is what is in any way hidden from the reader of romance fiction; on the contrary, it is what faces such a reader every time she *is* such a reader—there on the page, without dissimulation. It is not so much an intrusion into romance discourse as one of the many things adjacent to it, and therefore not at all external to it; what it represents is more like one of the possible margins of romance, and thus a fracture constitutive of romance. What it suggests is that romance is not a unitary discourse which defends itself against external distractions and detractions, but something which is already divided, multiple, full of clashes and incompatibilities. This is the very condition of its existence as a formation within which Gerty and others find a place.

Take the opening description of Gerty. After a paragraph of sentimental scene-setting, we are told that "The three girl friends were seated on the rocks, enjoying the evening scene and the air which was fresh but not too chilly" (*U* 13.9–10). But only two of these three friends are named immediately, and for the first few pages the focus is entirely on Cissy Caffrey and Edy Boardman, and the young brothers they are minding. The narrative moves to Gerty only once her name is mentioned by another. Just like the Stephen of the *Portrait,* called up by and in a story, or the Stephen of "Telemachus," whose interior monologue bursts into flow at his glimpse of himself in Mulligan's mirror (*U* 1.134–37), Gerty enters the narrative when she is invoked, called on from somewhere else. But this time the invocation has a marked and deliberate disingenuity: the narrative is *pretending not to know* this place it has carefully prepared by skirting discreetly all around it:

—I know, Edy Boardman said none too amiably with an arch glance from her shortsighted eyes. I know who is Tommy's sweetheart. Gerty is Tommy's sweetheart.

—Nao, Tommy said on the verge of tears.

Cissy's quick motherwit guessed what was amiss and she whispered to Edy Boardman to take him there behind the pushcar where the gentlemen couldn't see and to mind he didn't wet his new tan shoes.

But who was Gerty?

Gerty MacDowell who was seated near her companions, lost in thought, gazing far away into the distance was, in very truth, as fair a specimen of winsome Irish girlhood as one could wish to see. (*U* 13.71–81)

And what is revealed by this knowing disingenuity is a carefully posed and knowingly disingenuous Gerty, gazing far away into the distance as if herself gazed at from afar. Whether or not she is yet aware of the man looking at her from the rocks, that gaze which already transfixes her belongs to the very sentence in which she is seen, to the genre in which she sees herself as if seen and presents herself as "as fair a specimen of winsome Irish girlhood *as one could wish to see,*" which is to say as she could wish to be seen. Nausicaa's Art, according to both Gilbert and Linati, sums up the dynamic of the tableau in a word: painting. Gerty sees herself as seen, and as being seen to be seen. The chapter paints her in the act of being painted.[11]

This complicates what is essentially a *novelistic introduction* to a character. An introduction: that is, a function of narration rather than of character, because it is a matter of the narrative's addressing itself *as if* to one who does not already know. We are introduced to Gerty *as if* we do not know her;[12] but in fact we do, even before *Ulysses,* in that we are already familiar with just those genres and discourses on which she models herself, and that is where the pleasure of the joke lies. This *as if* with its knowing stance of not knowing has exactly the same dynamic as Gerty's pose for the unseen painter, or romance novelist, or that interesting older man in the rocks. Gerty poses as if for the approving gaze, and at the same time as if that gaze were not there: the role of the imagined onlooker which Bloom will come to occupy (that is, which he will find already there for him) is to play it as if it were not a role which pure happenstance had led him to fill, but as something unique, there for him alone—which is to say, as another role (*For him! For Raoul!*). Let us again note the proximity of this *as if* to the fetishistic disavowal: *I know that this is not the case, but nevertheless I will behave as if it were.*

What we have, then, is not a private fantasy with its source in a single fantasist. We have an entire machinery of stagecraft which produces a number of different pleasures, and displeasures, none of them necessarily heading in convergent directions even in a single participant. Nobody is fooled, nothing is hidden. The fantasy of winsome Irish girlhood and its attractions is Gerty's only because it is already inhabitable and indeed inhabited by all sorts of other subjects who, like Gerty, find themselves and their pleasures there. Such as, at very least, Bloom.

Consider. Bloom already knows well the idioms on which this fantasy draws. He is an advertising man who now works for a metropolitan daily and was previously a salesman for a large department store (though Ned Lambert disparagingly refers to him as having been "a traveler in blottingpaper" (*U* 6.703)). He would seem to be the main buyer of books for his wife, whose favorite reading is that sexually charged form of the romance, the bodice-ripper, and he seems to be quite familiar with the genre. (There are no samples of it on his own bookshelves downstairs in the living room at Eccles Street [*U* 17.1362–1407], but these are books one neither displays to visitors nor keeps; for the moment, they belong upstairs by Molly's bed, and once consumed they will go back into circulation again. Bloom's bookcase seems to contain no fiction at all—Shakespeare, of course, is that very different thing, Literature.) Only a few hours ago, with a connoisseur's eye he was carefully selecting Molly's next title from the stalls in Merchant's Arch. What makes him decide on *Sweets of Sin* is a passage at which he randomly opens: "*All the dollarbills her husband gave her were spent in the stores on wondrous gowns and costliest frillies. For him! For Raoul!*" (*U* 10.608–609). *Sortes Homericae:* another window has opened, from one game into another. A wife, a lover, a husband: the gift of the book will no doubt be a pointed comment to Molly, one which both says *I know, you know I know, I know you know I know* . . . and imposes complete silence by its indirection. Bloom has already today put himself into an important role in a romance, or in several—or rather, as his continuing reading makes clear, moved through a number of the roles and pleasures on offer:

> —*You are late, he spoke hoarsely, eying her with a suspicious glare. The beautiful woman threw off her sabletrimmed wrap, displaying her queenly shoulders and heaving embonpoint. An imperceptible smile played round her perfect lips as she turned to him calmly.*
> Mr Bloom read again: *The beautiful woman . . . .*
> Warmth showered gently over him, cowing his flesh. Flesh yielded amply amid rumpled clothes: whites of eyes swooning up. His nostrils arched themselves for prey. (*U* 10.615–21)

Whose flesh yields here? The fragments of the *Sweets of Sin* narrative suggest its heroine's, but the previous sentence has Bloom's flesh cowed and thus presumably ready to yield. The heroine's excitation passes to Bloom, who has to master his "troubled breath" (*U* 10.638) before he can speak. Personal pronouns are momentarily lost as we move from "her queenly shoulders and heaving embonpoint," "her perfect lips," "his flesh," to the bare "flesh" and "whites of eyes swooning up." This fantasy traverses a number of bodies, and produces somewhere between Bloom and the heroine something like an indeterminate body of pleasure of indefinite extent, both and neither his and hers. The very space of the shop and its rheumy owner take on these attributes too: just as those fat pears and shamefaced peaches of an earlier section of "Wandering Rocks" transfer Boylan's anticipation of Molly, surely we may take the effects of the shopman's coughs, "bulging out the dingy curtains" (*U* 10.632–33), as metaleptically belonging more to those (whose?) rumpled clothes amid which flesh is indeed yielding amply. Almost at the very end of "Nausicaa," those frillies will also metamorphose into Gerty's glimpsed knickers, not to mention Molly's drawers, in an extraordinary mixture of other fantasies which are not simply Bloom's own, pleasure and fear mixed, sweets and sin: *Sweets of Sin,* Molly and Boylan, Molly and the young Lieutenant Mulvey, and Bloom's Turkish dream of the night before (*U* 13.1240–42):

> O sweety all your little girlwhite up I saw dirty bracegirdle made me do love sticky we two naughty Grace darling she him half past the bed met him pike hoses frillies for Raoul de perfume your wife black hair heave under embon *señorita* young eyes Mulvey plump bubs me breadvan Winkle red slippers she rusty sleep wander years of dreams return tail end Agendath swoony lovey showed me her next year in drawers return next in her next her next. (*U* 13.1279–85)

It is easy, then, to see the "quiet gravefaced gentleman" (*U* 13.542) with those "wonderful eyes" so "superbly expressive" (*U* 13.414) as a role into which Bloom would more than willingly place himself. Indeed, looking again at where we have been, we may come to suspect that everything here is very easily inverted to become distinctly a part of *Bloom's* imaginings:

> She was pronounced beautiful by all who knew her though, as folks often said, she was more a Giltrap than a MacDowell. Her figure was slight and graceful, inclining even to fragility but those iron jelloids she had been taking of late had done her a world of good much better than the Widow Welch's female pills and she was much better of those discharges she used to get and that tired feeling. The waxen pallor of her face was almost spiritual in its ivorylike purity though her rosebud mouth was a genuine Cupid's bow, Greekly perfect. (*U* 13.81–89)

This has all the exteriority of any of the interior monologues. The rapidity of its citation and collation—advertisements and testimonials, novelistic description and homely wisdoms—emphasizes its distance from the psychologism of interior and personal experience, to the point where Gerty appears a collage of sometimes quite incongruous or conflicting parts. That discharge also suggests what we already know to be Bloom's prurient fascination with the female body and its flows.[13] Even the very phrasing seems to be full of small Bloomian signature-effects. Bloom is an advertising man himself: during the day he often shows an appreciative eye for the advertising which surrounds him, and his interior monologue is steeped in it; later in the night, he will offer Stephen his views on what makes a good ad and what doesn't (*U* 17.585–610). The comically loose association of fragments of knowledge which makes Roman Cupid Greekly perfect is more suggestive of the autodidacticism of Bloom (that Romanly Greek Ulysses) than it is of all-but-uneducated Gerty. The tumbling structure of that jelloids sentence, the awkward repetition and sometimes minimal or awkward punctuation ("had done her a world of good *much better* than the Widow Welch's female pills and she was *much better* of those discharges she used to get and that tired feeling"), the rosebud which is also a bow—all these foreshadow "Eumaeus." And if that chapter's catachreses, orotundities, and syntactic tangles suggest it is in a sense *My Experiences in a Cabman's Shelter,* the story Bloom imagines himself writing, then "Nausicaa" is in the same sense "*The Mystery Man on the Beach,* prize titbit story by Mr Leopold Bloom," both of them at the rate of one guinea per column (*U* 16.1230–31, 13.1060–61).

Above all, there is one recurrent factor which seems to point to Bloom rather than Gerty: neither Gerty nor the narrative appears to know, or register, that she is lame. The hinge point of the chapter, that massive change of apparent focalization from Gerty to Bloom midway through, happens when this can no longer be ignored: Gerty simply gets up and walks away.

> Slowly, without looking back she went down the uneven strand to Cissy, to Edy, to Jacky and Tommy Caffrey, to little baby Boardman. It was darker now and there were stones and bits of wood on the strand and slippy seaweed. She walked with a certain quiet dignity characteristic of her but with care and very slowly because—because Gerty MacDowell was . . .
> Tight boots? No. She's lame! O!
> Mr Bloom watched her as she limped away. Poor girl! That's why she's left on the shelf and the others did a sprint. Thought something was wrong by the cut of her jib. Jilted beauty. A defect is ten times worse in a woman. But makes them polite. Glad I didn't know it when she was on show. Hot little devil all the same. I wouldn't mind. (*U* 13.766–76)

Bloom can very quickly decide he could find that lameness exciting too—the object no doubt of another possible fantasy. But it has not been *this* fantasy, with the fetishistic concentration on the "wellturned foot" we have previously associated with Bloom (*U* 5.118). That "languid queenly *hauteur* about Gerty" of which we are told in the very first description of her is above all "unmistakably evidenced in her delicate hands and higharched instep" (*U* 13.97–98): at her feet, had she been born a gentle-woman, patrician suitors would vie with one another (*U* 13.99–104), and her beau ideal would lay "a rare and wondrous love" (*U* 13.209–10).

> Her shoes were the newest thing in footwear . . . with patent toecaps and just one smart buckle over her higharched instep. Her well-turned ankle displayed its perfect proportions beneath her skirt and just the proper amount and no more of her shapely limbs encased in finespun hose with highspliced heels and wide garter tops. (*U* 13.164–71)

Gerty's shoes mark the rhythm of the fantasy. The occasion for first eye contact is when the children's ball rolls under her skirt and she kicks it back (*U* 13.352–70). She swings her foot so that Bloom can see "the bright steel buckles of her shoes" (*U* 13.424–25); as their eyes meet again and her breath catches, she increases the speed of the swing (*U* 13.515–16), all the while glad she put on her good stockings, of which she will expose more and more (*U* 13.425–27, 499–505). The fantasy hinges on that fulcrum of the knee, with the arc of the bright buckle beneath it.

No wonder then that when the brute facticity of her lameness intrudes into it, the fantasy itself begins to limp ("because—because Gerty Mac-Dowell was . . .") and then all in a moment collapses altogether, to fall into the familiar syntax and tonalities of Bloom's interior monologue. The effect of this startling and sudden collapse is to make Gerty appear in retrospect as a mirror in which another's desire had been reflected all along. It is as if the looking glass had only now been made visible by the crack in it, which calls another and this time familiar subject into the narrative: Bloom. Everything which has happened so far in the chapter now shows itself in another light: everything which at first appeared to be Gerty now also works as Bloom. Every sentence now reveals itself, in retrospect, as capable of a double reading. (Joyce would hardly have ap-proved of any comparison with Henry James, but perhaps the only other thing quite like this are the labyrinths of *The Turn of the Screw* and *The Sacred Fount*.) If *Ulysses* is like "the progress of an immense sandblast," with each successive chapter reinventing its own technique and that of the novel itself, then "Nausicaa" enacts that sandblast in the space of a single chapter, here on Sandymount beach, building itself on sand just so that it may abruptly cave in on us.

Before the collapse—the Uncle Charles Principle suggests—we read the romance as characterizing Gerty, who has learnt its diction from her favor-ite reading and now loves to see herself in its terms. Indeed, the textual machinery of this free indirect discourse hardly has need of the exquisite sensitivity Kenner rightly admires in other passages, where the smallest flicker of a word may align itself with the gravitational center of a proper name: here, the comedy is broad, even obvious in its satire. But what the collapse reveals is that all along, and even unnoticed until now, this narration has *also* been responding to the pull of a more distant body and name: the man over in the rocks, and the name *Bloom*, which will not even be mentioned until his orgasm is over and the fantasy has at least for one of its fantasists achieved its aim. The narrative appears to have been responding to at least two gravitational centers. Not just successive centers, for that would be nothing more unusual than a shift of focalization: what the collapse emphasizes in its rewriting of everything that has gone before is that they *now appear to have been simultaneous*. The one textual space seems to be inhabited by at least two centers which are both incommensurate (there is no common measure of sexual difference) and interpermeating: Gerty and Bloom; Gerty watching Bloom, and Bloom watching Gerty; Gerty watching Bloom watching Gerty, and Bloom watching Gerty watching Bloom. *Sweets of Sin:* I know you know, and you know I do, and I know that too. Through this window, everything is transparent and clear; in this painterly tableau, everyone is transfixed in the light.[14]

These Gertys and Blooms multiply out along the lines of sight. When we first see her posing in abstracted concentration, Gerty is performing, behaving *as if* seen: performing herself for herself, she is also monitoring that performance, watching herself performing herself for herself. The man in the rocks does not appear to have come on the scene yet, but the dynamic is already complete without him. She is "gazing far away into the distance" (*U* 13.80), somewhere out of the frame of the picture and the narrative: a non-focus rather than a place, as it can be anywhere she turns as long as it is uninhabited. What she is looking at in this empty, abstracted gaze is exactly the place from which she is herself seen, that empty position which is nowhere in the field of vision but from which everything is organized and comes to take on its sense. The very first sentence of her description emphasizes that slippage between seeing and being seen, as that gaze into the distance comes back onto her from somewhere just as non-specific, to make her "in very truth, as fair a specimen of winsome Irish girlhood *as one could wish to see*" (*U* 13.79–81). Because it is essentially open, this position of sight can be filled in any number of ways, not necessarily commensurable: it is the place from which Gerty sees herself, lost in winsome thought on the beach, the place from which the man on the rocks sees her, the place from which she sees him watching her, or from which he sees her watching him watch her performance for him. This place from which one sees and is seen is the mobile, serial, empty site of *address*. It is significant, then, that the first description of Gerty should be initiated by the rhetorical question, "But who was Gerty?" (*U* 13.78). A question, even a rhetorical one, is directed, from somewhere to somewhere else: it foregrounds an address which in this case is both explicit and at the same time quite non-specific. It draws attention to itself as an event, in a way a statement does not; it suggests a situation of not knowing, even if, as here, that ignorance should be feigned or a detour. What the question does is not only confirm the existence of a character whom we are now to take in retrospect as having been there all along, and who has just before this been mentioned for the very first time, in dialogue. It also, and again in retrospect, suggests some sort of principle of selection, which has withheld this until now: a choice *not* to see, a position from which certain things will not have been seen.

Along with much narratological theory, the Uncle Charles Principle is a *characterological* description of free indirect discourse. It sees character in terms of the accretion of attributes around a name: as an object whose descriptors and characteristics, once they have been determined as *appropriate*, can then be transferred elsewhere within the narrative. For Barthes, as for much classical narratology, character is described by its attributes, as is any object. What he calls the *informants* of a narrative may just as easily apply to a setting as to a character (Barthes 96). That these characteristics might be without apparent unity, enigmatic, even contradictory, is not an obstacle: that can simply be read as affirming the inexhaustible complexity and depth of this object, the individual and *psychological* human being. Those two apparently distinct levels of text, narration and character, would correspond to observing subject and observed object, in strictly external arrangement: we can say that character may inflect narration, but that is only because we can already recognize what properly belongs to character and does not properly belong to narration.

But what do we do when the narrative we are examining refuses from the beginning to make any clear distinction between the one who observes and the object of that observation? When it is the infinitely refracted serial event of *seeing* within which both seer and seen exist only as countersignatures to each other, and where to be observed is inseparable from seeing oneself observed, which is to say inseparable from both seeing oneself *as if* observed, and from, simply, *seeing oneself*? This *oneself* is structurally taken out of itself in going through the detour of the other, *as seen by* the other, caught in an irreducible series of overbiddings: *I see you, I see you looking, I see myself seen, I see myself seeing you seeing me, I see you seeing this* . . . It is impossible to separate a Gerty who performs for herself, a Gerty who performs for Bloom, a Gerty who sees herself perform for Bloom, a Gerty whom Bloom sees performing, a Gerty who sees Bloom watching her perform, and so forth. With "Nausicaa," narration and character, observer and observed, are abyssally internal to each other. We no longer start from stable and objectifiable centers around which attributes can cluster, but from an impersonal action—a seeing, a knowing, a *telling*—within which unstable points of address invert themselves at almost infinite speed, and where addresser is already addressee, indeed is only addresser by virtue of being already addressee. *Gerty* and *Bloom* are names for this unstable and rapid oscillation between both ends of the gaze, the one who sees and the one who is seen, addresser and addressee.[15] Indeed, the monitoring of the performance—the game of adjudication—is strictly indistinguishable from the performance and its scopophilic pleasures. The pleasure lies not simply in seeing or in being seen, but in this rapid oscillation from one to the other: being seen to see at the same time as seeing the other being seen, and seeing oneself being seen by the other.

Shari Benstock and Bernard Benstock suggest a broadening of the Uncle Charles Principle to include:

> the capacity for extending narrative influences to include inanimate, mechanical, spontaneous, even organic processes. Such items as cakes of soap, newspapers, clouds, gulls, Elizabethan dance steps, not to mention Homeric correspondences, have the power to structure narrative form, provide images and echoes, and determine the progress of plot at any given moment.

They propose instead "The Benstock Principle":

> *Fictional texts that exploit free indirect speech* . . . *establish the contextual supremacy of subject matter, which influences the direction, tone, pace, point of view, and method of narration.* . . . [I]t is important to understand that what is at stake here is . . . a method for establishing, *within the confines of the textual narration,* the sources of its telling. ("Benstock Principle" 18, emphases in original)

But narratological informants already work this way, whether the object around which they accrete is inanimate or a character. What if, as in "Nausicaa," *character* is no longer objectal to the exact extent that it is bound up with the seriality we have been examining, no longer to be described in the classical narratological terms of the accretions of properties and attributes around a series of proper names or pronouns? The Benstock Principle does not extend the Uncle Charles Principle, it only reiterates its basis in a concept of character as objectal and already filled with a content whose very substantiality is able to influence what lies around it. What "Nausicaa" shows is not how a text can respond to the gravitational centers of a number of embedded subjects, but how it produces and works through a series of unstable and multiple positions, all of which can be occupied in a number of ways. Breen is marked by the postcard, not it by him.

We need to distinguish this from two influential ways of thinking through position, in and out of fiction. One of these is the idea of *subject-position,* found in various forms across much ethnographical, ideological, and post-Foucauldian analysis, where subjectivity is seen as something imposed from outside in a series of inhabitable *positions of subjectivation,* and the main question for the theorist is how the individual comes to assume, experience, and live those positions as their own. The second is the cognate form in narratology: the Greimasian distinction between *actant* and *acteur,* the role and the one who fills it (Greimas 5). In both cases, subjectivation is produced within a structure, as its determinate effect: subjectivity is given a content, something which comes to it from elsewhere but now belongs to it and is the set of its properties and attributes. In both cases, this is still to see the subject as objectal, with an objectality which is *given* it, from elsewhere. In this respect, it is essentially perfectly compatible with Q. D. Leavis's position, despite the obvious gap which separates her politics from that of most arguments about subjectivation. For Leavis, Gerty's subjectivity comes to her from elsewhere too. But for Leavis, that is precisely what is wrong with her and even makes her "dangerous": subject-positions are all you have left to you when you don't have a strong personality of your own. Whichever way it goes, it is to see subjects as substantial; they have and are defined in terms of a content, whether this is their own or comes to them from elsewhere.

"Nausicaa" suggests something else. What we have here is not the imposition of a content, the filling of a vacant space or two with something authentic or not, but a series of positions whose only content is an infinitely fast rhythm of oscillation: *I see you, I see you seeing, I see myself seen, I see myself seeing you seeing me . . .* If character as narratology conceives it is objectal and substantial, the accretion of attributes and the discovery of properties, then what "Nausicaa" presents us with is instead a *subjectality* of empty spaces and the oscillation among them. We can call this a position only on the understanding that it is indeed empty: it remains a promise to be fulfilled rather than a gap to be filled, even when it is occupied by the objectality of an *acteur*. This is the sense in which, for Lacan, the place precedes the object (Žižek, *Sublime* 194). Poe's "The Purloined Letter" sets up its deadly trap because the role of detective can be defined from the outset only in terms of those other roles of victim and villain. From the very beginning, what the detective cannot police, what will be stolen from him, what he begins to undo as soon as he acts, is the stability of that subject-position in which he acts, the role of detective itself (Lacan, "Seminar"). This is why Baldick finds it so easy to turn Leavis's rhetoric back on her, with a simple reversal of signs. It is also why *parody* and *satire* are altogether inadequate terms for what the middle chapters of *Ulysses* are doing: in their very excessiveness, the roles of address in the text are far too unstable to sustain the distance satire and parody need. If the proper names "Bloom" and "Gerty" are the points around which character can condense, in all its narratological objectality, then subject-ality finds itself figured in the text in a very different way: as the ellipsis of that uneasy moment where the fantasy seems to unravel and we become aware that it is no longer simply Gerty's—indeed, has not been all along, for everything that has just been read has now everted itself. At the very center of the chapter, what we have is not character but the point of collapse—and indefinite proliferation—of such a fantasy, marked by hesitation, ellipsis, and the unreadable silence between paragraphs: that momentary unease and destitution in which Bloom—and Gerty and reader—*can no longer be that:*

> She walked with a certain quiet dignity characteristic of her but with care and very slowly because—because Gerty MacDowell was . . .
> Tight boots? No. She's lame! O!
> Mr Bloom watched her as she limped away. (*U* 13.769–72)

Bloom as the object of description is rightly a cause of critical wonder: an entire genre of Joyce criticism, after all, is concerned with reconstructing the details of June 16 or the Blooms' life together.[16] But the *subjectality* of *Ulysses* is found in the moments of occlusion in this plethora of detail: in Bloom's inability to register until much later the information Molly must have given him in "Calypso" about the time of Boylan's visit; in his avoidance of Boylan and Boylan's name and the endless distraction of his day; in Stephen's inability to mourn his mother, and Bloom's recurrent mourning for son and father; in Bloom's fall through nonsense into sleep, as his consciousness at last winks out in the large dot which concludes "Ithaca"; in the increasingly great differences between the chapters, where each new chapter reinvents what has gone before; in the sexual difference which structures not only "Nausicaa" but *Ulysses* itself, where the last of the stylistic disjunctions between chapters comes to stand for sexual difference itself, and Molly's soliloquy does not so much sum up what has happened as recast it, without any possible synthesis, in a radically different perspective from across that sexual divide; in the asyndetic nature of the hypotheses the text is forever asking one to draw—and all this mirrored in the endless puzzles and enigmas of the text.

Peering into Mulligan's cleft mirror, dreadful bard Stephen sees just such a hall of mirrors: "As he and others see me. Who chose this face for me? . . . It asks me too" (*U* 1.136–37). Whose mirror is it? Mulligan and Stephen trade quotations, Mulligan from the epigrams preceding *The Picture of Dorian Grey,* Stephen from *The Decay of Lying:* Caliban not seeing himself in the mirror, and the cracked looking glass of a servant. Mulligan's, Stephen's, Wilde's, Caliban's, a servant's? In the brothel, Stephen looks into a mirror and sees the paralytic face of Shakespeare, that "mirror up to nature" as Lynch calls him—citing Hamlet, whose father's spirit is in turn the figure of that "playwright who wrote the folio of this world and wrote it badly" (*U* 15.3820–29, 3852–53, 9.1047). The mirror as the empty place of the father: before there is anything to reflect in it, there is a mirror, and what comes to be reflected in it, in this empty hall of reflections, will be the father. What can such a hall of cracked mirrors show? If the Art of "Nausicaa" is painting, this is not Joyce's first portrait.

4

In the Marketplace

As the *Portrait* progresses and as Stephen works his way through the broody adolescence of the artist as a young man, aesthetics comes increasingly to dominate the novel as a topic. By the fifth chapter—which at about one-third of the entire book is also considerably the longest—a good part of the action has become discussion, or the movement between or framing of discussions. Stephen argues Irishness with Davin, the "peasant student" (*P* 195), Aristotle, Aquinas, and tundishes with the dean of studies, Irishness and aesthetics after a lecture, aesthetics and the state of God's fingernails with Lynch, and finally belief and dissent with Cranly. Talk has become the main action, and one way or another most of it has to do with aesthetics. And this raises a number of critical problems.

First of all, although most critics might be in broad agreement about Stephen's, or Joyce's, sources for his aesthetics,[1] there is considerable disagreement about how faithful Stephen, or Joyce, might be to these sources.[2] Then, questions of faithfulness aside, there are also disagreements about whether the *Portrait* provides a cogent argument about aesthetics or a series of fragments.[3] And above and beyond that, there is the question of how we should take this aesthetics within its fictional framework. The simplest way, and the one with the most obvious problems, would be to read it all as self-commentary, as if what Stephen says is what both the *Portrait* and Joyce endorse as a framework in which to be read.[4] But clearly what Stephen says is the utterance of a character in a novel, and that hardly needs to have the consistency of a treatise on aesthetics—particularly when it would seem to be an important part of the book's meaning that despite his determination this character is *not yet* the artist who could write this portrait, or sum it up. We must, minimally, take that *not yet* seriously, and the promise which structures it. That nail-paring God of creation is doubly recessive: too late or too early, either the god of a creation still to come, or, once "the mystery of aesthetic . . . creation is accomplished" (*P* 233), withdrawn and silent, leaving behind barely a "thumbprint, mademark or just a poor trait of the artless" (*FW* 114.31–32), let alone a readers' guide.

To read Stephen's discussions of aesthetics as a framework for the *Portrait* would be to ignore this internal temporal dimension of the promise, and to treat them as the reflection within the book of a set of principles or a philosophical argument which lies outside the book but can be reconstructed from those reflections: governing its development, largely unseen but felt everywhere in it, guiding and adjudicating. To read this way would be to fill out the silences and complete the gaps, working towards that ideality of which the *Portrait* is an exemplification: to strive to make the gaps vanish, and to drag that absentee god back into the picture. But what if the *Portrait* is in some way *about* those gaps, *about* the incompletions and provisionalities of such frameworks? That would be to put aside questions of *aesthetics* (whether Stephen has an aesthetics, what it might be, what it owes to others, whether it is philosophically coherent, whether it accurately describes what he is doing in the *Portrait,* whether it is also Joyce's and to what extent, and whether that in turn accurately describes what *Joyce* is doing in the *Portrait*), and to ask instead questions about what I shall instead call *aestheticizing.*[5]

"For my purpose," Stephen assures the dean, "I can work on at present by the light of one or two ideas of Aristotle and Aquinas. . . . I need them only for my own use and guidance until I have done something for myself by their light. If the lamp smokes or smells I shall try to trim it. If it does not give light enough I shall sell it and buy another" (*P* 206). This is not a philosophical framework, but an act of improvisation. Stephen is making do with what he has in order to go somewhere else, the outlines of which are not yet even clear, but might—if the lamp trims well—become so as things progress. If this is the basis for an aesthetics, it is so only in an oddly provisional sense in which we can already see that recessive god of creation: Stephen needs them "*only . . . until* I have done something for myself by their light." That impossible green rose blossoms in the place of the countersignature. The light the lamp sheds comes only in part from that "garner of slender sentences from Aristotle's poetics and a *Synopsis Philosophiæ Scholasticæ ad mentem divi Thomæ*" (*P* 191) which Stephen admits to himself is the extent of his inheritance; it is reflected through Aquinas and Aristotle, but comes from a future which does not yet exist: if Aristotle and Aquinas cannot carry that light, time to buy another lamp. Stephen *aestheticizes:* he *makes aesthetics,* in the sense of an art of making do which is inseparable from all sorts of things, many of them not aesthetic. If the aesthetic is a thinking about art, a way of systematizing certain of its effects, then aestheticizing names the ways in which from the beginning such thinking finds itself embedded in all sorts of other things, infused with them and finding in itself ways of systematizing and negotiating them, and of playing and adjudicating all sorts of other games. Aestheticizing is a matter of a certain social role Stephen has already taken on himself ("You are an artist, are you not, Mr Dedalus?" [*P* 200]), this studied composure which is his prickly negotiation of love, authority, family, and friendships—in short, of all those nets he will finally declare his intention to fly past. Stephen's disavowal to the dean is not a proposition but a parrying. Through it, an uncountable number of pages in the future, we hear Stephen with Garrett Deasy, and behind that again Joyce selling paralysis to Grant Richards. It is a move in a game, a number of games: between an older man and a younger, a teacher and a student, an Englishman and an Irishman, a priest and an apostate. It says all sorts of things: *You are older, a priest, and a Jesuit, Aristotle and the church fathers are yours before they are mine, but look, I am doing, or hoping to do, something new with them, something you have never done; they are mine, I take them from you; but I submit myself to your examination, I answer you in your terms, perhaps seeking your approval as the bright pupil, the one who has learnt his lesson so well that he now supersedes the master, and will soon ask for the master's recognition of his own mastery; and I do this with such a slender garner, and admit this to you, either so that you will marvel all the more, or so that I am already defended against your disapproval; if I impress you, if you marvel at what I do with so little, imagine what I could do if I had your knowledge of them to draw on; or perhaps that knowledge has now become oddly redundant and useless, now that a young poet with only a fraction of your knowledge of it can produce this; and if what I am doing fails to impress you with its knowledge of Thomist and Aristotelian aesthetics, what difference does it make, because as I have told you from the outset these are of interest to me only in as much as they give me what I need; unlike you, I am not tied to them, or tied at all; I ask for an approval I do not need; and if I do not have that approval, I already have my defenses against refusal.* All these are conjunctions rather than a framework: Stephen's aestheticizing speaks aesthetics, but as a speculation which inhabits the gaps between all sorts of disparate and contingent things, including those between aesthetics and the novel.

Between one sort of novel and another. By its final chapter, with Stephen reinventing himself as artist, the *Portrait* not only is a *Bildungsroman* but also reinvents itself as a novel of ideas. If the *Bildungsroman* is above all about promise, what we get in its collision with the novel of ideas is the *staging* of ideas, and of promise: an aestheticizing. The *Portrait* is very careful to embed these in novelistic time, place, and situation, to link them with the ways of operating which the characters have available to them within those situations; it shows these ideas at work within a diegesis which is not necessarily at all that of conceptual development. These ideas have effects which cannot be reduced to or predicted from the ideas themselves. Stephen can propose that art is "the human disposition of sensible or intelligible matter for an aesthetic end," but whether it is or not will have little bearing on whether Lynch will actually stay around to hear him say it:

—If I am to listen to your aesthetic philosophy give me at least another cigarette. I don't care about it. I don't even care about women. Damn you and damn everything. I want a job of five hundred a year. You can't get me one. (*P* 224)

In the *Portrait,* ideas unfold as narrative events: dialogue is not just the working-out of a truth, it is argument, sparring, stakes and weapons. Ideas are weighed up against all sorts of things which are not ideas: banal things, too, like cigarettes. Everything is yet to come: the question is not whether Stephen's aesthetics is fragmentary or coherent, but whether it is an aesthetics *of* the fragmentary and the coherent, and of the asyndetic edge between them; of windows, through which all sorts of unexpected things come, perhaps to be swept away into different regimes altogether, perhaps even to invent new regimes; and of the unforeseen shouts (but also the traffic, the bustle of the marketplace, and a long fine needle of shivered glass) in the streets through which Stephen and Lynch walk. An aesthetics, in other words, of aestheticizing.

As Maud Ellmann points out in an important essay, Stephen's aesthetics relies heavily on a distinction between literature and "the market place" (192–94). The marketplace is above all the site of exchange, where all sorts of things flow across and over a number of surfaces; but the work of art would by contrast seem to be a withdrawal from all such exchanges, refusing them in favor of a hoarding by which the work can, at least for the moment, be detained as pure and apart.

On the one hand, for Ellmann the marketplace is characterized by emissions and incorporations. First, there is a movement of expulsion of the foreign or of waste. In the *Portrait* this is generally marked by tense and copious expressions of disgust: Stephen's sins, for example, which memorably "trickled from his lips, . . . festering and oozing like a sore" (P 156). This abjection is particularly intense where sexuality is involved, as we find in Stephen's encounter with the prostitute, and with his fascination with the fact of E—— C——'s menstruation, that "strange humiliation of her nature" which is displaced into those other all-but-disembodied flows of the villanelle: the smoke, the cries, the "chalice flowing to the brim" (P 242–43). Ellmann argues that these expulsions work synecdochically. Most obviously, they work as a purgation of the part from the whole, in a sort of sacrifice, which finds its most intense expression in Stephen's repentant self-mortifications early in the fourth chapter, in which "Each of his senses was brought under a rigid discipline": to mortify sight he forces himself to walk with eyes downcast, to mortify hearing he exercises no control over his breaking voice and makes no attempt to flee painful sounds, and so on. But this process of purgation is synecdochic in a further and rather unsettling way, in that the expelled part comes to stand for *the whole which expels it*, and "the subject is dispersed into the fragments and the waste that stand for him" (Ellmann, "Disremembering" 193). The whole is both what expels and what is found to be expelled: what is set up is a precarious rhythm of abjection before the boundaries of the body.

As well as expulsion, though, the marketplace is also the site of all sorts of movements of incorporation. These are metaphorical rather than synecdochic: in them, something is transformed into something else. And here too the signs of abjection become acute. If the dregs of that third cup of watery tea, the crusts of fried bread, and the dark pool of the dripping jar which open the fifth chapter are disgusting, it is because they are on their way to Stephen's mouth. Incorporation threatens to undo the work of expulsion, as if there is always the danger that what has already been so carefully expelled from the body will surreptitiously be returned into it: this is a body which is always worried about eating shit, or its own words. Often as not, Stephen's elaborate self-mortifications involve a deliberate and passive incorporation of these threatening exteriorities: he "made no attempt to flee from noises which caused him painful nervous irritation such as the sharpening of knives on the knifeboard . . . suffered patiently every itch or pain . . . [and] left parts of his neck and face undried so that air might sting them" (P 163). They even admit a sly quotient of perverse pleasure when it comes to the sense of smell, that most direct contact with the effluviant:

To mortify his smell was more difficult as he found in himself no instinctive repugnance to bad odours, whether they were the odours of the outdoor world such as those of dung or tar or the odours of his own person among which he had made many curious comparisons and experiments. (*P* 163)

Disturbing possibilities open. If purgation corresponds on the religious level to sacrifice, then incorporation is Eucharist, but a sacrament which one can never be sure is not tainted. And if the suspicion of that taint is a source of pleasure, how far are we from that very pleasure of the tainted which Stephen hopes to have purged?

It is hardly surprising, then (and here we reach that *on the other hand*), that the hoarding by which the work of art attempts to remove itself from the marketplace should appear a rather tenuous and unstable possibility, one which is haunted by the anxiety that it might already be invaded from within. Hoarding is, after all, an economic term, one which belongs in and makes sense only within the framework of the marketplace. One hoards only what could be circulated, dissipated, used. What is not capable of circulation is not hoarded, it is just inert massive presence. There is no hoarding without exchange, which is its prior condition; what is hoarded must retain its value as exchange *in* the hoarding if it is not to collapse into mere massiveness. This means that it is constituted as hoarded value only through an incessant affirmation of its circulability, which cannot afford to relent for an instant. What is hoarded is always in principle hoarded only because it is what *could* circulate, and is at every moment being held back by force from the circulation which alone makes it hoardable. Hoarding is a vigilance.

In this respect, we can leap ahead of ourselves for a moment and juxtapose hoarding and exchange with that other Dedalean pairing, the static and the kinetic. Hoarding is not at all the absence of exchange, in the way in which the static might seem to be the absence of motion; on the contrary, it is a deflection and containment of motion, a constant and wary counterforce which is always actively trying to judge itself one jump ahead of the movements it tries to contain. Hoarding, then, does not for an instant stop exchange and circulation. Rather than being the zero point of circulation, it is its infinite acceleration and virtualization, a singularity produced within the flows of exchange. What is hoarded is the valuable itself: rather than being a withdrawal from value, hoarding is a strategy within the marketplace for the acceleration of value, the affirmation of exchange: it is a withdrawal only to incorporate all the more deeply. To close off this momentary leap ahead of ourselves, then, might the pairing of the static and the kinetic also work the same way? What if the static is not the proper state prior to the kinetic and its abuses, but a tense and vigilant acceleration of the kinetic? And if hoarding is an acceleration, should we expect it to have something to do with the infinite speed of subjectality? We shall return to these.

So: by its own logic, the hoarding which, according to Stephen, literature performs, cannot be just set against the flows of the marketplace. The very affect of the idea perhaps says this: the outgoing and incoming flows of exchange are attended by deep anxiety, even abject disgust, over and over. Yet if literature were simply the putting-out-of-play Stephen proposes, and once and for all, why would this involve any anxiety at all? As it is, once it is made, that distinction between art and the marketplace has to be repeated, not only occasion by occasion, but also within itself: even within art one must be careful to distinguish between proper and improper art, between—and here we glimpse that second pairing again—the static aesthetic emotion and the kinetic emotions excited by the pornographic or didactic arts (*P* 222). In each case, the anxiety comes from the double bind of the demand, its simultaneous necessity and impossibility. Hoarding seeks to remove itself from the marketplace, to which it cannot thus afford to remain in debt. But hoarding depends on—is—exchange: literature cannot but be in debt to the marketplace; once the distinction is made, literature cannot help but find again, this time within it, the marketplace.

But we must not be too hasty here. This finding itself again in the marketplace does not mean that literature's hoarding is nothing more than illusory or self-deception, just the result of faulty reasoning, or naïveté from someone who may be an artist sometime in the future but for the moment is certainly a rather young man. That would be to affirm a distinction between a real world of the marketplace and the illusory positing of some sort of outside to that, and this is exactly what is not happening here. Literature is not to be set in opposition to the marketplace: the epiphanic shout, after all, will be in the street, surrounding him as he passes through the heart of the Hibernian metropolis in "Aeolus."[6] Sustained by that very marketplace to which it is in debt, literature is itself a sort of speculation, and, to start with, in the most vulgar sense of that word. What it aims at is a surplus, a profit even. The relationship of the two is not mutual exclusion across an unbreachable wall, but regulation across a semi-porous membrane. Hoarding does not prevent flows: it *selects* carefully from them according to certain criteria: certain flows are allowed in one direction, others in the reverse direction are not. Hoarding is an accumulation. It involves a vigilance on boundaries, a series of decisions on what to let pass:

> His father's whistle, his mother's mutterings, the screech of an unseen maniac were to him now so many voices offending and threatening to humble the pride of his youth. He drove their echoes even out of his heart with an execration: but, as he walked down the avenue and felt the grey morning light falling about him through the dripping trees and smelt the strange wild smell of the wet leaves and bark, his soul was loosed of her miseries.
>
> The rainladen trees of the avenue evoked in him, as always, memories of the girls and women of the plays of Gerhart Hauptmann. (*P* 190)

The condition for that famous fingernail-paring God of artistic creation begins to look somewhat like Maxwell's demon of boundaries, engaged in an incessant sorting operation by which strongly negentropic, directional, and highly complex local structures begin to emerge out of the happenstance of chance meetings.

It is a model which will turn up elsewhere, of course. If *Portrait* suggests it as part of a logic of the aesthetic, then—to take an example which is not just one example among many—as we have seen, Freud will also use just the same function of sorting as a crucial part of his description of the psyche. From as early as the Freud-Breuer *Studies on Hysteria* of 1895, we find the psyche pictured according to a "principle of constancy," a "tendency to keep . . . excitation constant" (272) in a homeostatic system:

> the cerebral elements, after being completely restored, liberate a certain amount of energy even when they are at rest; and if this energy is not employed functionally it increases the normal intracerebral excitation. The result is a feeling of unpleasure. . . .
>
> . . . We can understand the tendency in warm-blooded animals to keep a constant mean temperature, because our experience has taught us that temperature is an optimum for the functioning of their organs. And we make a similar assumption in regard to the constancy of the water-content of the blood; and so on. I think that we may also assume that there is an optimum for the height of the intracerebral tonic excitation. (272–73)[7]

By the time of *Beyond the Pleasure Principle* (1920), Freud will have postulated his famous animalcule, whose cortex is specialized to perform the double and essentially selective function of protecting the sensitive interior from the ravages and intensities of external stimuli, and at the same time admitting certain of those stimuli as the organism's necessary perception of the world in which it has to live and die. It is again a boundary which functions as boundary only because its separation is never and must never be complete. Its cost is a necessary blurring of the very inside and outside which must be kept so separate: the outer cortex takes on itself that death from which it has to protect the inner elements, to become what Freud calls "a crust . . . which would at last have been . . . thoroughly 'baked through'" (*Beyond* 297). The choice of figure is telling, as if the faint disgust of abjection against the improper and the breaching of the proper always haunts the very constitution of the subject: consciousness as scab.

Body and psyche, psyche *as* body. There is something quite complex and intriguing going on here. The metaphor of psyche as a little animal is being used to *describe* processes of regulation across a threshold. If we are to take a very familiar concept of metaphor, it is describing an unfamiliar form of this regulation (the psychic) in terms of a more familiar one (the physiological). So we have, to begin with, a metaphor *of* what happens when we get thresholds, and transferences across those thresholds—from the biological to the psychological, from neuroanatomy to psychoanalysis. But there is a twist here, an involution of metaphor into itself. Selective transference across thresholds, from one domain to another (minimally, from the familiar to the unfamiliar), is, after all, *exactly what metaphor itself does, to begin with*, its very definition: metaphor *as* thresholds and transferences. What happens when the very process of metaphor is itself used as metaphor? We may doubt that it can even be sufficient to describe it as metaphor any longer, because now that it is at very least the metaphor *of* metaphor, the *truth* of metaphor, can it be distinguished from the truth of truth (Derrida, *Post Card* 415)? This now somewhat undecidable figure of regulation across a threshold, then, itself comes to cross conceptual boundaries as it leaps the mind-body split.[8] Through this window and the shout which traverses it, it is no longer entirely possible to make a strict distinction between what might be internal to such a figure (the ways in which it functions within a given discourse, or text, or discipline) and what might be external to it (the ways in which it connects or is echoed in other perhaps quite distant texts, discourses, and disciplines—*A Portrait of the Artist as a Young Man* and *Beyond the Pleasure Principle* now appear in subterranean communication). It is the very permeability of that membrane between inside and outside which has made such a figure possible in the first place: or, quite simply, has made figuration itself possible.

Exchange always yields some surplus, something which spills over even the very terms of the original exchange.

So we have Stephen's drama of an art which holds itself aloof from the marketplace by which it is nevertheless made possible. The excessive metaphorics of exchange this involves necessarily plays itself out across a number of surfaces in one and the same movement, or rather, more accurately, maps out a number of such surfaces in its rhythm. Thus there is Stephen's walk, in which the mundane Dublin through which he travels is overlaid and remade by literature:

> The rainladen trees of the avenue evoked in him, as always, memories of the girls and women of the plays of Gerhart Hauptmann; and the memory of their pale sorrows and the fragrance falling from the wet branches mingled in a mood of quiet joy. His morning walk across the city had begun, and he foreknew that as he passed the sloblands of Fairview he would think of the cloistral silverveined prose of Newman, that as he walked along the North Strand Road, glancing idly at the windows of the provision shops, he would recall the dark humor of Guido Cavalcanti and smile, that as he went by Baird's stonecutting works in Talbot Place the spirit of Ibsen would blow through him like a keen wind, a spirit of wayward boyish beauty, and that passing a grimy marinedealer's shop beyond the Liffey he would repeat the song by Ben Jonson which begins:
>
> *I was not wearier where I lay.*
>
> (*P* 190)

A walk across town is also a trajectory through the works of those writers the young Stephen admires, which in turn becomes a sort of calligraphy written across Dublin by Stephen's feet: Dublin, by Hauptmann, Dublin by Newman, by Cavalcanti, Ibsen, Jonson . . . : signed; countersigned S. Dedalus. One after another, these ghostly signatures overwrite the "so many voices offending and threatening to humble the pride of his youth." They are what reduce the voices of his parents' authority to the inarticulate, yoking "his father's whistle, his mother's mutterings" with "the screech of an unseen maniac" (*P* 190). The Dublin which has made Stephen is now itself remade as the Dublin he has signed as Literature. (Buck Mulligan's ambiguous pronouns will catch it exactly when later on, in *Ulysses,* he will promise Haines that Stephen "proves by algebra that Hamlet's grandson is Shakespeare's grandfather and that he himself is the ghost of his own father" [*U* 1.555–57]. That Haines momentarily understands this "he himself" as meaning Stephen is of course the very elision Stephen would himself wish to make, returning to him by a circuit of mistake and mishearing.) Stephen overwrites place, origin, progenitors, transposed at least for the moment from the sordidness of his home life. We must take this in a way which is not simply figurative, and not least because it is the question of the literal and the figurative which is involved here in the metaphorics of exchange and in these names which can be read across Dublin.

There are at least three series here, in this walk. The first is geographical, or topographical. Stephen is walking through the streets of Dublin. On the level of the story narrated, Stephen's trajectory is of course continuous, and it is even narrated in a plausible order if Stephen is seen as beginning from the Joyce family's own address in Fairview at the time. But the series is somewhat more complex than that, as the tenses and iterative frequency of its narration may suggest. Those "rainladen trees of the avenue" are in the past tense of the surrounding narration, but the passage through the sloblands, along the North Strand Road, by Talbot Place, and across the Liffey is modal: he "foreknew that as he passed the sloblands of Fairview." The passage is doubled and redoubled by its iterative nature: Stephen foreknows because it has already happened this way, many times before. The moment narrated goes backwards and forwards into other repetitions: it stands at the center of a doubled temporal loop. This series is both spatial and temporal; or rather, it is both horizontal (a journey across the surface of Dublin) and vertical (the repetitions of that journey), where the latter disarranges the sequentiality of the former. This doubling means that the series is now no longer governed by the order of the walk: it is the series of memory, reaching ahead of itself as it reaches back, scattering the linear trajectory into an instantaneous simultaneity of all its points.

The second series is literary. Hauptmann, Newman, Cavalcanti, Ibsen, Jonson: separate names which in themselves lay no claim to any sort of narrative progression through European literature, but forming again a simultaneous and doubled series of memory which does not depend on the sequence of the particular passage Stephen is describing across the city. But these two series, the geographical and the literary, are nevertheless linked. Again, it is by memory, in a doubling and redoubling which already characterizes both of the initial series. Those "rainladen trees of the avenue" *evoke* Hauptmann, the Fairview sloblands *evoke* Newman. Or rather, not simply Hauptmann or Newman, for those trees "evoked in him, as always, *memories* of the girls and women of the plays of Gerhart

Hauptmann." The subtle difference that word *memories* makes is important: it opens up the evocation of the girls and women of the plays to an
evoking of memory itself, a vista of other reminiscences ("as always"),
remembering *other occasions of remembering*. Beyond its given content at
any particular point, remembering remembers remembering: before it is a
memory of trees or silverveined prose, it is an iteration, a reactivation, of
the empty movement of iteration itself, in return on itself.

And there would seem to be no necessary connection between the two
series. We are not told why it should be that Stephen remembers such-and-
such a writer at such-and-such a place—why the provision shops of the
North Strand Road should recall the dark humor of Guido Cavalcanti, or
the marinedealer's shop Ben Jonson. It is hard to see any specific likeness
being suggested (how for example would the sloblands be like Newman's
silverveined prose? or cloistral?) in any of the cases given; it is as though
the repetition of examples suggests and confirms that likeness is indeed
not the governing principle here. Or rather, it is not *necessary* that there be
any particular reason for the two series to be pinned together as they are
at these particular points; there may indeed be reasons, many of them, but
what is important here is simply the fact that they *are* conjoined, laced
together one onto the other by a thread of utterance.[9] *This* place, *this*
writing: this writing is what this place, for whatever reason, has previously
brought to mind, and will again: this is the way the chains of the signifiers
of two different series interlace.

That is, from the intersection of these two series in all their iterability
we have the outline of a third series, marked by and arising in the contingency that marks their intersection: a comportment. We can give this series
the name the text itself does: simply, Stephen. This is to see Stephen in
other terms than the characterological or psychological terms of a person-
age, even if a fictional one. It is to see things in terms which predate that,
and by means of which it will be possible to say that there is a character
called Stephen, who thinks thus and acts thus. Stephen as intersection
comes before and calls up that later figure, that host of later figures who
inhabit the name and the readings of the name. This is not (at very least,
not yet) a Stephen who redeems the squalor of the urban through art, or
who imposes his vision on the world, or even who through an act of will
brings disparate worlds together. This Stephen is as yet no more than the
precarious moving point of a repeated series of intersections, these and a
thousand others. Like the infant Stephen at the very beginning of the *Portrait,* nothing more than the point of traversal of a clamor of other voices,
this Stephen too, striding across Dublin, is interpenetrated by words, by

places, in what is almost a topological eversion. In place of a Stephen who in his passage lays claim to Dublin, we have a Stephen traversed by the city, and across whose very body Dublin will write itself. This is a Stephen who is already HCE, the sleeping giant who is also Dublin, and whose culminating monologue in III.3 is the intersection of all sorts of series: the response to and echoing of the accusations of civic guilt, the story of the wooing or rape of ALP, of the building of Dublin, of the Viking invasions, of the Irish diaspora, of the path of the Liffey as it heads to the sea (*FW* 532.06–554.10).

Which way does it go, which is within what? The figure is that peculiar one Derrida calls double invagination ("Living On" 97–103), whereby an apparent subset is seen to contain the whole. Such a figure—and here it is, again, precisely figuration and figurality which are in question—comes about because of the instability of boundaries. This is not at the level of some sort of threatened psychotic collapse of what should have been firm and clear from the beginning. It is rather a matter of the serial and asyndetic nature of all boundary: the sheer contingency of that necessary meeting, and the unstoppable multiplication and subdivision of that meeting across the entire series. Stephen's passing through Dublin is also Dublin's passing through Stephen. Its sights, sounds, and smells permeate him, as do the writings with which they are juxtaposed—the marketplace and literature—to find a new and unstable synthesis. Stephen is subject in as much as he is this precarious point of intersection.

Hence the *Portrait*'s complex and often-noted use of free indirect discourse, which does not so much express a subject as map out its emergence within a language which is not its own. Hence also the importance of the third-person narration of the book, which thus avoids any claim to that impossible central place of an originary voice. The very language of *Portrait* is always from somewhere just off to one side of Stephen, who is never—and this is true even of its dialogue—simply its source or point of emission, but rather an inflection, a curvature, a tonality: the lisp of the green rose. This is emphasized by the distinction between narration and focalization which the book carefully maintains. As many commentators have pointed out, *Portrait* gives the effect of a single source of light, a world in which everything grows progressively hazier and attenuated in proportion to its distance from Stephen. But the correlate of this is that Stephen is not the source of that light, which is shed *on* him from elsewhere, somewhere off unseen on what is a periphery precisely because the dazzlement of that source prevents us ever seeing beyond it. If Stephen speaks, it is because his words come to him from elsewhere, passing across and over him like that "keen wind" which is the spirit of Ibsen.[10] In this respect, *A Portrait of the Artist as a Young Man* is an anti-*Bildungsroman*: it is not about the gradual unfolding of the germ of selfhood from within, but about what comes to produce but never fill this empty, folded interiority. Stephen is the unstable set of signature effects generated by and in such a collision of series. He is first of all a name for the flickerings and swerves within a language which can never be anything but borrowed, not because of a deep and irredeemable inauthenticity of language or the subject, but because this borrowing is its very possibility. (We recall his confusion over the dean's use of the word *funnel* for an object Stephen has always thought of as a *tundish*. Stephen thinks of the word he knows as Irish, and the dean's word as the imposition of colonialism; only later does he find out to his annoyance that it is actually the Irish survival of an Elizabethan English word, now obsolete in England [*P* 274].) Within the contingencies of these meeting series, there is hollowed out that third series which manifests itself as a series of *comportments*. We have the "rainladen trees of the avenue" and the "memories of the girls and women of the plays of Gerhart Hauptmann," and at their intersection, "the memory of their pale sorrows and the fragrance falling from the wet branches *mingled in a mood of quiet joy*." The windows of the provision shops on the North Strand Road refract the "dark humor" of Cavalcanti into a smile, the Ibsen wind on Talbot Place invests Stephen with "a spirit of wayward boyish beauty."

The most elaborate example of this series of comportments—and of this section's use of free indirect discourse—is to follow, as Stephen passes the marinedealer's, and repeats to himself

the song by Ben Jonson which begins:

I was not wearier where I lay.

His mind, when wearied of its search for the essence of beauty amid the spectral words of Aristotle or Aquinas, turned often for its pleasure to the dainty songs of the Elizabethans. His mind, in the vesture of a doubting monk, stood often in shadow under the windows of that age, to hear the grave and mocking music of the lutenists or the frank laughter of waistcoaters until a laugh too low, a phrase, tarnished by time, of chambering and false honor, stung his monkish pride and drove him from his lurkingplace. (*P* 190–91)

"Search for the essence of beauty," "turned often for its pleasure to," "the dainty songs of the Elizabethans," the "frank laughter of waistcoaters": the diction is forced, an exercise in style and deliberate archaism whose very derivativeness marks out the effect we call "Stephen" as much as a "repaired" marks out Uncle Charles. In their preciosity, the words stand out as something tried on for the occasion, like an unfamiliar suit of clothing—like, in fact, that archaism "vesture" which both *belongs to* and *is* itself that monk: like clothing, the monk is a role Stephen can put on or take off as he desires. So too no less is the seeker after "the essence of beauty"; the next paragraph will tell us of his feeling that "the spirit of beauty had folded him round like a mantle" (191).

But this is not to imply an "authentic" Stephen at the heart of all these "inauthentic" masks and vestures. Far from it. It is as if the generative machinery behind this is not a personality, a Stephen whom we already know: this newly aesthetic Stephen, seeker in Aristotle and Aquinas, is after all unfamiliar to us before this point. What we are seeing is the generation of all this out of a series of possible dictions and even ways of filling the empty structure of a sentence. After the Jonson song we have two sentences which begin almost as formal variants:

His mind, when wearied of its search . . .

His mind, in the vesture of a doubting monk . . .

They start off identically and continue in each case with a prepositional phrase ("of . . .") which emphasizes a common doubt, a search for what is not there, and thus has to be sought elsewhere. Between those two points, the "his mind" which begins each sentence and the seeking or doubting which follows it, we have what appears, at least, to be something different in each case. In the first, the sentence takes up the "wearier," which has already been offered it by the Jonson poem immediately before, and puts it on, like vesture, tries it out: wears it—and passes it on.

wearier → wear → vesture

Perhaps it is possible to trace here a series like that of "throwaway" in *Ulysses,* where the sheer contingency of a signifier is forever subdividing and multiplying itself to generate a loose but insistent web of meanings across the text. That "wearied" will after all turn up again in the chapter as a strongly generative word, as we shall see, especially as Stephen begins to phrase the villanelle to himself. The final diary entries of the novel will multiply these tryings-on of comportments, that sense of Stephen watching himself try on roles—as indeed will *Ulysses,* from the moment of Stephen's initial glimpse of himself "as he and others see me" in Mulligan's shaving mirror (*U* 1.136), to the self-conscious brooding on the beach in "Proteus," and to the phantasmagoria of "Circe"; and in this sense of the trying-on of a number of *stylistic* comportments, the *Portrait* already anticipates the middle chapters of *Ulysses.*

"Stephen" is the name *A Portrait of the Artist as a Young Man* gives to a particular set of effects it stages across a series of reflexive addresses like these. That is, it is not just that the *Portrait* is staging a series of roles attached to that name—the wearied and self-denying seeker of beauty, the improbable "doubting monk" in a Merrie England of mocking lutenists and laughing prostitutes—but that it is also *staging its own staging of those roles*. Bloom watches Gerty watching him watch her . . . Stephen is not just the aggregate of those roles, but the impossible, invisible point from which they seem to be played as roles: the virtual point of an optics. Stephen is nowhere and everywhere in the text, not so much its principle as its effect, a looking at looking or a remembering remembering: a *turning,* as the text has it, from "the spectral words of Aristotle or Aquinas" to "the dainty songs of the Elizabethans," from seeker of beauty to doubting monk, from first sentence to second, and within the second from monk to overhearer of the pleasures of others. And in this turning and its doubling and redoubling of stagings, "Stephen" becomes in turn the site for a sly and persistent pleasure, which seems not so much to inhabit the roles themselves as lie, again, in the slippage among them. Even the monk's stung pride becomes a sort of pleasure, much as the younger Stephen, taking on the role of Edmond Dantes, Count of Monte Cristo, can take pleasure in his "sadly proud gesture of refusal": "Madam, I never eat muscatel grapes" (*P* 65).

The taste of grapes, the love of Mercedes, the waistcoateers and the chambering: these are the sorts of sensuous pleasures which Stephen will shortly declare to Lynch as too kinetic, too mingled with the marketplace to be truly aesthetic. And yet there is a certain surplus of pleasure here in this renunciation which is inseparable from watching oneself renounce, a nice little profit to be turned.[11] *I have renounced pleasure, and from that I can draw pleasure.* That very renunciation performed in the name of the aesthetic cannot escape being a maneuver of the market: a hoarding, in short, which temporarily removes itself from circulation only in order to reap the profit of that removal. This is what the free indirect discourse of the *Portrait* works to emphasize: the very words out of which Stephen emerges here on the page for us, and the very words out of which both his aesthetic theories and his comportment of artist emerge, are themselves words which come to him only through the marketplace of a language in all its history and social circulation. The weariness of his mind is offered him by a Jonson poem; not wearied of ardent ways, he will incorporate it and work it into his own poem in turn. It is as if Stephen is a device a poem has for making another poem. Or rather, what we have here is quite precisely the Lacanian definition of the signifier as that which represents the subject for another signifier (Lacan, *Écrits* 316; Žižek, *Sublime* 104). Stephen takes on the wearied phrase as his own, bestowed on him, the mandate of Literature itself. If the Elizabethan age he invokes can stand for Literature in this way, as it will in much of the discussion in the library in *Ulysses,* it is not only a vision of a particularly kinetic and sensuous England, but also a highly clichéd and market-soiled one, both in the details it gives and in the diction of the offer. In the terms Stephen has set up, the very emergence of the aesthetic is marked by this paradox. Its very possibility is given it by what it must refuse; but for it to refuse the marketplace would be to forgo its own possibility.

So, in these intersections, the subject emerges as a series of roles. Or *vestures,* as the text would have it: in that word, *Stephen* flickers out as a momentary effect, not first of all, as the Uncle Charles Principle would have it, because we know already that this is the sort of word Stephen would use if he were to describe things, but because the word itself is marked with a certain difference which distances it from the classically distantiating tone of third-person novelistic discourse. It is this distance which we take as *synecdochic* of Stephen, with all the deep ambivalence Ellmann gives that term. The word appears to come from Stephen, it works as if emitted by him, it is a part which comes to stand for the whole; it sets up a distinction between what is properly Stephen and what is not, one which is unstable and thus stands to be a source of anxiety, even perhaps abjection as it perilously inverts itself: the vesture of the monk, after all, is to wear the stinging of pride as pleasure. What is lost may also stand to turn a profit elsewhere, expulsion to become incorporation, synecdoche to become metaphor, when these roles are already like clothing, to be tried on or exchanged at will. And again, as Derrida has already pointed out, the metaphor of clothing is metaphoricity itself, metaphoricity redoubled, the metaphor *of* metaphor (*Post Card* 415). The "essence of beauty" Stephen seeks is not something hidden away in depths: it is "folded him round *like a mantle.*" Beauty's *essence* is like a covering, which both conceals and promises the revelation of a truth. Beauty is not what is hidden, but this very game of hide-and-seek which slips between the truth and the metaphor, the literal and the figurative: a mantle, whose wearing effects a tenuous distinction sustained only in its own collapse. Or a comportment, around the name of Stephen: "wrapped up in yourself," as McCann will accuse (*P* 191).

The very possibility of the subject, then, is bound up with the question of metaphor and synecdoche, and thus with what Ellmann calls incorporation and emission. Here, it is worth recalling Lacan's thesis on the "metaphor of the subject," as Slavoj Žižek reworks it (*For They Know Not* 48–49). There are two complementary ways, Žižek argues, in which the subject can be seen in terms of metaphor, each of which has its own commonsensical, self-evident experience of subjectivity. In the first, the subject is seen as "the last, ever-elusive Signified of the signifying chain." The subject transcends the signifying chain, so the closest relationship any signifier can have to the subject is as a metaphor: *like* but not *the same as* the subject, pointing obliquely to it but always missing, misrepresenting it even as it represents it as faithfully as it can. This is the commonplace feeling that our deep subjectivity is quite beyond words. The second way of seeing subjectivity in terms of metaphor seems at first to be opposed to this. Here, the subject is not the ultimate reference point beyond all language, but steeped throughout language, "a name for the different ways the described state of things is always-already presented from some partial, biased position of enunciation." If a naïve communications theory would like to see language exclusively in terms of the conveying of information, then subjectivity would reside in all those features which refuse to let language be just "a neutral tool for designation of some objective state of things" (49). That is, subjectivity is here a matter of the functions of address, of the positions of addresser and addressee provided within the text and the slidings among them, and in particular, of all those little stylistic opacities which act as signature effects. From the point of view of our straw communications model, all these can be seen only as pure noise, but as we have seen these *comportments* arise out of the contingent meetings of multiple and autonomous series. Those flickerings of "Stephenness" within *Portrait*'s polyphony of free indirect discourse do not name a subject which transcends them and which would be their original source; they name the serial structure of signification, whose asyndetic overlappings, gaps, excesses, redundancies are subjectality itself.

The first of these two ways tends to think of subject as substance, even if it can retain that substantiality only by being pushed off into the unreachable. Here, the signifier of this distant subject tends to collapse into what Lacan calls the "metonymy of the object": that is, in this case, *synecdoche*, in which the signifier stands for a part of the transcendent whole. The second relation is far more radical in its implications, though, for with it the signifier stands not for an absent plenitude, but for a gap, a hiatus, a silence. This is why Žižek can say that "[t]he 'original metaphor' is not a substitution of 'something for something-else' but a substitution of *something for nothing:* the act by means of which 'there is something instead of nothing'" (*For They Know Not* 50). Metaphor in this sense counts Zero as One. As such, it is the originary figure, accounting not only for metaphor in its ordinary sense ("something for something-else") but also for metonymy and synecdoche: "the metonymic sliding from one (partial) object to another is set in motion by the metaphoric substitution constitutive of the subject: the 'one for another' presupposes the 'one for nothing'" (*For They Know Not* 50). A metonymy of the object and a metaphor of the subject, then. Do we not have here Ellmann's description of the marketplace, with its synecdochic flows outwards and its metaphoric flows inwards? Metaphor is the relationship "towards the substanceless void which is the subject" (*For They Know Not* 50), while synecdoche-metonymy constitutes the relationship to the object. And both are unstable. There is no simple boundary between them any more than there was between the other pairings we have encountered. The void of the subject is constituted in the intersections of the event, in all its materiality and contingency; the object is close to the abject. Metaphor and metonymy are the asymmetric names for what happens *across* the juxtapositions of series which have concerned us here: names for the production of a tenuous subject of gaps, and the no less tenuous substantiality of the world against which this subject finds itself placed. The two overlap nevertheless in this asymmetry. One of the effects of this metaphoricity is after all that feeling that the subject is indeed a thing, even if one which is inscrutably deep and unreachable by words. The subject is at one and the same moment an interruption or hiatus of or within flows, and the production of a sort of phantom substantiality. The site, in other words, of a hoarding.

We are left, all the time, it would seem, with a number of disparate series, and between them the contingent space of their meeting. This space, if we can even call it that, is profoundly empty, in the sense that its regimes of exchange are not given before the event. But there is minimally an incessant and instantaneous traversal of this space, a crossing-over from one series to another. It is in this *rhythm* between series and in its immeasurable rapidity that the subject arises as a phenomenon of boundaries. But they are boundaries which are brought into being only by such a rhythm, and which are thus transgressed in and by their very postulation as boundaries. The *Portrait*'s entire rhetoric of transgression begs to be seen in this light, from first to last: from the infant's guilt as he hides under the table from the words and figures which invoke him as subject and demand from him response, to the young man's decision to fly by the nets of nation, family, and religion. It is also the rhythm of pleasure and disgust in their sheer proximity; the text swings from one to the other: at times finding one nestling in the other, as with Stephen's first encounter with the prostitute; at others juxtaposing them across a literal and typographical gap, like the one between the bird-girl epiphany at the end of chapter IV and the fried-bread-and-dripping breakfast which opens chapter V.

It is also, of course, the dynamics of the distinction Stephen wishes to make between art and the marketplace, which as we have seen is postulated on its own dissolution. We find in him an incessant oscillation. In the midst of his doubts, an acquaintance with "nobility" and "the spirit of beauty" allows him to be "glad to find himself still in the midst of common lives, passing on his way amid the squalor and noise and sloth of the city fearlessly and with a light heart" (P 191). But then, just a few pages later, there will be the disturbing recollection of Cranly, which will turn all of this yet again to threat:

> the nightshade of his friend's listlessness seemed to be diffusing in the air around him a tenuous and deadly exhalation and he found himself glancing from one casual word to another on his right or left in stolid wonder that they had been so silently emptied of instantaneous sense until every mean shop legend bound his mind like the words of a spell and his soul shrivelled up, sighing with age as he walked on in a lane among heaps of dead language. (P 193)

The "heaps of wet rubbish" and "mouldering offal" in the waterlogged lane behind the terrace in which Stephen and his family live (P 189) have transposed themselves in this rhythm—Stephen's walking—into the "heaps of dead language" of another lane. The very echoing of the phrases in their assonance (*wet . . . dead*) and scansion (*rubbish . . . language*) underlines the bringing-together of the series of city and literature. Stephen is here most clearly a creature of this empty, serial language which, before it serves to express any inwardness, is the rhythm of a passage through the streets:

> His own consciousness of language was ebbing from his brain and trickling into the very words themselves which set to band and disband themselves in wayward rhythms:
>
> *The ivy whines upon the wall*
> *And whines and twines upon the wall*
> *The ivy whines upon the wall*
> *The yellow ivy on the wall*
> *Ivy, ivy up the wall.*

Did any one ever hear such drivel? Lord Almighty! Who ever heard
of ivy whining on a wall? Yellow ivy: that was all right. Yellow ivory
also. And what about ivory ivy?

The word now shone in his brain, clearer and brighter than any
ivory sawn from the mottled tusks of elephants. *Ivory, ivoire, avorio,
ebur.* One of the first examples that he had learnt in Latin had run:
India mittit ebur; and he had recalled the shrewd northern face of the
rector who had taught him to construe the Metamorphoses of Ovid
in a courtly English, made whimsical by the mention of porkers and
potsherds and chines of bacon. He had learnt what little he knew of
the laws of Latin verse from a ragged book written by a Portuguese
priest. (*P* 193–94)

Stephen is somewhat late on a scene already occupied by a chattering and
banal language. It is with a slight shock, followed immediately by saving
and sharp disdain, that he realizes the doggerel which *has already* been
going through his head, and for which he seems to have been the passive
and quite unaware site. His reaction is one of disgust. Something unclean
which should have been kept at a certain distance has come too close, has
found its way almost into his mouth, and the first impulse is to spit it out
again. And with this everything immediately everts itself, as that very
selfhood becomes an outward, excretory flow into the thing which is now
greeted with disgust: "[h]is own consciousness of language was ebbing
from his brain and *trickling* into the very words themselves."[12]

The invasive words move according to their own logic and time as they
"set to band and disband themselves in wayward rhythm": the verbal
mechanism of that Elizabethan fantasy is now brought out onto the very
surface, free as the ivy doggerel seems to be from all but a minimum of
sense. Whatever continuity it might have does not come to it from any
unities of the ego, but from the combinatories of the letter: not from an "I"
or a will, but from an *i* and an *ll* and their repetitions and accretions which,
like ivy itself, will grow and fasten onto whatever is at hand. Within the
verse itself, there are of course *ivy, whines,* and *twines,* and the five *wall*s
whose *ll* will in the fourth line be absorbed by this growing and now
ye*ll*ow ivy. The shock of delayed recognition and disavowal will not be
enough to stop the process, as the very disavowal itself continues this
banding and disbanding ("Did any one ever hear such dr*i*vel? Lord Al-
m*i*ghty!"). And almost as soon as the disavowal is made, it too will be
dismissed, for what Stephen finds in these apparently senseless colloca-
tions is an unexpected interest, something indeed quite usable, that ye*ll*ow

ivy ("that was a*ll* r*i*ght"). From now on in this sequence, just as it was the word rather than the concept of *paralysis* which has previously filled the young narrator of "The Sisters" with fear, it will be the word itself which shines in this brain from which the "consciousness of language" has just recently ebbed, and where the signifier itself is "clearer and brighter" than the thing it stands for and has now eclipsed. The combinatory continues apace, without change: all that has changed is that Stephen now no longer shuns it ("Yellow ivory also. And what about ivory ivy?"). Indeed, given that what formally distinguishes poetry from prose is precisely its structuring according to the signifier, how could he? At the moment when it might be tempting to see Stephen as coming into his own, as becoming in however jejune a way a poet, it is not because he has suddenly found a voice and starts to speak stammeringly of what lies within, but simply because he is affirming the impersonality and contingency of a language which arrives at him after the event. Banality has become mandate. Now it is the signifier itself which will proliferate and generate its series: *ivory, ivoire, avorio, ebur;* India *mitt*it ebur; O*vi*d, not by chance the poet of *Metamorphoses;* Latin *v*erse, and va*ri*ant *i*n *carmine vates* ("the poets"—not only Ovid!—"transform in their verses"); the signatures of the brothers *I*n*v*erar*i*ty on his "timeworn Horace," on verses which seem to have *"lai*n a*ll* those years in my*rt*le and *la*vender and *v*er*v*a*i*n"—all of which will culminate, across the span of another forty pages, in Stephen's *v*illane*lle* (*P* 193–94).

Of course, all this is not simply to be taken as Stephen's intention. Intention is not the point here. What we have is a repetition which began before intention or even awareness could latch onto it, and by which intention is largely dragged along: the ivy has been whining in Stephen's head for a while before he hears it. It makes no more sense to rephrase the question as a matter of *Joyce's* intentions, as what we have here is a staging of the serial structures in which subjectivity itself arises: subsisting only on boundaries, indeterminately inside or outside, neither simple accident and thus to be dismissed from the arena of meaning, nor yet meaning itself, for what is at work here is a repetition on a smaller scale than that of the word, breaking up the word into its component letters and sounds and rhythmically regrouping them. For all its obvious differences, in *A Portrait of the Artist as a Young Man* we are not all that far from the processes which *Finnegans Wake* will elaborate into a structural principle: the collision of all sorts of preverbal figures, the chance striking of sense out of these, the generative functions of rhythm.

And this rhythm which underlies the possibilities of subjectivity, and of the aestheticizing in which a young man is perhaps becoming an artist, is something Stephen's aesthetic engages with from the outset. We see it mused on again in the walk which counterbalances the one we have just been reading, in the arguments Stephen conducts with Lynch as the two of them head across town on foot, in a long and important sequence which carries them from University College to the National Library, south of Trinity College (*P* 221–35). Again, we shall have to pay particular attention to the ways the argument is *performed* in the fiction. The text meagerly but significantly records their passage through the city: the canal bridge, Sir Patrick Dun's hospital, Lower Mount Street, Merrion Square, the Duke's lawn (*P* 224, 226, 228, 229, 233)—part of Stephen's earlier path to classes that morning took him in almost the reverse trajectory. Two sites of learning, then, connected by a loop, and between them the urban hubbub of the city. It is a juxtaposition rather like the one which informs the two central chapters of *Ulysses*, "Scylla and Charybdis" and "Wandering Rocks": the most cerebral and the most physical chapters, the most static and the most kinetic, art and the city, the library and the labyrinth. While Stephen may want clearly to separate out such groupings, the narrative framing of *Portrait* nevertheless offers a continual and multiple blurring of their boundaries. In the college, the arguments Stephen and his confreres make are all about politics and nationalism, and on the library steps at the other end the talk is all about jobs and earning money: the arguments on aesthetics are left for the streets, where Lynch, like Mulligan after him, will turn Stephen's examples into opportunities for bawdiness, and the urban setting itself will, as we shall see, furthermore interrupt in all sorts of sly ways.

There are some quite elaborate patternings here. At beginning and end of this round trip from Trinity College to University College and back, two closely interrelated encounters stand like bookends. Echoing the endings of chapters II and IV (which themselves mirror each other and stand as opening and conclusion to Stephen's religious fervor), these too will be encounters with women. On his way to classes in the morning, along Grafton Street near Trinity College and the Library, Stephen has met a flowergirl and brusquely rejected her approaches (*P* 198–99). On the Library steps at the other end of the round trip, he will see the young woman with whom he is in love, standing silently among her companions as he is among his (*P* 234–35); but he remembers the jealousy aroused by her speaking and laughing with Father Moran, for which he has already dropped out of the Gaelic League classes (*P* 219), and neither of them addresses the other. In each case, the (non-)meeting is framed by commerce. In the first, this comes from the suggestions of prostitution it carries, and Stephen's "wishing to be out of the way before she offered her ware to another, a tourist from England or a student of Trinity," both of whom will presumably have the money to afford it (*P* 199). In the second, Stephen's mind has "emptied of theory and courage," and is filled with the voices of students around him, which reach his ears "as if from a distance in *interrupted pulsation*": chatter of careers now the exam results are known, and how "There's plenty of money to be made in a big commercial city" (*P* 234: my emphasis). What's more, the two episodes are balanced against each other so that the second retrospectively rereads the first. That Stephen is so clearly troubled by E—— C—— on the second occasion seems to indicate that his apparent failure to give her a thought on the first—even as he is passing through the very area of the city in which he must expect he will meet her that afternoon—can be read as a careful repression. What is left of it on the surface of things is his displaced impatience and shortness with the flowergirl.[13] If University College is connected with Stephen's studies, the Library and Trinity College would appear to be associated here, one way or another, with the amorous.[14] Far from being the havens for an art removed from the marketplace, the endpoints of that return trip would seem to be marked by the kinetic and improperly aesthetic emotions Stephen associates with the pornographical and didactic (*P* 222).

But things are more complex yet. That first meeting is already doubled when it occurs, for Stephen has just this moment been remembering *another* encounter, the one Davin has told him about: the peasant woman's invitation. Memory is again as ambivalent, serial, and multiple as it was earlier, when those "rainladen trees of the avenue evoked in him, as always, memories of the girls and women of the plays of Gerhart Hauptmann" (*P* 190). Here, the woman in the story is already multiplied out in an indefinite hall of reflections. By the time the flowergirl arrives on the scene, the place for her has already been prepared: the Irish woman who offers something to the stranger. The two incidents are hinged together as Stephen strides down Grafton Street:

> The last words of Davin's story sang in his memory and the figure of the woman in the story stood forth, *reflected in other figures* of the peasant woman whom he had seen standing in the doorways at Clane as the college cars drove by, as a type of her race and his own, a batlike soul waking to the consciousness of itself in darkness and secrecy and loneliness and, through the eyes and voice and gesture of

a woman without guile, calling the stranger to her bed.

A hand was laid on his arm and a young voice cried:

—Ah, gentleman, your own girl, sir! The first handsel today, gentleman. Buy that lovely bunch. Will you, gentleman?

The blue flowers which she lifted towards him and her young blue eyes seemed to him at that instant images of guilelessness; and he halted till the image had vanished and he saw only her ragged dress and damp coarse hair and hoydenish face. (*P* 198: my emphasis)

The series will continue. Alone in his room, with the words of the villanelle forming in his mind, Stephen will be angry at E—— C—— for her failure to salute him on the Library steps and for her flirtation with the young priest, and will place her in the same series:

Rude brutal anger routed the last lingering instant of ecstasy from his soul. It broke up violently her fair image and flung the fragments on all sides. On all sides *distorted reflections of her image* started from his memory: the flowergirl in the ragged dress with damp coarse hair and a hoyden's face who had called herself his own girl and begged his handsel, the kitchengirl in the next house who sang over the clatter of her plates with the drawl of a country singer the first bars of *By Killarney's Lakes and Fells,* a girl who had laughed gaily to see him stumble when the iron grating in the footpath near Cork Hill had caught the broken sole of his shoe, a girl he had glanced at, attracted by her small ripe mouth as she passed out of Jacob's biscuit factory, who had cried to him over her shoulder:

—Do you like what you seen of me, straight hair and curly eyebrows? (*P* 239: my emphasis)

To underline it, there is even the repetition of the same words in the description of each:

He had told himself bitterly as he walked through the streets that she was a figure of the womanhood of her country, *a batlike soul waking to the consciousness of itself in darkness and secrecy and loneliness,* tarrying awhile, loveless and sinless, with her mild lover and leaving him to whisper of innocent transgressions in the latticed ear of a priest. (*P* 239–40: my emphasis)

As in "The Sisters," it is the words which fascinate. They sing in Stephen's mind and bring forth this series of types of "her race and his." Their fascination is not due to their signified meaning (just what *does* that repeated phrase mean?), but to the trying-out of a diction, a comportment. Stephen wears them as a vesture: being no less angry or bitter, but watching himself, in angry or bitter fascination, *being angry or bitter as a poet might*. The peasant woman, the flowergirl, those endless figures of the womanhood of their country—and now E—— C——, jealousy for whom we may suspect has been behind this series all along. There will shortly be another term to add to the series.

Stephen passes through the marketplace his art would disdain, and in the rhythms and slippages of this *aestheticizing on his feet,* we glimpse other series, other factors at work, layered in together by these rhythms: jealousy and sexual desire, say, the vestures of a monk, or a poet. Sometimes this rhythmic interlayering may lead to something disruptive or disturbing, as it will just at the very moment when Stephen is about to analyze the aesthetic in terms of rhythm.

Before Stephen and Lynch even begin their walk and the discussion, there is that small framing action we noted earlier. Stephen has taken "a packet of cigarettes from his pocket and offered it to his companion," saying "I know you are poor"; Lynch has responded by damning his "yellow insolence," but nevertheless accepts the gift (*P* 221). The exchange is important, for it places Lynch under an obligation to Stephen which, being poor, he can repay only in the way Stephen asks of him: by being a listener. Stephen's juxtaposition of art and marketplace is played out to a bought audience. It is clearly a familiar routine for both parties. Stephen wastes no time in pleasantries after Lynch accepts, starts in almost immediately on his definitions of the tragic emotions of pity and terror, and simply rides over Lynch's protestations. He has obviously rehearsed for the occasion: the definitions are balanced, symmetric, paired, not at all improvised. As clarification, he will give an example of what is *not* tragic—of the misuse of the word in the marketplace, in fact, and in a story which takes place on the streets:

> —Pity is the feeling which arrests the mind in the presence of whatsoever is grave and constant in human sufferings and unites it with the human sufferer. Terror is the feeling which arrests the mind in the presence of whatsoever is grave and constant in human sufferings and unites it with the secret cause.
> —Repeat, said Lynch.
> Stephen repeated the definitions slowly.
> —A girl got into a hansom a few days ago, he went on, in London. She was on her way to meet her mother whom she had not seen for

many years. At the corner of a street the shaft of a lorry shivered the window of the hansom in the shape of a star. A long fine needle of the shivered glass pierced her heart. She died on the instant. The reporter called it a tragic death. It is not. It is remote from terror and pity according to the terms of my definitions.

—The tragic emotion, in fact, is a face looking two ways, towards terror and towards pity, both of which are phases of it. You see I use the word *arrest*. I mean that the tragic emotion is static. Or rather the dramatic emotion is. The feelings excited by improper art are kinetic, desire or loathing. Desire urges us to possess, to go to something; loathing urges us to abandon, to go from something. These are kinetic emotions. The arts which excite them, pornographical or didactic, are therefore improper arts. The aesthetic emotion (I use the general term) is therefore static. The mind is arrested and raised above desire and loathing. (*P* 221–22)

So the tragic emotion is an arrest, it is static. But it has phases: it looks both ways, towards the sufferer and towards the cause. It oscillates between at least two positions, each irreducible to the other. Stephen's definitions suggest in their symmetry that this is one and the same process for both pity and terror: all that is different between them is the direction in which each aims. This stasis of the true tragic or dramatic emotion which comprises them is thus not frozen and motionless but a rhythm, an extremely rapid oscillation from subject to cause, pity to terror and back, without ever approaching or abandoning either pole, which would be to lapse into the improper and the kinetic. The static is necessarily a tension maintained against what would disturb it from outside, a homeostasis which turns out to be not the absence of movement but its acceleration and virtualization.

And in this virtualization, the tragic emotion is also profoundly impersonal, as opposed to the improper and invariably personalized desires called up by kinetic art, for which all movement is to be seen as coming from or back to the self: possession, loathing, flights to or away from. Stephen's very choice of terms emphasizes that. Personal pronouns characterize his descriptions of the kinetic, which is a matter of "our flesh," "our eyelid" which blinks as the fly approaches "our eye" (*P* 223); or "your flesh," Lynch's, aroused by the Venus of Praxiteles (*P* 222). In the aesthetic emotion, on the other hand, there are simply the bare articles: "the mind is arrested," beauty induces "an aesthetic stasis, an ideal pity or an ideal terror" (*P* 223). Personality is not the question here. It is not a matter of the "you" or "us" or even "I" (though Stephen will admit gen-

erously that "we are all animals. I also am an animal" in polite parenthesis
[*P* 223]). It is a question of "the mind," which is produced in and across
that rapid subjectal rhythm of stasis: impersonal, as that definite article
suggests. The static is neither personal nor expressive of a person, inasmuch as it is static: what it expresses is beauty, which is precisely this
impersonal rhythm. It is the state of the subject as pure oscillation across
a mark, that "slow and dark birth" of the soul of which Stephen has just
spoken to Davin, "more mysterious than that of the body" (*P* 220), and
which, as oscillation, is also and at the same time the process of its own
dissolution. "Beauty expressed by the artist," says Stephen,

> cannot awaken in us an emotion which is kinetic or a sensation
> which is purely physical. It awakens, or ought to awaken, or in-
> duces, or ought to induce, an aesthetic stasis, an ideal pity or an ideal
> terror, a stasis called forth, prolonged and at last dissolved by what
> I call the rhythm of beauty. (*P* 223)

The aesthetic is not a representation, but the name for a *genesis*, that
moment of intersection of a number of series in their contigency which
Stephen will define as rhythm: "the first formal aesthetic relation of part
to part in any aesthetic whole or of an aesthetic whole to its part or parts
or of any part to the aesthetic whole of which it is a part" (*P* 223). Rhythm
is synecdochic: it belongs to the marketplace before the chaste retentions
of Literature, and as dismembering and emission before remembering and
incorporation (M. Ellmann 193).

And the genuinely aesthetic stasis is "called forth" by this "rhythm of
beauty," that "first formal aesthetic relation." But it *need not* be. Beauty
"awakens, or *ought to* awaken, or induces, or *ought to* induce": there are
all sorts of vicissitudes in play here, where the very expression of beauty is
subject to contingency. It *ought* to induce that stasis, but it *need* not; and
Stephen admits this from the beginning.

There are at least two ways in which we could read that. The first
would be to see this expressed beauty as something which lies behind all its
manifestations, and whose tenuous emergence into visibility would be the
proper business of the artwork—but for all that, the artwork is unable to
guarantee this emergence, which is subject to all kinds of unforeseeable
vicissitudes both in the artist's execution and the reader's engagement. The
artwork expresses something prior and transcendental in the mundane,
and the physical form of the artwork and the circumstances of its composition and reception are all essentially later accretions. The ideal exists
behind or beyond or before the artwork, which strives to reveal it to us, to

present us with an eternal Idea beyond the world of appearances. It is familiar, banal, and, as we shall soon see, something Stephen will refuse.

But what if, on the other hand, we read quite literally the suggestion that the rhythm of beauty is "the first formal aesthetic relation"? That is, that before this rhythm, there is no prior and transcendental Idea, and that the aesthetic whole is itself a product of that relation? In the beginning is the rhythm. From this arises much of the complexity—and the dilemma— of the *Portrait's* aesthetics, which the novel plays out through Stephen and even behind his back. If Stephen wants to define art against the marketplace, and then refine that further by distinguishing a proper against an improper art, then *the proper* becomes intensely problematic. What should by rights be the principle *behind* this aesthetics, some set of fixed conditions by reference to which one can declare what is or is not genuinely art, becomes a sort of shorthand for an effect of rhythm. It can define itself only against an *im*proper which it is forced to keep in its sights as a perpetual rejection, and which thus secretly informs it everywhere, at its heart.

Pity and terror are phases of the tragic or aesthetic emotion, says Stephen. I define pity thus. I define terror thus. Repeat, says Lynch, who insists on paying fairly for his cigarettes. And the example Stephen gives is a *negative* one, of the *im*proper: this is what the proper is *not*. The horrible story is allowed to hang there, suspended, fascinating: no example of the proper follows it, to dispel the kinetic emotions this thin sliver of story has introduced. Invoking the improper at the very moment which claims to dispel it, it even makes the improper linger. As if *the proper* were simply, all along, another name for the improper. And what is this improper story about, this story which reintroduces the improper into the argument? Precisely about the introduction of the improper, of something which penetrates improperly into the heart.

Improper, because it is clear that the story is intensely sexualized: the death is a horrible parody of the sexual act. It immediately takes the place prepared for it in that peasant woman–flowergirl series, but inverts a number of its signs. The directly or indirectly sexualized encounter the young woman with a male stranger becomes the chaste meeting with the longlost mother; the sexual(ized) encounter turned down becomes a non-sexual encounter turned intensely and grotesquely sexual; instead of a refusal, we have the reluctant heart finally penetrated; instead of the moral, or moralistic, refusal, we have a rape; and instead of the aesthetic refusal of the pornographic and the didactic, we have something violently sexual and the uneasy feeling that this is a fantasized staging in which, with a distant and obscene enjoyment, someone is being taught a lesson. . . . Doubly, triply improper: something intervenes violently, in all directions at once. The lorry intrudes violently into the hansom, the glass intrudes into the heart, the story brings with it everything the aesthetic would exclude. The story doubles itself, performs in a displaced way what it describes, describes what it does, acts out that describing, and describes that describing. It not only sets out the intrusion of the improper and the sexualized nature of that intrusion, but the way in which one intrusion stands for or does the work of another. The shaft of a lorry shatters the thin membrane of the window, and then, in turn, a long fine needle of that shivered glass enters the girl's heart—as if what kills *is* the doubling. *Multiply* improper, then: in this doubling and redoubling, there can be no counting the story's improprieties.

And it is a found story, to hand, like the shout from the hockey field. Not Stephen's invention, it is something he read in the papers, and which may originally have carried none of the resonances it has for Stephen. So much the better that it is agentless: *this is not my story, I am not doing this, it is a newspaper report, the blind mass of a lorry, the frangibility of glass.* Everywhere Stephen turns, he finds the reflection of his own distinctly kinetic emotions in what comes to hand, already there, laid out across the world, ready for him to encounter.

This is not to argue that Stephen's aesthetics is nothing more than confused adolescent feelings of sexuality. This is not a choice between a genuine aesthetics and young lust, one or the other: that would, after all, be exactly the distinction between static and kinetic, proper and improper, which Stephen's theory itself cannot sustain. It is *both,* and more, articulated in many different series at the same time: aestheticizing before it is an aesthetics, a comportment produced at the intersections of series; an improvisation with what is at hand. Throughout, a recurrent series of incidents has provided a number of momentary, unstable positions Stephen comes to inhabit, or feels unable to inhabit, or tries on as vesture, or hangs suspended between: swooning sinner, renouncer of muscatel grapes, acolyte whose sacrificing hands upraise the chalice, visionary striding far out over the sands, masturbator waking from odorous sleep, franchisee of the spiritual-heroic refrigerating apparatus. They are not exclusive: Stephen can be one, or the other, or many, or all of these. They only appear to be successive; they are inhabited with a furious simultaneity, so that the progression of the narrative is not a trajectory from one actant to the next, but a process of eversion: the acolyte sacrifices himself, the renouncer swoons with pride, the aesthetician is kineticist. When the words themselves empty out in order to bear the fervency of desire, when metaphor turns into the stammered repetition of a comportment leaving only the bare repeated form, . . . *like* . . . , . . . *like* . . . , . . . *like* . . . , when everything is elsewhere, in what it is like or what enfolds it or yields or flows around it or over, where do the roles begin or end?

> Her nakedness yielded to him, radiant, warm, odorous and lavish-limbed, enfolded him like a shining cloud, enfolded him like water with a liquid life: and like a cloud of vapour or like waters circumfluent in space the liquid letters of speech, symbols of the element of mystery, flowed forth over his brain.
>
> *Are you not weary of ardent ways* . . .
>
> (P 242)

Stephen is none of these and all of them, most Stephen when he disappears in the infinite speed of movement from one to another. This is why the last of the roles the book prepares for him—the only one before which the narrative can at last and for a few brief pages devolve into the first person—is simply the bare reprisal of a being-elsewhere: exile.

Neither is it the case that the proper is some sort of illusion, a false category the young Stephen still needs to draw on. What is happening is much more complex than that. The proper, the static, the properly aesthetic, the subject—all are indeed produced in that rhythm of seriality, but *as what is already excluded,* the last Signified of the signifying chain. The proper, with its invocations of the personal pronouns and distinctions between mine and yours, belongs from the beginning to the *kinetic,* to those desires and loathings which urge us to possess or abandon. The static is no more than the vast acceleration of the kinetic, and the proper which informs it is a sort of remnant of the processes of rhythm: something which is always and already off somewhere to one side, just as the free indirect discourse ensures Stephen is from the very beginning. Rather than the statement of a banal platonism, then, we can read the qualifications by which beauty "awakens, or *ought to* awaken, or induces, or *ought to* induce, an aesthetic stasis" as arguing just this. Long before one reaches those last signifieds of the proper, the static, the subject, everything is diverted, snatched away on other tracks, in other series. Without that shuttling, nothing at all would happen, kinesis or stasis: the very condition of the stasis is a rhythm.

Stephen elaborates on rhythm in his gloss on Aquinas's three "qualities of universal beauty": *integritas, consonantia,* and *claritas,* or, as Stephen translates them, *wholeness, harmony,* and *radiance.* Again, we must pay particular care to the way in which the argument is performed in the fiction, set as this sequence is on the streets, surrounded by the hubbub of that very marketplace from which the aesthetic must and cannot disengage itself. Again, a window opens:

Stephen pointed to a basket which a butcher's boy had slung inverted on his head.

—Look at that basket, he said.

—I see it, said Lynch.

—In order to see that basket, said Stephen, your mind first of all separates the basket from the rest of the visible universe which is not the basket. The first phase of apprehension is a bounding line drawn about the object to be apprehended. An aesthetic image is presented to us either in space or in time. What is audible is presented in time, what is visible is presented in space. But, temporal or spatial, the aesthetic image is first luminously apprehended as selfbounded and selfcontained upon the immeasurable background of space or time which is not it. You apprehend it as *one* thing. You see it as one whole. You apprehend its wholeness. That is *integritas.*

—Bull's eye! said Lynch, laughing. Go on.

—Then, said Stephen, you pass from point to point, led by its formal lines; you apprehend it as balanced part against part within its limits; you feel the rhythm of its structure. In other words the synthesis of immediate perception is followed by the analysis of apprehension. Having first felt that it is *one* thing, you now feel that it is a *thing.* You apprehend it as complex, multiple, divisible, separable, made up of its parts, the results of its parts and their sum, harmonious. That is *consonantia.*

—Bull's eye again! said Lynch wittily. Tell me now what is *claritas* and you win the cigar. (*P* 230)

The first phase of aesthetic apprehension involves the boundary, which allows the object to appear against its background. For this to happen, there must be an incessant oscillation across that line, whose rhythm is in effect that very boundary. The object is apprehended in its wholeness, as *one* thing, in this rhythm. But the rhythm is also immediately doubled, and redoubled: it marks out not only the object seen but (as Lynch has already affirmed) the subject seeing, and also, and by exactly the same process, the parts within that whole.

So far, all this would seem to be readily compatible with a sort of platonism. If this were the case, having perceived the object one would now judge it harmonious according to the way in which its various parts combine to attain an ideal proportion, by the ways in which its complexity is nevertheless productive of a unity which would always be supraphenomenal, and an ideal against which one would judge the phenomenal. But this is quite explicitly not what Stephen argues:

> The connotation of the word [*claritas*], Stephen said, is rather vague. Aquinas uses a term which seems to be inexact. It baffled me for a long time. It would lead you to believe that he had in mind symbolism or idealism, the supreme quality of beauty being a light from some other world, the idea of which the matter is but the shadow, the reality of which is but the symbol. I thought he might mean that *claritas* is the artistic discovery and representation of the divine purpose in anything or a force of generalization which would make the aesthetic image a universal one, make it outshine its proper conditions. But that is literary talk. I understand it so. When you have apprehended that basket as one thing and then have analyzed it according to its form and apprehended it as a thing you make the only synthesis which is logically and aesthetically permissible. You see that it is that thing which it is and no other thing. The radiance of which he speaks is the scholastic *quidditas*, the *whatness* of a thing. This supreme quality is felt by the artist when the aesthetic image is first conceived in his imagination. The mind in that mysterious instant Shelley likened beautifully to a fading coal. The instant wherein that supreme quality of beauty, the clear radiance of the aesthetic image, is apprehended luminously by the mind which has been arrested by its wholeness and fascinated by its harmony is the luminous silent stasis of aesthetic pleasure, a spiritual state very like to that cardiac condition which the Italian physiologist Luigi Galvani, using a phrase almost as beautiful as Shelley's, called the enchantment of the heart.
>
> Stephen paused and, though his companion did not speak, felt that his words had called up around them a thoughtenchanted silence. (*P* 230–31)

But that is literary talk. I understand it so. Stephen is not setting an ideal world of essence against a fallen world of the material, but explicitly rejecting that way of going about things. Neither is he looking for a divine purpose within or behind or before the work, or the universality which would let it "outshine its proper conditions" in a sort of aesthetic immortality. All that, says Stephen in a peculiar reversal of the value he seems until now to have placed on the term, is just "literary talk." Such a suspicion is not completely new in the *Portrait*. In a sense, we have seen it already in his confessions that he is really only working on "one or two ideas of Aristotle and Aquinas" (*P* 202), that he is "so poor a Latinist" (*P* 194), with "only a garner of slender sentences" from a few meager sources, one of which is a crib (*P* 191). Stephen is not particularly respectful of tradition as the transmission of a prior truth. One does not have to know all of Aristotle, little bits will do, and Aquinas "uses a term which seems to be inexact" anyway, "rather vague." If Aristotle and Aquinas give light, it is not because they *contain* truth: their relation to truth, and their value to him in this, are far more complex than that. The problem is not how to be true to sources (if the lamps smoke, trim or sell them), but how to use them, and towards ends which have not yet taken shape. Tradition is not something one observes, but produces; before it comes from a past, it reaches back from a future which has not yet occurred; its tense is the future perfect of what *will have been.*

What then is this radiance, this unorthodox—and Scotian rather than Thomist—*quidditas*, the *whatness* of a thing by which one sees "that thing which it is and no other"? We know what Stephen has said it is not: an essence which precedes and informs the thing, or the apprehension of the ideal as it manifests itself in the shadow of materiality. On the contrary, we know that it comes *after* the thing: after the apprehension in a synthesis as *one* thing, and the analysis of its form as *thing, claritas* returns us by another act of synthesis to something like the place where we began. But not quite. Where the first step, *integritas*, functions as a postulation in order to get the whole process going (the "synthesis of immediate perception"), now *claritas* functions as retrospective affirmation of that, in the light of the analysis that has just been effected as *consonantia*. It is after the event, and yet affirms what is and has been *already* the "supreme quality felt by the artist when the aesthetic image is first conceived in his imagination." But it is not just an elaborate return to the content of an authorial intention, something placed in the work at its inception and now, at last and above all vicissitudes, conveyed to its intended destination. *Claritas* is curiously empty of content. Its point is not content at all, but bare affirmation: "it is that thing which it is and no other," whatever that thing might be. It redoubles the affirmation the artist has already made at the moment of the work's conception, once the work's specific content or intention are put aside. It does not matter if the artist should have begun with a set of intentions which were to change in the course of the work or even never to be realized: what is being affirmed is neither the purity of the development of an intention nor the teleology of achieved purpose, but that the thing is what it is. But the work of art is not *yet* what it is: what that is comes to it from a future which has not yet arrived. What *claritas* affirms is the original openness to contingency which precedes and opens the ground for any particular content of intention. This is one of the things we can hear in Stephen's brusque retort in *Ulysses,* when librarian Eglinton suggests that in marrying Anne Hathaway Shakespeare might have made a mistake:

> —Bosh! Stephen said rudely. A man of genius makes no mistakes. His errors are volitional and are the portals of discovery. (*U* 9.228–29)

Far from being a direct and faithful transmission of an essence, this *claritas* partakes in all the paradoxes of destination: a *quidditas* which arrives after the event, as it were, as symptom or promise. What is affirmed is the contingency and *non*-necessity of its arrival, and the constitutive role of the vicissitudes of transmission. This is why beauty "awakens, or *ought to awaken,* or induces, or *ought to induce,* an aesthetic stasis" (*P* 223): there can be no guarantees. And this opens up a possibility which is not explored in the *Portrait,* but will be in *Ulysses* and *Finnegans Wake:* that in this fortuity, this debt to two irreducible series, in principle the rhythmic subdivision of the very *first* stage, *consonantia,* is capable of being carried out in a number of ways which are not necessarily reducible to each other. The thing which is apprehended would not be a single whole, but potentially *a number* of wholes according to the particular rhythm of subdivision.

In its affirmation of an empty intentionality without content, Stephen's argument about *claritas* is close to Kant's on the "purposiveness without purpose" of the work of art, but with a significant difference. What Stephen has chosen as his example is not a work of art at all, not even the simulacrum of one (like the accidental likeness of a cow, hacked in fury from a block of wood [*P* 232]),[15] but something altogether banal, which the market just happened to offer—a basket: certainly, one which at this moment is no longer fulfilling its function of container for marketable goods, but quite unaestheticized, symbol of nothing (unlike all those figures of Irish womanhood who seem to disappear almost immediately into the symbolic, "as a type of her race and his own" [*P* 198]): just a basket. This entire process of apprehension, ending in "the luminous silent stasis of aesthetic pleasure," is not limited to the art object.

This is the *epiphany*. It happens when, as the earlier version of this exchange tells us, the object's

soul, its whatness, leaps to us from the vestment of its appearance. The soul *of the commonest object*, the structure of which is so adjusted, seems to us radiant. The object achieves its epiphany. (*SH* 218: my emphasis)

This soul leaps *from*, not from beneath or behind, the vestment of appearance. It is impersonal, the soul of the object itself which radiates, and the most banal, the most vulgar of objects—the kinetic itself—is capable of revealing it. In the earlier novel, Stephen tells Cranly "that the clock of the Ballast Office was capable of an epiphany," leaping out from "the catalogue of Dublin's street furniture" (*SH* 216). Epiphany blurs irreparably that boundary between art and the marketplace. Stephen will elaborate after his "thoughtenchanted silence":

—What I have said, he began again, refers to beauty in the wider sense of the word, in the sense which the word has in the literary tradition. In the marketplace it has another sense. When we speak of beauty in the second sense of the term our judgment is influenced in the first place by the art itself and by the form of that art. The image, it is clear, must be set between the mind or senses of the artist himself and the mind or senses of others. If you bear this in memory you will see that art necessarily divides itself into three forms progressing from one to the next. These forms are: the lyrical form, the form wherein the artist presents his image in immediate relation to himself; the epical form, the form wherein he presents his image in mediate relation to himself and others; the dramatic form, the form wherein he presents his image in immediate relation to others. (*P* 231–2)

Here it is no longer quite clear just what belongs to literature and what to the marketplace. Everything Stephen has just said has been using beauty "in the wider sense of the word, in the sense which the word has in the literary tradition." But it has "another sense" in the marketplace, and when we speak of it in that second, less wide sense, we find other things to take into account. Now it is no longer a matter of the ontology of the epiphanized object, or the phenomenology of the perception of the work. It is a question of exchange. The image, the work, is in a space *between*, set minimally "between the mind or senses of the artist himself and the mind or senses of others," where a window opens and a fortuitous, unpredictable exchange may leap between series. Literature is already in the market-place when at the heart of literature one already finds the short-circuit of the epiphany, where all exchange rates become infinite.

In this marketplace, art "*divides itself* into three forms" according to its mode of exchange. The three forms Stephen outlines—lyrical, epical, and dramatic—seem to mark out that narrative progression from artist to other, and from earliest to latest: the most highly developed art is the one which has most distanced itself from its creator, culminating of course in the famous nail-paring God of creation. At a first reading, it may seem that what this passage is arguing is that art begins with the self, and only after a long and difficult passage which is both historical and personal—the progress of an art's finding itself as much as of an artist's finding himself as artist—can it arrive at a sublime indifference. But we recall Stephen's ear-lier discussion of the tragic (which he elides with the dramatic): the two tragic emotions of pity and terror unite the mind respectively with the sufferer and the cause. From the beginning, what drops out of the equa-tion is the state of mind of the artist and along with it any question of personal expression: the "mind or sense of the artist" are of interest only inasmuch as they unite themselves with what is quite foreign to them, and it is this union-in-foreignness which is the measure of the properly aes-thetic. The *im*proper arts are the ones which urge or excite; the properly aesthetic is what arrests. The dramatic gives full rein to the intensity of emotions such as pity and terror only by withdrawing from any question of self-expression. The lyrical is not simply the expression of a self which is already there, but considerably more impersonal than that might imply: the self that is supposedly being expressed occurs only as a sort of ghostly effect. The lyrical form "is in fact the simplest verbal *vesture of an instant of emotion, a rhythmical cry.* . . . He who utters it is more conscious of the instant of emotion than of himself as feeling emotion" (*P* 232: my empha-ses): as we have seen in chapter 2, the cry has already been countersigned elsewhere with the Name of impersonality itself. What is there first of all is this instant of emotion: the event, which is not quite yet subjective or objective, active or passive, the emotion of which could only be described in a sort of middle voice: an "it feels," in the sense of "it rains": "*there is an emoting, a feeling cry,*" rather than "I feel, I shout." Or rather, what is there is the *vesture* of this instant of emotion: something to be tried on, a bare place, but in the traversals of which alone an "I" can arise. Raising itself above a background, the cry is rhythmical in its structure even if it should be only a single sound. The lyrical *is* self-expression, but only in a new, inverted sense: not the expression in words of a self which precedes words, but the product, the drawing-out or ex-pressing of a self in and by a cry which need no longer even be words. With the cry, some sort of larval subject flickers up into momentary existence, not its source but invoked in, called up, apostrophized by the cry in this mysterious "birth of the soul." With the epical form, this "personality of the artist"—which, we note, is already and from the beginning an effect of the process, "passes into the narration itself, flowing round and round the persons and the actions like a vital sea." "[A]t first a cry or a cadence or a mood and then a fluid and lambent narrative," this personality "finally refines itself out of existence, impersonalizes itself so to speak" (P 233). But we *began* with the impersonal, and a cry which was not yet personalized. It is as if the dramatic, that "purification" of the static "from the human imagination" is the rediscovery of the originary inhuman at the heart of the human, the preindividual at the heart of the individual. Refining oneself out of existence, one discovers the constitutive traces of the radically other. With *Ulysses*, that inhuman and impersonal site of the cry will be seen to be already the possibility of the social, the political, the ethical. But it is in *Finnegans Wake* above all that we shall see in most detail that apostrophic calling-up at work; and it is to *Finnegans Wake* that we now finally turn.

5

The War within Providence

HCE has been tried, and as the four judges have been able to "do no worse than promulgate their standing verdict of Nolans Brumans" (*FW* 92.36–93.01),[1] the reprobate "left the tribunal scotfree" (93.03). "And so it all ended" (93.22).

But of course it hasn't. In *Finnegans Wake,* to speak, to document, investigate, analyze, are never ways of getting rid of the need for further speech, documentation, investigation, or analysis. They are instead its proliferation, and the guarantee of its further proliferation. Even if we could somehow establish incontrovertibly the truth of what happened that night in Phoenix Park, we would still be left with the question of what it means, in the Lacanian sense of the *Che vuoi?:* I know what you have said, but what do you mean by it? what should I understand you as wanting to say by it, what do you want me to understand by it?[2] *Nolens volens:* that is precisely what the court has refused to comment on, and precisely what continues to fascinate. No sooner has HCE left the court than he is confronted by the twenty-eight "chassetitties belles conclaiming: You and your gift of your gaft of your garbage abaht our Farvver!" (93.19–20); no sooner are we reassured that this is how "it all ended" than there is the call for old Kate to produce the letter once again, so that it can all be gone over once more in the light of that judgment: "Ask Kavya for the kay. And so everybody heard their plaint and all listened to their plause. The letter! The litter!" (93.22–24). The case is closed: now everyone can go off and speculate, even the judges: "So there you are now there they were, when all was over again, the four with them, setting around upin their judges' chambers, in the muniment room, of their marshalsea, under the suspices of Lally, around their old traditional tables of the law like Somany Solans to talk it over rallthesameagain" (94.23–27), as gossipy as anyone on the steps of the courthouse, but all "accourting to king's evelyns" (94.28).

On the one hand, this fascination is quite external to what the letter says, or to the particular judgment the court hands down, or to the true story of what happened in the park. Even if the letter is just litter after all, it is no less an event, the occasion for those plaints and plauses of all—perhaps all the more purely so for the absence or invisibility of content. What fascinates about the letter and ensures its endless proliferation and return is that it cannot be reduced to a content it would convey on the level of enunciation. What fascinates is what it *has not yet* said: not in the sense of a definite but yet undiscovered content, a secret it would finally reveal if seen from just the right angle or in all good time, but in the far simpler sense of an *always more*. Whatever is said about the letter, or whatever the court's judgment might be, there is always more to be said: leave the court, and there on the steps the gossip begins again, because it has never really left off for a moment. This is not because the letter is inexhaustibly rich. On the contrary, what we do glimpse of it in the various fragmentary and sometimes contradictory versions of it scattered around the *Wake* suggests its banality: chat about relatives and presents and cakes, for the most part with barely a breath of scandal. That *always more* is simply because the letter's meaning, banal as that might be, is always to an extent beyond itself, yet to come, arriving at it from a future its content cannot begin to guess at—and all that history-to-come on which any text lays the wager of its meaning includes the gossip on the steps as much as the learned commentary of Law or Critic. What fascinates is what escapes, and the endlessly repeated attempts at "the capture of uncertain comets chance-drifting through our system" (100.33–34), as the *Wake* has it, echoing not only the schemas' Symbol but also the precise function of that symbol in the "Ithaca" chapter of *Ulysses*.

On the other hand, though, this externality is right at the heart of the message itself. Everywhere, the sheer content of whatever it is that does, after all, get said, is divided against itself by this externality, which marks it with gaps, contradictions, hesitations, stammers. Whether or not HCE did anything reprehensible in the park, "the spoil of hesitants, the spell of hesitency" (97.25) which characterizes his speech suggests the pressure of something guiltily hidden, a "tittery taw tatterytail" (97.26). A stranger out for a stroll merely asks him the time, and is deluged with denials of any wrongdoing (35.01–36.34). Everything points towards something unbearable and obscene, and which HCE cannot recognize under his own words. What do these slips of the tongue want from *him*? Confession? Far from making peace with oneself and in that recognizing what one truly is, confession only doubles the gap of desire: what did I mean by confessing? what did *he* mean by confessing? Confession can only be yet another spur for gossip. The most intimate conversation of self with self is mediated by a vast externality, whose figure is what we should not be too hasty to refer to as the *circularity* of the *Wake*. To make the final "the" (628.16) and the initial "riverrun" (3.01) into contiguous words of the one sentence, after all, we have to leave the book and pass, in potential, through everything in the world that is not *Finnegans Wake*. If the *Wake* is circular, it is as an indefinite openness across a breach whereby the apparently external intrudes into the text.[3] And this is not limited to first and last words. One of the effects of the monstrous polyglottal overdetermination of every word of the *Wake* is that the path from *any* word to the next may require us to make a detour of indefinite and fractal extent.

HCE might have "left the tribunal scotfree" (93.03), but its verdict changes nothing. Only a few pages later, he will be back in his watery tomb. Perhaps worse: the Lough Neagh of his pretrial imprisonment (76.21–22) seems to have been exchanged for an even more secure site "under leagues of it in deep Bartholoman's Deep" (100.3–4). No doubt it is the immense water pressure which collapses that "Lough Neagh" into those "leagues": here in the deeps and Chinese whispers of sleep, words implode into their components, "mush spread" (98.24). In the proliferation of which the court's judgment is only a part, in the many forms of the letter, in the gossip which both letter and judgment provoke rather than quell, HCE is buried as effectively beneath words as water: "The latter! The latter! . . . He lay under leagues of it" (100.2–4). The verdict (such as it is) has been handed down. HCE has left the court to the jeers of the "twofromthirty advocatesses" (93.12). And everything, now it is all ended, still remains to be done, or carries on regardless. Call for the letter.

If the letter's meaning is essentially yet to come, it is never simply there, in the hand or on the page; the letter is always something to be invoked, summonsed, called on, called into being. Either it is somewhere else—lost, undelivered, held up in the mails, stolen or redirected, or in someone else's keeping—or when we actually do seem to have it, there in front of us, it turns out to be fragmentary, or damaged beyond any more than partial legibility, or a clever fake, or somebody else's reconstruction or commentary all along. It is not so much something which exists—already there, waiting to be read—as something which is invoked, called into being: "The letter! The litter!" (93.24); "The latter! The latter!" (100.2); "Ask Kavya [old Kate] for the kay" (93.22–23); "Now tell me, tell me, tell me then!" (94.19); "Do tell us all about. As we want to hear allabout. So tellus tellas allabouter" (101.2–3).

Call for the letter: the letter is what is called *for,* called *up,* to be cited and passed on: to hear allabout is to retell allabout. Claudette Sartiliot points out that in both English and French, one of the meanings of *citation* is a summons to appear in court; the one who is called up as expert witness is in that very appearance put under the law's scrutiny, so it is no longer clear which is judge and which the judged (22). Who is looking at whom? In this very invocation, we have something of the inextricable bond between Bloom and Gerty on the beach. Indeed, the authorship of the letter is uncertain, apparently multiple, though there would seem to be a definite feminine inflection ("Of eyebrow pencilled, by lipstipple penned" [93.25]), and contributions in one form or another from all the family (94.5–9), as well as from a host of others the *Wake* will do little more than name:

> Borrowing a word and begging the question and stealing tinder and slipping like soap. From dark Rasa Lane a sigh and a weep, from Lesbia Looshe the beam in her eye, from lone Coogan Barry his arrow of song, from Sean Kelly's anagrim a blush at the name, from I am the Sullivan that trumpeting tramp, from Suffering Dufferin the Sit of her Style, from Kathleen May Vernon her Mebbe fair efforst . . . (93.25–32)

As these are the names of popular songs and their writers or singers (Moore's "Lesbia Hath a Beaming Eye," Kathleen Mavourneen for whom "It may be for years and it may be forever," Dufferin's "Lament of the Irish Emigrant," and so on: McHugh 93), this is indeed borrowing a word or two, perhaps even stealing thunder. A sigh and a weep, a beaming eye, an arrow of song, a blush, the wish that God save Ireland, the absent loved one ("I'm sitting on the stile, Mary"): all of them are themselves figures or examples of address, call, invocation—as indeed is so common in song. We examine the content of those borrowed words, and at the heart of it we find ourselves left again with externalities, and the invocation outwards towards an absent other. We go to sources, and we find destinations, the pleas and flatteries (the Anglo-Irish "plausy") of a multitude in which plaintiffs and listeners are not easily distinguished: "everybody heard their plaint and all listened to their plause" (93.23–24). From the filiating story of its son arises the hubbub of the city: "And that was how framm Sin fromm Son, acity arose" (94.19). Everyone seems to have contributed to this story, or invoked it, these "sibspeeches of all mankind" which "have foliated (earth seizing them!) from the root of some funner's stotter" (96.30–31).

What we have here in the letter and the host of voices which tell, retell, and call for the telling of HCE's story is yet another version of that collective enunciative assemblage we have seen at work in *Portrait* and *Ulysses*. As there, this assemblage is not the sum total of the utterances of already-constituted individuals; it is something preindividual and as yet impersonal, within which subjects will come to be assigned and distributed. In this, that collective "we" cannot be additive, only subtractive: while it is an affirmation as much as Molly Bloom's *oui,* it is also what is left over, the waste from what has been bibbed:

> *We're all up to the years in hues and cribies.*
> *That's what she's done for wee!* (103.5–6)

In the emergence of that tentative and subtractive collective subject, we perhaps have the familiar shape of the gnomon again, that L in the middle of A P, "our weewee mother" (598.34) making music at her chamber pot: "let *naaman* laugh at Jordan" (103.8–9: emphasis added). The language of *Finnegans Wake* is a vastly accelerated form of free indirect discourse, in which the puns and portmanteau words afforded by some sixty languages ensure the unprecedented density of what is actually uttered, or stuttered. But there is more than compression at stake here.

I have argued in the third chapter that the true radicality of invention in *Ulysses* lies not so much in the interior monologue (which in itself leaves untouched the basic representational functions of a psychologistic or realist fiction), but in the book's thoroughgoing use of free indirect discourse and its instabilities of address. This in particular is accelerated enormously in the *Wake:* if the meaning of any given *Wake*word may slip among three or four or more possibilities in a given sentence, so too may the apparent functions of address. *On the one hand,* this means all positions are subject to an apparently unconstrained and quite uncontrollable multiplication. The letter is written by ALP, but also by Issy, or by either of the two sons, or perhaps even the father. But even granted that, the family of which the various versions of the letter speak doesn't always seem to be the troubled Earwickers we have seen in the rest of the book. Sometimes it is as if the entire letter is a graft from elsewhere, assembled together out of many contributions, perhaps even the hue and cry of all Dublin. At others, or at the same times, it may be a fake, with the mother's signature forged by one or the other of the two sons or the daughter. It may even be the accidental and improbable result of some sort of blind natural process as it incubated in its "mudmound" (111.34) into an apparent "whyacinthinous riot of blots and blurs and bars and balls" (118.28–30), like the flower whose petals bear the letters of the Greek word "woe" in the blood of the murdered Hyacinth—one of ALP's roles is after all that of nature herself, Gaea Tellus ("So tellus tellas allabouter," 101.2–3).

Let us use Joyce's term for it, which is quite precise: even if ALP should after all turn out to be the letter's true author—whatever that might mean—what are we to make of something written by *plurability* itself? And even if we decide on the irrelevance or impossibility of the question of "who in hallhagal wrote the durn thing anyhow" (107.36–108.1), what are we to make of a letter which remains no less *signed in the name of plurability*? When that very attestation of the uniqueness and authenticity of an utterance is performed by a name which in its turn names the instability of all these?[4] (We can turn it around: what are we to make of a *Wake* signed by a name which in *Wake*se becomes all sorts of things inauthentic [shame, sham, joke, reprobate Shem] and non-unique [choice]? As the court hearing finishes, the "chassetitties belles" abuse the departing HCE: "You and your gift of your gaft of your garbage abaht our Farvver!"; their salvo of names concludes with that of the abused father of this text, the one we are reading: "Skam! Schams! Shames!" [93.19–21].)

This alone is complex enough. But *on the other hand, plurability* goes further than an unconstrained multiplication of those who may have contributed to the letter and those who may be its recipients. That is to leave the arrow intact by multiplying it: to start with a message which travels from a sender to a receiver, from one already-constituted subject to another. In short, it is again to think of what is happening here in terms of the vector of communication. Of course, we rapidly find we can no longer be sure just how many subjects are involved at each end of this arrow. Nevertheless, while we might have a host of possible senders and receivers, they still seem to respect and slot neatly enough into one or the other of two basic *roles*, addresser and addressee. The arrow remains intact: all we have done is shift a level, from personages outside the message to roles within it, from subjects to subject positions, and from communications theory to semiotics. What we have is accretive: it begins with that unitary arrow, and adds it to itself, over and over, so that the most complex situations can in principle be analyzed into familiar and stable elementary components: the message, where it is coming from, and where it is going to. The multiplication of the arrow, no matter how unconstrained it may be, does not disturb this.

*Wake*an plurability goes still further. Call for the letter: ALP is invoked as "the Bringer of Plurabilities" (104.1–2). But which way does it run here? On the one hand (again), ALP is, as her name says, plurability itself.

Wherever she goes she brings that plurability with her to where there has been none before, making all things possible in the largesse she distributes to her many children (209.18–212.19). As pure and unstinting giving, she is *source itself*—or more accurately, sourceless herself, she is the very possibility of there being source and address. On the other hand, though, the genitive suggests just the opposite: ALP is plurabilities' mere bringer, its functionary. Rather than being sender or source herself, she is on the other end of the arrow, as receiver of a plurability which provides her possibility as much as anyone or anything else's, and as the intermediary trusted with its delivery: not so much will to be done as rill to be run (104.2–3). And she is not even its first receiver, for she only responds to an address already directed at her, from those very children who await the bounty their address implies they already have, before the event. Plurability not only multiplies but confounds the positions of addresser and addressee, the one who writes and the one who delivers, Shem the Penman and Shaun the Post, suggesting something which predates both, as their very possibility. This is why plurability and ALP can only ever be invoked.

Wake language is indirect discourse accelerated to something close to its limits, at its most insistent: that *free* indirect discourse which Deleuze and Guattari see as being "of exemplary value." Language, they suggest,

> does not operate between something seen (or felt) and something said, but always goes from saying to saying. We believe that narrative consists not in communicating what one has seen but in transmitting what one has heard, what someone else said to you. Hearsay. . . . The "first" language, or rather the first determination of language, is not the trope or metaphor but *indirect discourse*. (*A Thousand Plateaus* 80, 76–77; quoted in Donoghue 25)

If we were to characterize this as hearing what has been said *and then* saying what has been heard, we would have no more than the loop of communication again: from the mouth of one to the ear of the other, then from the mouth of the other back to the ear of the one. But accelerate that process so that the "then" collapses into simultaneity, and there is no time at all between *hearing what has been said* and *saying what has been heard*. Hearsay, sayhear: what one says is already what has been said, what one hears has already been heard. At the heart of saying is a hearing, and a hearing-somebody-else-say; saying is already, from the outset, somebody else's saying, somebody else's hearing: in short, a collective assemblage. As we have seen, this is already the comedy of *Ulysses:* Bloom is a thirsty sponge for other('s) words; we hear all sorts of other voices behind and within and beyond him; "Bloom" is not the name of an originating source so much as of a particular refractive index. A collective assemblage, say Deleuze and Guattari, is not built up from individuated utterances, or from uttering individuals; it is preindividual and impersonal, and assigns and distributes subjectivities which may be partial and quite unstable, unconstrained by semiosis and "slipping like soap" (93.26–27) across addresser and addressee alike.

This happens insistently and in a particularly complex way in the *Wake*. "From dark Rasa Lane a sigh and a weep" (93.27): is this sighing and weeping something the letter has borrowed from Rasa Lane (and from Mangan, and the dark Rosaleen of his song), or is it part of the plaints and plauses, begging the question, a plea for the key to "The letter! The litter!" (93.24)? Does it belong to where the letter is coming from, or where it is going to? The one is forever flipping over into the other. Rasa Lane, or Rosaleen, sighs and weeps; the letter quotes this, and even dutifully acknowledges the source, so on the one hand this Rosaleen, or Rasa Lane, becomes yet another signatory to the letter. But Rosaleen is also the one addressed rather than the one addressing: "O my dark Rosaleen," enjoins Mangan's song, "do not sigh, do not weep!" where—to complicate matters still further—Rosaleen is being enjoined, as addressee, *not* to be addresser in such a way: *do not* sigh like that, *do not* weep, even in the very way this song itself sighs and weeps; be silent, erased. Rasa Lane, or Rosaleen, is addressed purely in order to be silent, or silenced. Say nothing: *tabula rasa*. But in this saying nothing, lend your voice, such as it is, these wordless sighs and weeps; countersign this letter, right here, with your name; say nothing, addresser; become addresser by saying nothing, simply by being addressed. This Rasa Lane–Rosaleen is invoked by nothing more than a name. Multiplied out into a list the name again dominates this sentence: Lesbia Looshe, Coogan Barry, Sean Kelly, Suffering Dufferin, Kathleen May Vernon. And all of these names call up songs, and all of these songs themselves work on prosonomasia or its variations[5] (the personification and invocation of speech in prosopopoeia, the vividness of prosopographia's description of the dead or the purely imaginary): "Lesbia Hath a Beaming Eye," "God Save Ireland," "There is a green island in Lone Gougabe Barra / Where Allua of songs rushes forth like an arrow," "The Memory of the Dead," "I'm sitting on the stile, Mary," Kathleen Mavourneen, even—*en abyme*—"from Timm Finn again's weak tribes, loss of strenghth to his sowheel" (93.35–36), each of them with the same shifting instability of addresser and addressee.

The plurability of the *Wake*, then, is more than a polysemy of content, even if that should be unconstrained. It involves also the instability of the very positions of utterance, in an acceleration of those processes of free indirect discourse we saw at work two chapters ago, in "Nausicaa." Source everts itself into destination, destination into source. And if this multiple and divided letter is also everywhere associated with ALP, who is earth mother ("tellus tellas allabouter" [101.2–3] and "Mother of us all" [299.3]), its signature—the name of plurability itself—is no more origin than was that earlier name of a Father, countersignature to a shout in the street. Rather than giving us the letter and its effects as familiar mythical and maternal archetypes, the *Wake* suggests ways of thinking through those figures in terms of effects of signature and address, and of the "lifewand [that makes] the dumb speak." Before it is about the "Quoiquoiquoiquoiquoiquoiquoi!" of what is said, it is about the act of speech which "lifts the lifewand and [makes] the dumb speak" (195.5–6). The *Wake* inverts mythopoeia into prosopopoeia.

The topography is familiar now. If ALP lies behind the letter, in the past, as source to be reconstructed, that is only because she is also somewhere after the letter, still to come, "a little lady waiting" (102.22–23)[6] whose arrival promises if not explanation then at least countersignature. In most of her key appearances, she is a tonality or an inflection rather than a presence, and most famously in the river language which burbles its way through the pages and drowns out the voices of the washerwomen in the Anna Livia chapter (196–216). ALP is the subject of gossip in both senses: like her husband, she is the topic for gossip, but she is also herself "giddgaddy, grannyma, gossipaceous Anna Livia" (193.3–4). The very personification of gossip, gossip itself, she is that collective assemblage of enunciation from whose "waters of babalong" (103.11) voices will emerge, and subjects gradually but never entirely stably coalesce.

We can see in this how far Joyce is away from the Heideggerian question of authenticity, where in *Being and Time* the epitome of the inauthentic is the "idle talk" of *das Man* (218–19, 296). Anna Livia's gossipaceousness is closer to what the early Lacan calls "empty speech," that phatic dimension before communication of any content in which the speakers recognize each other in language, as speakers. Empty speech is empty not because it talks of trivialities or untruth, but because whatever it talks of just functions like the swapping of a password, the content of which is perfectly indifferent as long as we both recognize it as password, and in it, each other. Empty speech is thus something like the purest speech, as in it I am purely the subject of enunciation: a speaking instant, the *event* of speaking.[7] Hearsay. As event, this empty act points out minimally to a series of other events, past and future, in a double debt: the response this password invokes, or is yet to invoke, and in that response the recognition of what I have, perhaps unknown to me until now, already been. Who chose this face for me, which I glimpse in the flash of an offered mirror, this face I do not yet quite ever know for it is always as others yet to come see me? (*U* 1.136–37). Surrounded, like the reader of the *Wake,* by language it does not yet understand but which insistently addresses it, the child repeats, and in that repetition alone perhaps learns: "Words which he did not understand he said over and over to himself till he had learned them by heart: and through them he had glimpses of the real world about him" (*P* 64).[8] (*No hope,* says the light in the old man's window; *paralysis,* says the boy.) And ALP is not just what one invokes, or what responds: she is invocation itself, in all the instability of its address. She is the one addressed ("Wery weeny wight, plead for Morandmor!" [102.18]), and in this has already addressed us, for "we list, as she bibs us" (103.10). As the last lines of the book suggest, before there is really anyone or anywhere, there is a call, from elsewhere—*elsewhere itself* calls ("Far calls")—and only with that call is there one who answers, someone somewhere called up ("Coming, far!" [628.13]).[9] Empty speech is empty, just as gossip is gossip, because it is pure responsivity.

The recognition this responsivity invokes is marked everywhere in the *Wake* by its use of grammatical and narrative person. No other texts of Joyce's—indeed, few texts of any sort—use first-person *plural* narration quite as much as *Finnegans Wake.* It is there in the first abruptly beginning sentence, as a place to take us as readers by surprise and bring us back to somewhere we have apparently already been: that is, not only to Howth Castle and Environs, but to these unfamiliar words themselves, marked off as already ours in the uttering as if from our own mouths: "rivverrun, past Eve and Adam's, from swerve of shore to bend of bay, brings *us* by a commodius vicus of recirculation back to Howth Castle and Environs" (3.1–3). And it is there on the last page, lines before the end, as ALP and the text together dissolve: "*We* pass through grass behush the bush to. Whish! A gull. Gulls. Far calls. Coming, far! End here. *Us* then. Finn, again! Take. Bussoftlhee, mememormee! Till thousendsthee. Lps. The keys to. Given! A way a lone a last a loved a long the" (628.12–16). Between those points, virtually every page somewhere calls up the collective "we," or the demand for response of a "you," the caesura of a rhetorical question. It is a responsivity which is also thematized everywhere in the *Wake,* when the question raised by the scandal is how to respond to it, and the very scandal itself comes from HCE's preemptively guilty response to a question the Cad never asked (35.1–36.34). If the letter promises to be a response to this scandal (at least in some of its guises), then the question it raises in turn is how to respond to the letter. Scholarly investigation by a busy professor, perhaps, the findings to be reported in a public lecture which in turn will be full of its own exasperated responses, provoked as much by the lecture as the letter. All of this, in turn yet again, finds its own response in a vast formation of criticism, publication, pedagogy, discussion, reading groups, mailing lists, and symposia, in what cannot be anything but what Derek Attridge calls an industry without limits (*Joyce Effects* 168–71), for the simple reason that it is a responsivity without limits.

This bidding to which we list, and which imbibes us in all sorts of ways, is what the letter chapter of the *Wake* (I.5) will elaborate. Not for the first time, a chapter will take in and swallow up the rest of the book. This will be, again, a matter of the name: of invocation, prosonomasia, and a place marked by a name which is yet to come and which, in the coming, will already be plural, even no name at all:

> In the name of Annah the Allmaziful, the Everliving, the Bringer of Plurabilities, haloed be her eve, her singtime sung, her rill be run, unhemmed as it is uneven!
> Her untitled mamafesta memorialising the Mosthighest has gone by many names at disjointed times. Thus we hear of . . . (104.1–5)

And again, this name is connected with memory. It memorializes and brings into memory—and in a disjointed time, this may be something rather different from the recall of a past.

Once again, ALP is invoked rather than present: "In the name of Annah the Allmaziful." To invoke the name—to call on, by name and in the name of—is at the same time to invoke the law. As with all performatives, the invocation calls on the law in order to work as invocation in the first place: *I invoke you in the name of the law; the law invokes you, and I invoke the law which invokes you in its name; I invoke the law by which you are invoked as you.* The law underlies the name and gives it its performative force; in turn, the name is what allows the law to appear, the way in which it is manifested: the link between *nomen* and *nomos* may, as so often in the *Wake,* be more than just a pun. For all that—or rather because of it—this invocation of the name does not quite coincide with the law. As we have seen, ALP and the letter are invoked after the courtroom deliberation, after the verdict which lets HCE off scotfree and which sets off also the renewed hubbub of gossip and hearsay. It is as if the invocation were associated not so much with the law's decision as with all the ways in which that decision still leaves things open. Even once we had determined the matter of what the law says and enacts (even if that should be determinable), we would once more be left with the still unanswered and unanswerable question of the *Che vuoi?*—what does the law *want?*—and with the suspicion that it is already bound up with what Žižek calls an "obscene enjoyment."[10] And we would no less be left with the question of what will be done with the law after the event, *nolens volens,* and how its decision will be used in all sorts of games other than the law's, and in ways which are not themselves legislatable. Whatever the court decides, it acts like the empty password of responsivity: more grist for the rumor mill in the unhemmed, uneven loops of plurability.

To invoke ALP is also to invoke her *as* "mother of us all," or "mother of the book" (50.12), or "Annah the Allmaziful," or even "Bringer of Plurabilities." To invoke is necessarily to invoke *as:* to invoke a role or function, not some bare thing in itself. At the very instant ALP is being called on *as* absolute authenticity, the ground of all things, what is invoked is actually a role, behind which she again recedes. ALP, source and mother of all, appears only in a series of appositions. Again we meet the logic of plurability. The absolutely real and non-figurative appears only *as:* as "Bringer of Plurabilities," as "Mosthighest," as *figure,* always arriving from elsewhere. We can read the *Wake*'s final monologue as ALP's disappearance into that elsewhere, with the "mother of the book" (50.12) invoking her own origin, both so near ("Onetwo moremens more" [628.5–6]) and yet calling across a vast distance ("Far calls. Coming, far!"). All that remains of this origin in the text is that unreadable gap of externality between last and first pages of the *Wake,* which one can traverse only backwards. ALP is origin only inasmuch as she is too early or too late: *too late* in that when the book begins (and the shape of the book dares one to begin it anywhere) that separation has already taken place, and has already been lost; and *too early* in that the very form of invocation calls up what is not yet here, and which is still only a promise. An immeasureable silence divides the last and first sentence of the *Wake* from and within itself, never simply within the book or outside it, but before, after, and within every point of the text.

ALP is not simply a source, a principle of continuity, or a primal unity. As plurability, she is a disjunction at the heart of things, and is the rhythm with which these disjunctions are incessantly articulated against each other and dissolved (Kristeva 26). She does not *exist* as being so much as *insist* as a proliferation before or behind being: the anachrony of being, as

Derrida will say of the Platonic *khora*, or being *as* anachrony. That is to say, she is not a constant principle underlying her many invocations, so much as *what is always called in the same way* (*"Khora"* 94, 98). Always a bountiful giver, she is divestiture itself. Divesting herself of everything, her sole property is to be propertyless, and thus to be nothing but a receiver of everything, a matrix in which even that maternity which is most her own comes from elsewhere, as "mother-in-lieu" (220.22–23) or nurse.[11] Called up from his sleep on Howth Hill the giant HCE proclaims his endless benevolence to ALP in a massive, self-satisfied, and grandiose justification of his actions (532.6–554.9). Over and over, he insists, he has showered her with gifts (548.18ff). But the massive and barely concealed violence of this manic escalation makes it clear that ALP is no more than the occasion for a circuit which returns everything to him with interest, a way of calling up his own glory in even more splendor: "if I was magmonimoss as staidy lavgiver I revolucanized by my eructions: the hye and bye wayseeds I scattered em, in my graben fields sew sowage I gathered em" (545.32–34). Whatever ALP is invested with by invocation has come from elsewhere and has already passed on to others. If ALP is a origin, it is a strange deflected one which engenders and owns nothing: deflection itself, articulated in the circuit of an always incomplete return.

This is why ALP's "untitled mamafesta" is both unnamed and proliferates its namings, multiplying them as soon as she is invoked, and why what we are bid to list to can only be a *list*.

> Her untitled mamafesta memorialising the Mosthighest has gone by many names at disjointed times. Thus we hear of, *The Augusta Angustissimost for Old Seabeastius' Salvation, Rockabill Booby in the Wave Trough, Here's to the Relicts of All Decencies, Anna Stessa's Rise to Notice, Knickle Down Duddy Gunne and Arishe Sir Cannon, My Golden One and My Selver Wedding, Amoury Treestam and Icy Siseule, Saith a Sawyer til a Strame, Ik dik dopedope et tu mihimihi, Buy Birthplate for a Bite, Which of your Hesterdays Mean Ye to Morra? Hoebegunne the Hebrewer Hit Waterman the Brayned, Arcs in His Ceiling Flee Chinx on the Flur, Rebus de Hibernicis, The Crazier Letters* . . . (104.1–14)

There is of course more, much more: at almost three pages, this is one of the longest lists in a book enamored of them.

And from the outset, we are warned about this list. Its entries are what "we hear of" (104.5): there may be more we haven't heard of, and those we have may have reached us in a number of less than reliable ways. We might expect (or hope) the letter to have the relative stability of an object, but these burgeoning, gossipy names are still as much rumor as the previous chapters' tales about HCE. Heard and overheard, they would seem to have undergone all sorts of vagaries and distortions in their travels. As commas seem to be used within names as well as to separate names, we cannot even be sure just how many there are (Tindall 99). At least one entry is explicitly tagged as illegible, or inaudible, where something has dropped out: "*An Apology for a Big* (some such nonoun as *Husband* or *husboat* or *hosebound* is probably understood for we have also the plutherplethoric *My Hoonsbood Hansbaad's a Journey to Porthergill gone and He Never Has the Hour)*" (104.15–19).[12]

Nevertheless, the list tempts us, as they do, to find some principle of order in it. Tindall points out that the list contains two easily overlooked semicolons among the hundreds of separating commas, and that we might take these as dividing the list into three, one for each of ALP's aspects, the girl Isabel, the old woman Kate, and the mother Anna Livia—"Anna was, Livia is, Plurabelle's to be" (215.24; Tindall 99). Overall this does seem to be the case, but one does not have to search far to find apparent anomalies.[13] The *Wake* both offers and withdraws the hypothesis, withdraws it in the very process of offering. Regularities accrete, to be sure, but they have the status of working hypotheses, tentative and open to revision. Because we already have "the plutherplethoric *My Hoonsbood Hansbaad* [etc.]," we can make an informed guess at what a plausibly gnomonic "nonoun" might be (104.16–18). But even if we have more than a plethora of evidence for the guess, it remains a guess: the list is not redundant, because there is always the possibility that the next element will surprise. The list is neither ordered nor unordered but asyndetic: from its bare juxtaposition without conjunctions, complex and unforeseeable regularities may arise. The names which make it up have come about at "disjointed times," for reasons which may be structurally quite independent and owe nothing to a common principle. "Unhemmed as it is uneven" (104.3), the list is frayed and without clear boundary. Non-homogeneous, it is a conglomerate, an aggregate of happenstance.

This list functions somewhat like the overture to the "Sirens" episode of *Ulysses:* it encapsulates and echoes episodes, phrases, words, and tonalities from all over the text of which it is part, but without necessarily bringing them into some thoroughly coherent order. If the letter is a sort of miniature of the *Wake,* it is easy to see this list of names as in turn a sort of miniature of the letter it prefaces. Its final entry, after all, encapsulates everything in the manner of the title of an eighteenth-century novel:

*First and Last Only True Account all about the Honorary Mirsu
Earwicker, L.S.D., and the Snake (Nuggets!) by a Woman of the
World who only can Tell Naked Truths about a Dear Man and all his
Conspirators how they all Tried to Fall him Putting it all around
Lucalizod about Privates Earwicker and a Pair of Sloppy Sluts
plainly Showing all the Unmentionability falsely Accusing about the
Raincoats.* (107.1–7)

But this is not *quite* a question of a text which knowingly and reflexively
represents its own processes, any more than Stephen's aesthetics did that
for the *Portrait.* Indeed, it is not quite a question of representation at all,
and for all the reasons we have been examining. ALP is not what is invoked, but invocation itself; there is no original ALP to be represented,
only a series of invocations of ALP *as* origin; like her story, she does not
even have an original name, but has gone by many; as *khora,* she is *what
is always called in the same way.* It would be missing the point to treat the
letter as paraphrasable content, the truth of which could then be applied
to the *Wake* as a whole. The content of Dennis Breen's postcard in *Ulysses*
remains inscrutable: what drives him to distraction is that it arrives, and
addresses him in that arrival. Essentially, the letter is empty. It says nothing. The letter is not a sign, if we are to take *sign* in its classical sense of the
union of signifying element and a signified meaning. Where letter, list, and
Wake meet and echo is in what they do not say so much as *perform,* on
that asyndetic and proliferating edge between order and disorder.
    Now this refusal of signification to the letter is precisely Freud's strat-
egy. What the analyst listens for is not the content of what is said, but for
the forms of the act of enunciation, and in particular of address. To this
extent, psychoanalysis is not a hermeneutics, in that its aim is not to reconstruct and thus free a subtle and buried content. Its questions are not *What
are you really saying?* but *To whom is this really addressed? Who is really
addressing it? What is the inter- and transpersonal network across which
these passwords are exchanged?* On the level of the dream analysis, the
unconscious desire at which the analysis aims is thus not at all the latent
dream thought beneath the manifest content: this, as Žižek insists (*Sublime Object* 12–13), generally turns out to be something quite banal, and
not even unconscious. The unconscious desire is carried in the dream-
work which links the latent and the manifest through the purely literal,
rebus-like manipulations of displacement and condensation. When Freud
meticulously recounts his patients' or his own waking memories of their
dreams, he is not concerned, even as a starting point, with setting out a

faithful representation of the dream, but with the ways in which the waking recounting of the dream is already pervaded by the letter's processes of reworking.

No more than Freud is the *Wake* concerned with bringing to light a hitherto unseen or unread content. As Campbell and Robinson so amply show despite themselves, in its repetitive and overdetermined mythopoeia the decoded content of *Finnegans Wake* is so often just as banal and overfamiliar as that of the latent dream thought beneath the manifest content, and has just as little to do with the unconscious.[14] John Bishop asserts in *Joyce's Book of the Dark* that the *Wake* is not the representation of a dream at all, as it is so often taken to be, but is about *dreamless* sleep, "the same kind of nothing that one will not remember not having experienced in sleep last night" (43). What he focuses on repeatedly is the ways in which syntax and wordplay are forever denying, negating, or contradicting the apparent content, even in the text's very positing of that content. Seeking its "tumptytumtoes" to the west on the first page of the *Wake,* the sleeping giant's empty "humptyhillhead" sends out "an unquiring one" (3.20–21): an *unquiry* would have to be not only an inquiry into what is not, but an inquiry which *is* not, and which never gets made (Bishop 27–41). Without existence, without content which does not sooner or later undo itself, about nothing, "on the verge of closing time" (474.8), the *Wake* performs an insistent, clamorous calling-up out of a silence before meaning, a sleep beneath or before or emptied of dreams. This is the paralysis which three words introduced late in the piece into the first story of *Dubliners,* but what was there a flickering on the fringes of vision is here extended out to monstrosity when utterances unravel themselves and single words behave everywhere with the illegible and irreparable opacity of a stain. In the sleeper Bishop finds everywhere in the *Wake,* this paralysis is not so much represented as embodied, in the words themselves: before this sleeping giant is the "erse solid man" (3.20) whose recumbent form is spread out across the Dublin landscape from Howth Hill to Phoenix Park, it is spread out across the purely literal and empty—which is to say rhythmic—repetition of the signifier, from "humptyhillhead" to "tumptytumtoes," and from "Finn no more!" (28.34) to "Finn, again!" (628.14). Bishop reads literally—to the letter—and anachronically *across* the *Wake,* finding distant echoes and serial recurrences which precede and underlie the narratological, the characterological, or the psychological.[15] The *Wake* is not the *representation* of a dream: that is, the mad proliferation of its linguistic virtuosity does not find its own principle of economy by being pressed into the dutiful service of depicting with an unprecedented faithfulness a dream-thought which would nevertheless remain essentially and forever beyond words; it is not a realism of the night any more than *Ulysses* was a realism of the day. Since the first paragraph of *Dubliners,* Joyce's writing has explored the ways in which language is always and first of all something more than the communication of a signified meaning; *Finnegans Wake* adds its own warnings that "to concentrate solely on the literal sense or even the psychological content of any document . . . is . . . hurtful to sound sense" (109.12–15). For the same reason, the *Wake* is not even a *representation* of the unconscious processes by which such things as dreams, among others, are possible.[16] Instead, it *stages* those very processes before it speaks *of* them, reproducing and repeating them in Beckett's sense of a performative writing which is not *about* something but is *that something itself* (14).

More important than its content, then, what the list of names offers as a clue to both letter and *Wake* is simply its form. Asyndetic, it does not even have structure, though neither is it strictly *without* structure (lack is something we could determine only on the basis of being and properties). Instead, it proliferates into disjunct and uncountable series, within which we find all sorts of things: overlapping and sometimes contradictory commentaries, reconstructions of what the letter may or may not have said, opinions considered and baseless, wishes, and guesses. Some versions of the letter suggest the turmoil in the Earwicker household, and explicitly defend the erring HCE—"All schwants (schwrites) ischt tell the cock's trootabout him. . . . No minzies matter. He had to see life foully the plak and the smut, (schwrites)" (113.11–14). Others seem to give us little more than innocuous domesticity or the standard phatic links of the genre, a swapping of tesserae (a parcel of cakes, a born gentleman, a funeral, Christmas wishes, fondest love, dear thank you, XXXX . . .). Another version suggests that the letter might be to Issy, under her sometime petname, "originating by transhipt from Boston . . . to Dear whom it proceeded to mention Maggy well & allathome's health well . . . & Muggy well how are you Maggy & hopes soon to hear well & must now close it with fondest to the twoinns" (111.9–17). Any one of these yields multitudes. Do we read "Dear [whoever it might be], Maggy's well and so are all at home. How are you? Maggy hopes to hear soon from . . . ," or do we read "Dear [who is it? the letter will tell us straightaway:] Maggy, Well! All at home are well. How are you, Maggy? I hope soon to hear you're well . . ."? The syntax allows all sorts of conflicting senses, the internal repetitions and variations suggesting both more and less than a single letter, with no attempt to synthesize the divergences. It is not a matter of deciding which of these possibilities might be true, what it is really about, or who it is really from, but of attending to its plurability, the slippages in syntax and address through which the utterance breaks into hubbub.

This "mamafesta" of "Annah the Allmaziful" which has been invoked by many names is "a polyhedron of scripture" (107.8). "Proteiform" (107.8)—"proto-," "protean-," and "cuneiform"—it gives us an ur-writing whose proto-form is change itself. After chapters of speculation on what might have happened in Phoenix Park, on the swell of gossip and innuendo, on the court's deliberation and HCE's incarceration, the apparent fixity of the letter will turn out to be just as "deliquescent" (107.10), dissolving under our very eyes. Is it even the letter itself we are examining, or still that inventory (*bordereau*) of names by which it has been invoked?[17]

> Closer inspection of the *bordereau* would reveal a multiplicity of personalities inflicted on the documents or document and some pre-vision of virtual crime or crimes might be made by anyone unwary enough before any suitable occasion for it or them had so far managed to happen along. In fact, under the closed eyes of the inspectors the traits featuring the *chiaroscuro* coalesce, their contrarieties eliminated, in one stable somebody similarly as by the providential warring of heartshaker with housebreaker and of dramdrinker against freethinker our social something bowls along bumpily, experiencing a jolting series of prearranged disappointments, down the long lane of (it's as semper as oxhousehumper!) generations, more generations and still more generations. (107.23–35)

Our close inspection seems to be done with closed eyes, for only once we read with a certain lack of distinctness and a certain blindness to the letter, will those "stable somebod[ies]" of representation arise from the coalescence of contrarieties, and the familiar narrative effects of characters and events emerge from its chaotic, or khoratic, matrix, "as semper as oxhousehumper" (as McHugh points out, *aleph, beth,* and *gimel* are the Hebrew words for *ox, house,* and *camel*).

This inseparability of blindness from the very possibility of reading, indeed from the possibility of perception itself, is everywhere in *Finnegans Wake,* as Bishop argues throughout. Mythopoeic approaches such as Campbell and Robinson's read the presence of some sixty-odd languages in the *Wake* as an index of its universality, where the sleeping mind taps into a collective unconscious of transcultural archetypes and Earwicker becomes Everyman. But the plurability of the text diverges everywhere:

rather than drawing all of the text towards one radiating tale in a single common voice, it peppers it with blind spots and multiplies it into clamor. What the *Wake*'s plethora of Samoan and Provençal, Old Church Slavonic and Kiswahili, Persian and Shelta guarantees is that the only universal is an *inability* to read it, even for that "ideal reader suffering from an ideal insomnia" (120.13–14). To open *Finnegans Wake* is to find oneself blind and deaf. Something is written, there on the page, but it is unintelligible even as it is said, partly obliterated at the very moment it shows itself—and if anything even more puzzling in those rare moments where the text seems relatively straightforward and without its insistent portmanteaux. The *Wake* places that inability to read right at the heart of the very possibility of reading, not somewhere outside it as an accident ideally to be eliminated. So, for example, just before examining the *bordereau*, we have been advised, or warned, that:

> All's so herou [far] from us him in a kitcher[night]nott darkness, by hasard [thousand] and worn rolls arered, we must grope on till Zerogh [day] hour like pou [owl] owl giaours [blind] as we are would we salve aught of moments for our aysore [today] today. (107.20–23)

The brackets gloss the Arabic-English puns, which for those of us poor owls blind to Arabic are blind spots which are not so much represented as staged by the very fact of being in a language we cannot read. And yet once we do the translation (or, as I did, have McHugh do it for us), what we find is just a statement of that blindness we have been groping through, governed by hazard, looking for daylight. But if we are owls, that daylight can only blind us: to read the content clearly would in this sense be quite to miss the point when that darkness is a condition of our seeing anything at all.[18]

Part of the resentment for the incurred debt which Derrida suggests accompanies the pleasures of reading Joyce comes from this sheer unreadability at the heart of the legible: like Denis Breen with his postcard, we are insistently being addressed, but we do not quite know what it is which is being addressed to us or what it asks of us, only that it demands response and is forever tugging at our sleeve with confidences and adjurations and familiarities and asides: "Mind your hats goan in!" (8.9), or "You is feeling like you was lost in the bush, boy?" (112.3), or "Tell me something. . . . Isn't that terribly nice of them? You can ken that they come of a rarely old family" (560.22, 32–33), or "Well, here's lettering you erronnymously" (617.30), or "We feem to have being elfewhere as tho' th' had paſsed in our ſuſpens" (238.7–8). Before it can be about any universal "one stable somebody" with all "contrarieties eliminated," which is to say before those "traits featuring the *chiaroscuro* coalesce," *Finnegans Wake* is about the fractured and multiple collectivity of language, to which we have no choice but to belong, even if that should be in a singular destitution. Lacan's term for this asyndetic fracturing is useful, and succinct: the radical inconsistency of the big Other.

We are still inspecting that *bordereau* closely. Those traits coalesce and contrarieties are eliminated "in one stable somebody *similarly as* . . . our social something bowls along bumpily" (107.29–33: emphasis added). *Similarly as:* we are being offered a comparison. Or so it would seem: something similar to a comparison perhaps, as the catachrestic form "similarly as" is not *quite* that of a comparison. Before we make any consideration of its content, then, let us not be blind to the letter, which brings things together by rhythm, consonance, and a visual assonance as much as by sense, setting up an elaborate rhetorical balance across that now multiplied simile (see figure 5.1). Over and over, *Wake* sentences are structured like this.[19] As this chapter's invocation of the "tenebrous . . . Book of Kells" (122.22–23) suggests, and as the various draft versions bear out,[20] they develop by troping, and by troping of tropes: subsidiary clauses balloon within subsidiary clauses, and then within those, so that sometimes the only way to follow the structure of a *Wake* sentence is to keep one finger firmly on the grammatical subject until the verb arrives. This syntactical overbidding tends to empty the sentence out, to turn it into something of unclear sense but insistent address: whatever it says, it treats you as if you do and should understand it. What links *stable somebody* and *social something* is thus not only the conceptual affinity between signified meanings, but the melismatic repetition and elaboration of signifiers, and in particular of the letters which make them up. In this repetition, they are linked in a mutual debt of responsivity, a promise which can never quite be called in, with the one calling to the other across the sentence in an empty speech which is the bare exchange of *tesserae:* an *s*, an *l*, a *some-*.

Content belongs to the word, the sentence: here it is the letter we are reading, illegible because it is before content. "Drawing nearer to take our slant at it" (113.30–31), we find instead a writing which is a furious eventfulness of the intersections of all sorts of things: if we find we no longer even know what surface all this is inscribed on and over which we jolt, it may be because it is many surfaces, all at once. "One cannot help noticing that rather more than half of the lines run north-south in the Nemzes and

Figure 5.1

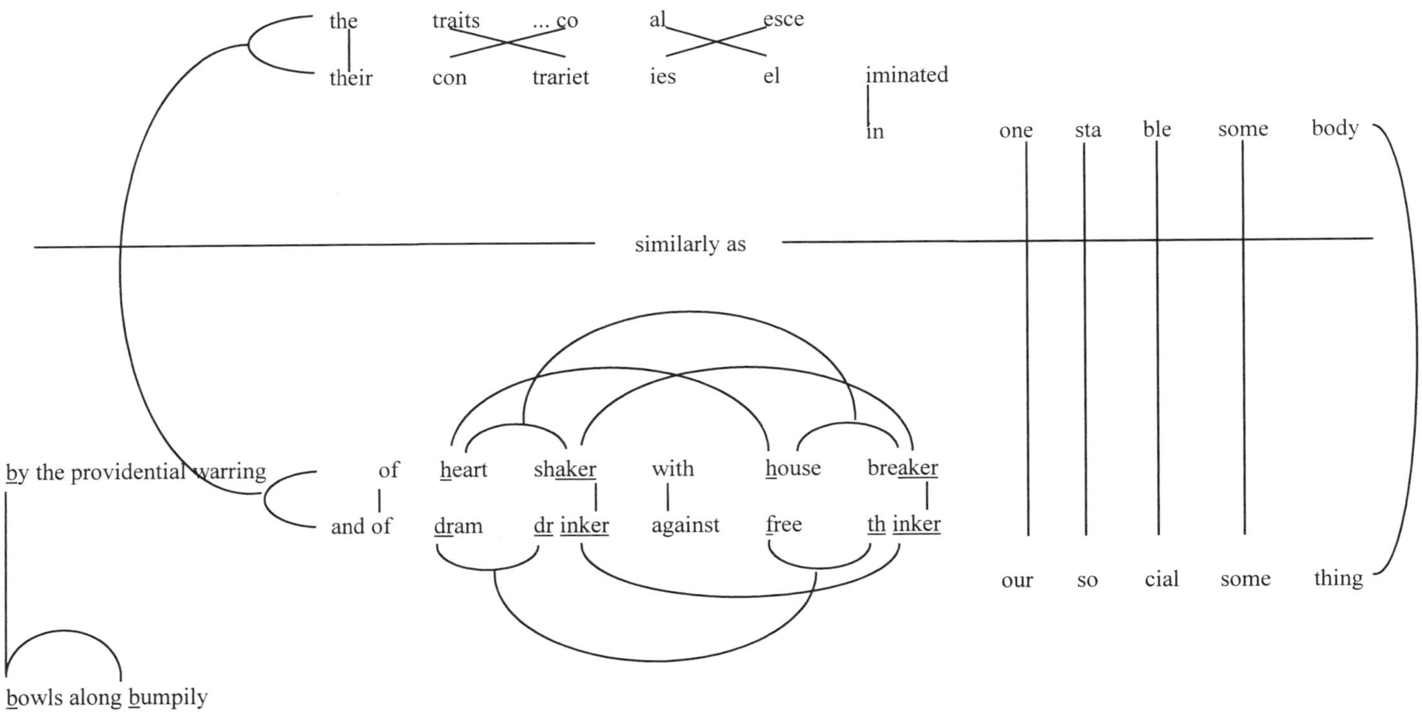

Bukarahast directions while the others go west-east in search from Maliziies with Bulgarad" (114.2–5); along the "ruled barriers," "the traced words, run, march, halt, walk, stumble at doubtful points, stumble up again in comparative safety" (114.7–9), as much choreography as calligraphy; we can no longer tell if the "cardinal points" are those of compass or document; some believe that "the intention may have been geodetic" (114.14–15). Boustrophedonic, with the movement of the ox at plough "writing thithaways end to end and turning, turning and end to end hithaways writing" (114.16–17), it maps out earth and language simultaneously, building Babel with its "lines of litters slittering up and louds of latters slettering down" (114.17–18). Stephen is making his way across town surrounded by the clamor of the marketplace, and the ivy is singing its high whiny song in his head (*P* 193). It is already well past ten, and somewhere else, a Leopold Bloom we have not yet met is doubtless also out on the streets, marking out other paths north-south and east-west. In the heart of the Hibernian metropolis, trams are slowing, shunting, changing trolley, right and left; "grossbooted draymen rolled barrels dullthudding out of Prince's stores and bumped them up on the brewery float. On the brewery float bumped dullthudding barrels rolled by grossbooted draymen out of Prince's stores" (*U* 7.1, 10, 22–24).

This geodesy is an earth-writing without content. It sets boundaries and limits, and defines insides and outsides, and thus opens the possibility of regulation of exchanges amongst them. It is what allows there to be a *hearth* (the "domestic economical" intention some suggest is related to the geodetic [114.15]), and with that, all the forms of *the proper* which will emerge unstably and again coalesce into the flux of the *Wake*: person, certainly, but at the same time family, nation, protocol, law . . . In its emergence and from the beginning, the proper is improper, in that it arises out of the marketplace and the hubbub which inhabits it. Its writing is not its own, but is "*inflicted* on the documents" (107.25) as a matter of violence ("the homeborn shillelagh as an aid to calligraphy" [114.12]), or a "raiding": "[t]hat's the point of eschatology our book of kills reaches for" (482.31–34). Everywhere, that gap within providence takes the form of a rhythm. The mark, the surface: an unstable, oscillating *chiaroscuro*.

In the proliferating repetition and excess of its patterns, the letter leads the dance of sense, just as it did with that ivy twining and whining on the wall. Recall Saussure's insistence on the arbitrariness of the connection between the two parallel but autonomous regimes of signifier and signified: there is "no internal connexion . . . between the idea 'sister' and the French sequence of sounds *s-ö-r*" which acts as its signifier (Saussure 67).

That is, the connection cannot be described in terms which are internal to either of the series it connects: it belongs neither to the conceptual logic of the signified meaning, nor to the regularities of the signifying phonemic or graphemic system, which is to say it belongs to neither side of the classical philosophical opposition of the sensible and the intelligible. What links thought and mark is sheer historical vicissitude. Even within a single language, the very possibility of its articulation *as* a language rests on the serial meeting of these two different and relatively autonomous regimes. The *Wake* multiplies this exponentially in its tropes-upon-tropes across any number of the potential sixty-something languages it invokes, and across both "stable somebody" and "social something."[21] In this passage, its word for such a meeting is *providence*. Language is layered against language, to produce an "[a]ccidental music providentially arranged by L'Archet and Laccorde. Melodiotiosities in purefusion by the score" (222.1–2).

Now *providence* is always double, one of those words which is forever undoing itself. On the one hand, the providential is the purely accidental: what happens to fall out, or in one's path, that kernel of the Real which is the luck of the draw by which one has what is at hand, and the thousand and one *hasard*s which bring the Arabic and English words together. This is providence as the unforeseeable and the unaccountable, beyond calculation. But *providence* is also the opposite of this, when it is the action of the guiding hand, even if one which reveals itself only in retrospect when it has already taken its place in a chain of causalities "down the long lane of . . . generations, more generations and still more generations." This providence is an appointment which can have been met only after the event, a meeting of disjointed times in that jolting series of "prearranged disappointments" in which history "bowls along bumpily" (107.32–34): the arrest, the symptom, granulated out down to the level of the letter. Providence is both of these meanings, the at-hand and the guiding hand: not their synthesis, for they have none, but precisely their "providential warring," the gap and irresolvable tension between them: the war *within* providence. It is the very instability which we have seen in the case of that great provider herself, ALP.

There is a gap within providence: providence is itself a gap, gnomonic perhaps, the very thing we earlier called the serial temporality of the Messianic, after Benjamin, or the "non-historical kernel of the process of historicization," after Žižek (*Plague* 49), or the radical inconsistency of the big Other, after Lacan. And that gap within providentiality repeatedly

deflects the question of what the letter might signify, and prevents it settling onto a stable signified meaning. Here, in this arrest, "thinking suddenly stops in a configuration pregnant with tensions" (Benjamin 254),
because thought, the signified, is not what governs this generative mechanism of the signifier and the tensions of its serial connectivity. On this
smallest of all scales, the Messianic arrest is the gap by which utterance
remains empty speech in that Lacanian sense: not filled with a present
meaning but always awaiting its meaning, as promise, in an exchange
which can never be completed.

There is an instant. It is one among countless many, so many and so
countless that we cannot even think of them as a succession of *now*s, even
an endless succession. There is nothing exceptional at all about this instant. But for there to be an instant, for it not to disappear totally, it must
be marked off somehow, *as* instant, and thus after all as exceptional. There
is a necessary and modest epiphany of what simply happens: epiphany is
that moment, both exceptional and utterly ordinary, at which the excep-
tionality of the ordinary reveals itself.[22] (It is tempting to say of the moment in general, but that "in general" is precisely what is put in question
in the epiphany.) The instant is minimally a rhythm, a *now* marked off
against a background. It is the utterly ordinary, the very texture of the
experience itself; but even in this utter ordinariness there is a force of
breaking with what came before, and of the non-necessity of the providential. What gives the instant this character is the event: something in all its
banality marks this instant irreducibly *as* instant. The instant is structured
as pure and impossible *mark;* which is thus to say that before there is even
anyone there to read it, indeed as a condition of the possibility that there
should be someone, anyone at all there, it has the structure of a *letter.*[23]
The letter is what marks, providentially, a certain intensity: *now, here,* that
minimal epiphany. It is not necessary that we know whether to call it
pleasure or pain, or some other affect altogether, let alone that we can say
whose affect this might be, or might eventually turn out to be. The intensity of the letter does not rely on or belong to a subject; it is what marks out
the possibility of there being a subject.

This is why the *Wake*'s characters, in the sense of its personages, are
also characters in the sense of *letters.* HCEs and ALPs of course multiply
throughout the text, but there are also the sigla, those letters of a strange
new alphabet: ⊓ , △ , ∧ , ⎾ , ⼢ . The sigla do not correspond one-to-
one with the personages, but incessantly combine and divide (⼢ combines
both ∧ and ⎾ , and all three, with ⊆ , are possible manifestations of ⊓ ,
which in turn is also found in all of its other orientations, ∃ , ⊔ , and ⊢ ;

△ is sometimes manifested as ᛕ or ⊣, the latter of which is in turn sometimes doubled by ⊢ or aggregated into ⬭ ; ○ and X are also aggregates, whereas neither □ nor ⊕ are attached to personages at all).[24] In this proliferation, the sigla are essentially empty, a series of differential markings without content—differences without positive term, as Saussure will say of the signifier (118).[25] In themselves, they mean nothing: as letters, below the level of the word, these marks in a new alphabet can take on meaning only from their relationships with each other. Hence their multiplicity (the letter can be conceived only in its serial articulation with other letters, and the infinitely rapid oscillation that articulation sets up) and their impersonality (rather than name an essential personality, they set up an algebra, a seriality, a rhythm which is also that of responsivity). What they break character down into is not the set of warring homuncular components a Jungian approach might suggest (the warring sons who are really the hero's own divided self, the wife who is his anima), but something quite non-human, a thorough *de*composition of the very idea of fictional character (we recall how much the letter is associated with the "orangeflavoured mudmound" [111.34] from which the hen digs it up, almost as if it had been generated in those processes of decomposition). The sigla are not even names: McHugh fittingly calls them "particles" (*Annotations* xi–xii), as if they are elemental or, better yet, inflections, like the "paper wounds" which "ad bîn 'provoked' ay ∧ fork, of à grave Brofèsor; àth é's Brèak—fast—table; ; acùtely profèššionally *piquéd*, to=introdùce a notion of time [ùpon à plane (?) sù ' ' fàç'e'] by pùnct! ingh oles (sic) in iSpace?!" (124.3, 9–12).

The sigla, then, are not essences or archetypes of character. Just as they themselves, as letters, take on meaning only from their interrelations, what they stand for in the characters is precisely what is invested on or in them from elsewhere. Before we have Stephen, and before there is something like Stephen's father or his mother or Dante, before even the moocow or baby tuckoo, there is a swarming of utterances which have already passed through the marketplace and many mouths, the swirling and hubbub of comportments and demands, and the responsivity of debt already incurred. *Sing, dance, apologize. You are a nicens little boy, not because of what you do or even what you are, but because you are addressed as one. Nicens little boy is now your debt.* Just as they were for the boy looking anxiously up at the dying priest's window, the doggerel words are already singing and answering to each other as Stephen makes his way across town, and the green rose blossoms into twining, whining ivy. On the strand at Sandymount, there is a watching going on, and an excitement;

somewhere in these are Bloom and Gerty, but also the *Lady's Pictorial,* iron jelloids, *Sweets of Sin,* a thousand unsolicited testimonials, 7 Eccles Street, and Miss Cummins, author of *Mabel Vaughan* and other tales. The relationship the sigla have to characters is that which the equally unpronounceable name signing the shout from the hockey field has to the boys whose voices make the noise. Sigla are the countersignatures from elsewhere by which there come to be such effects as Earwicker and Anna Livia, Shem, Shaun, and Isabel: not their essential individuality, but the impersonality of a debt which, passed on from one term to another within that minimal algebra, is forever unpayable.

The trigrams HCE and ALP too are both more and less than abbreviations for names. Not only are *Humphrey Chimpden Earwicker* and *Anna Livia Plurabelle* gloriously improbable names—which is in itself hardly an objection to anything in *Finnegans Wake*—but more significantly, neither of them are used anywhere in the *Wake* in those full and undistorted forms, though partial and distorted versions abound.[26] What the trigrams do, of course, is trigger a potentially endless combinatory of acrostics which countersign the text on almost every page. But they do this without discernible limit: their effect is not to bring all of the text under the propriety of a couple of proper names, but rather to blur the very boundaries of signature, and of the text itself. Thus, while the capitalization of the "Howth Castle and Environs" of the opening sentence (3.3) or the famous "Here Comes Everybody" (32.18–19) flags both of them as an obvious version of the proper name, there are other occasions in which the letters of what we might quite reasonably want to see as an occurrence of the trigram are neither capitalized nor initial: the entomological lusts of that "*e*ternal *c*himera*h*unter," for example (or perhaps it's "*e*ternal *ch*imera-hunter") (107.14), mark it out anyway as another version of HCE. We may even want to argue that a signature can be made up from an entirely internal occurrence of the three letters, as in that "affectionate large-looking ta*che* of tch" which is after all "the masterbilker here, as usual, signing the page away" (111.19–21). We may even want to see a signature in a repeated scattering of the relevant letters throughout a phrase, as in the letter's "round thousand whirligig glorioles pre*f*aced by (*a*las!) now il*l*egible *a*iry *p*lumeflights," especially as these are "ambiembellishing the initials majuscule of Earwicker" (119.14–17). But where would we choose *not* to see signature? Could we, for example, see it in reading across the end of one word and the beginning of the next, as in those "traits featuring the *ch*iaroscuro" (107.29)? It would again seem to be quite appropriate in this case, for we are told that these traits do coalesce in one stable somebody. Could we see it where only two of the three elements occur? One of Shaun's ripostes in chapter III.1 is a paragraph marked with initial *H*s and *C*s but not *E*s: "How are them columbuses?,," "Hobos hornknees and the coorveture of my spine," "My heaviest crux and dairy lot it is," "the Headfire Clump," and "Hagios Colleenkiller's prophecies" (409.11–30). The incomplete HC(E) is perhaps a signature in its very incompleteness, delaying the complete trigram just as the stammer which also marks the passage delays the complete utterance ("whowho"). Could we even read the famous final "the" as a signature effect in and because of its very incompleteness? Anna Livia is after all responding ("Coming, far!") to the "Far calls" of her father, the sea to whom she is returning. But as the moment of that return is also the moment of her death, it can never actually occur in her soliloquy; it remains asymptotic, something just after the end, figured in the stammered, insistent, and increasingly frequent repetitions of the partial signature awaiting a *c* it will never reach:[27]

> Coming, far! End *he*re. Us *t*he*n*. Finn, again! Take. Bussoftl*hee*, mememormee! Till thousendst*hee*. Lps. T*he* keys to. Given! A way a lone a last a loved a long t*he* (628.13–16)

We can note a similar and somewhat more obvious effect as the AL(P) signature too trails off into incompleteness ("*a lone a last a loved a long the*"—or perhaps to a paraphic completion which takes us to another signature altogether: "PARIS, 1922–1939"). Could we, or should we, in principle treat every occurrence of any two elements of the trigrams as at least potentially signature-effects? After all, the two-part names *Anna Livia* and *Humphrey Chimpden* are actually used in the *Wake,* while the full triple-deckers are not. Even if we were to decide to admit only full three-part acrostics (but on what grounds other than fiat could we do this?), would it matter how far the three elements were from each other? The answer to the question of who "sports a *c*hainganger's albert solemenly over his *h*ullender's *e*pulence" (126.13–14) is after all indeed HCE. Do the elements even have to be in the same sentence? ("his farced *e*pistol to the *h*ibruws. From *C*ernilius slomtime prepositus of Toumaria to the clutch in Anteach" [228.33–34]). Do they even have to be in adjacent sentences? Given that two of the letters of HCE occur in words as common as "he," "the," "they," "then," "there," "their," "here"—and even, just to confuse things, in "she," "her" and "hen"—surely *any* passage from the *Wake* is capable of producing the trigram if we are only willing to interpret broadly and wait long enough. As one of the objections runs, "why, pray, sign anything as long as every word, letter, penstroke, paper-space is a perfect signature of its own?" (115.6–8); wherever we turn, we "*Hear! Calls! Everywhair!*" (108.23), finding those signatures of all things Stephen declared himself here to read (*U* 3.2).

As with so many other aspects of the *Wake,* signature effects do not so much consolidate the text as overbid it into an anxiety which leaks out everywhere. There are constant injunctions which interrupt the letter chapter to demand what on earth the letter might be saying, and what if anything the principle of unity behind it might be. They mirror the anxieties attendant on reading the *Wake* itself, and in *Wake* criticism. In one of the seminal pieces of *A Wake Newslitter,* for example, Clive Hart argues on the one hand that there is a danger in "too great an insistence on the primacy of Joyce's intentions," as "there is nothing to suggest that he wants to hold the meaning of [*Finnegans Wake*] within rigid limits"; "ultimately, there is . . . no such thing as an incorrect reading of *FW*" ("Elephant" 2–3). On the other hand, though, "I must stress that I am not on my way towards a justification of *FW* as cloud-material onto which we readers can project whatever sense seems best suited to our psyches" ("Elephant" 3), as there are indeed certain principles of order in this "chaosmos" (118.21):

> anything in *FW* is indeed about anything else—*but only in the last of an infinite regress of planes of meaning.* The all-important question, in my view, is how to get these planes of meaning into the right order, and into the right perspective. I have no doubts, myself, that Joyce intends all the planes to be there. ("Elephant" 6: emphases in original)[28]

We see the tension acted out again in the juxtaposition of Hart's two great contemporary works of *Wake*iana, the 1962 *Structure and Motif in "Finnegans Wake"* and the 1963 *Concordance:* if the latter opens up a vista of potentially unlimited interrelationships within the text, the former strives mightily to contain that within what it sees as the structure of a *Wake*an equivalent of *Ulysses'* Gilbert and Linati schemas.[29] On the one hand, the *Wake* demands and sets in place an infinite connectivity; on the other, though, criticism and scholarship must draw, assent to, and even enforce such a limit, or anything goes: the question of the limit is inseparable from the question of the existence and limits of criticism itself. For Hart's *Newslitter* piece, those limits arrive as the six numbered "propositions about the reading of the book" with which he concludes: not the endpoints of an argument, but a set of principles on which an investigation can take place.

The Joycean temporalities of the signature ensure that meaning is structurally and necessarily something which is not yet entirely present, but is still to arrive. One cannot prove that "every syllable [of the *Wake*] is meaningful," as the first of Hart's principles has it, for example ("Elephant" 8), but one can work as though this were the case, and as though there were really only two types of syllable, those whose meaning is already known and those whose meaning is not yet known. As Hart says, Joyce "seems to have wanted meanings to accrete in his text by hindsight" ("Elephant" 5). Which is to say that there is a sense in which *reading into* is not only in principle indistinguishable from just *reading*, but is its very possibility. The point is not that the *Wake*, or any text, has no limits, but first of all that these limits are never established as a presence; everywhere, they leak into a future, an absolute future which will never remain anything but future. If limits produce meaning, they nevertheless cannot be expressed in terms of a set of general principles which would allow one to decide beforehand the *legitimacy* of a particular interpretation. In a word, they *resist principle*. Asyndetic, the limits against and across which the *Wake* is forever working are precisely those between the generality of principle and the happenstance of the specific. This incessant eversion from one to the other—from a Chapelizod publican, his wife, and their three children, to Here Comes Everybody and Haveth Childers Everywhere—is not allegorization or mythopoeia, both of which are firmly and knowingly on the side of generality and principle. It is logically prior to both: only once there is this asyndetic eversion can there be something like myth or allegory as a governing principle. We can say that *this* or *that* particular incidence of the letters H, C, and E, or A, L, and P, is more or less likely to make sense as a signature, but we cannot guarantee that as *Wake* criticism bowls along bumpily, its providential warring will not at some point in the future produce some sort of framework in which such an incidence will now make clear sense as signature—that every so often, "unexpectedly one bushman's holiday," it will throw up "a few spontaneous fragments of orangepeel" (110.27–28). One cannot say that *in principle* occurrences of the letters of the trigram which are separated by more than a certain crucial difference should not be considered as legitimate signature effects, for how would one determine a limit which is not yet present? What, indeed, does separation mean in the *Wake*, when every word in it stands to be connected instantaneously to others perhaps hundreds of pages away?[30] We can decide that in a particular case, and for now, there is no point in seeing a certain configuration as meaningful, but we cannot exclude in the name of a general principle the possibility of its *coming to mean*, for that possibility depends on the very providence that is not yet encompassed by the general.

This is why Hart is quite right to suggest that "every syllable is meaningful," while Campbell and Robinson are quite wrong when, in their *Skeleton Key*, they appear to exclaim the same thing: "*There are no nonsense syllables in Joyce!*" (360, their emphasis). *Finnegans Wake* is not already replete with the eternal verities of myth; it is an asyndetic machine for those meanings which, as Hart says, accrete by hindsight. There are no syllables which can be excluded from the possibility of making sense sometime in the future, though there are doubtless many we cannot make sense of at the moment, and perhaps many we never will. What might make sense of them is not what is already and archetypally known, but an intrusion from elsewhere, the swerve which lends "another cant to the questy" (109.1), or that "*portal* vein" of discovery through which "our wholemole millwheeling vicociclometer . . . receives . . . the dialytically separated elements of precedent decomposition" (614.27–34: emphasis added). This accretion of meanings is not the gradual excavation of what already lies buried and only awaits its gradual and patient uncovering, but a stuttering, jolting affair of bidding and overbidding. Each move in *Wake* criticism looks back: to different parts and aspects of the *Wake* (this text which makes such a problem of continuity and unity), and to different parts and aspects of *Wake* criticism (which, now that professors have been busy over it for over half a century, is of such a volume and complexity that few readers can claim overview). Each move involves a bid of summation, but the sum and what are summed are different for each case. And in this summation each move is also a bid on the future, opening up a different set of possibilities of response: development, refutation, debate, rewriting.

It may be, then, that the fact that neither the letter nor the *Wake* seems to do what it promises—exonerate HCE, shed light on his alleged indiscretion, or provide what Senn calls "the trite, hypolectic sense of 'understanding'" ("Linguistic Dissatisfaction" 212)—is by a twist of the tale precisely the point at which it does indeed illuminate after all. The letter's relation to HCE is precisely its non-relation: it is what remains to be done, to be remade at every stage; it keeps that promise open, as promise, refusing to appear to foreclose by the accident of whatever has actually arrived. And it is precisely because of this non-relation, this dehiscence, that the matter can never be closed, and the letter *can,* after all, be made to do duty for alibi, circulating, written, and overwritten at each stage, as chiasmic as the meeting between Bloom and Stephen. If there is always something accidental in the signature—"pee ess from (locust may eat all but this sign shall they never) affectionate largelooking tache of tch" (111.18–20)—then stain *is* signature in the very accident of its nature, a countersignature after the event, "on the spout of the moment." In claiming the letter for itself, the very stain is a "signing the page *away,*" sending it elsewhere, and in that very indirection marking it off "as a genuine relique" (111.21–22, emphasis added). To read is to (re)mark: to comment, and to write over; to send on elsewhere. And just as *stable somebody* and *social something* call and answer to each other across the sentence in which they are embedded, so too do the sigla and the apparently unprecedented processes of *Finnegans Wake* which they epitomize in fact echo, amplify, and formalize aspects of what this book has tried to show has been in Joyce's work all along: the work of the word as debt, promise, and countersignature.

Notes

Opening Accounts: Signatures and Countertimes

1. On Joyce's roles in the marketing of his work, see for example Dettmar, "Selling *Ulysses*."

2. To take only one of the more obvious indicators of such meetings, the Fifth International James Joyce Symposium in Paris, June 1975, included addresses by Jacques Lacan and Philippe Sollers; the Ninth, in Frankfurt 1984, included addresses by Jacques Derrida and Julia Kristeva. See Beja, "Synjoysium," and Herring, "The Frankforall Symposium."

3. Attridge and Ferrer report the story in their introduction to *Post-Structuralist Joyce* (11). Senn affirms it in a letter to *James Joyce Quarterly* 24.1 (115–16). See also the interview with Senn in the "Introductory Scrutinies: Focus on Senn," and "Instead of a Preface: The Creed of Naïveté," both in his *Inductive Scrutinies* (xii–xix, 1–5).

4. Benstock uses the phrase as the title of the first chapter of his 1965 *Joyce-Again's Wake*. Twelve years later, taking stock of *Finnegans Wake* criticism to introduce a *Wake* issue of the *James Joyce Quarterly*, he would suggest that at that time, "The mystery of *Ulysses* posits real solutions; the mystery of *Finnegans Wake*, mostly new frustrations" ("The State of the *Wake*" 238). Fritz Senn echoes this in the preface to his 1984 *Joyce's Dislocutions*: "When I started out, some thirty years ago, in the juvenile flush of those euphoric first unravelings of meaning, I hoped that within some decades we might jointly arrive at sufficient basic understanding (at the modest level of Roland McHugh's helpful *Annotations*) that would enable us to go beyond those resistant details and to make statements of more general import and validity, perhaps even in a scholarly way. We obviously haven't" (xi).

5. It should be clear that much of what I have to say on the signature is informed by Jacques Derrida's meditations on the topic, in texts such as "Signature Event Context" (*Margins of Philosophy* 307–30), *Signéponge/Signsponge*, "To Speculate—On 'Freud'" (*Post Card* 257–409), and *The Ear of the Other*.

1. Paralysis

1. As Bloom realizes in "Sirens": "Could make a kind of pun on that. It is a kind of music I often thought when she. Acoustics that is. Tinkling. Empty vessels make

most noise. Because the acoustics, the resonance changes according as the weight of the water is equal to the law of falling water" (*U* 11.979–83). See also *JJ* 154.

2. Thus in Sonnet 116, the *error* of "If this be error and upon me proved, / I never writ, nor no man ever loved" is a lack of fixity as well as of truth: love, the "ever-fixèd mark," and "star to every wand'ring bark," is what does not veer from its course, "even to the edge of doom."

3. Richards began The World's Classics in the wake of the success of Dent's Everyman series, as another set of cheap reprints of out-of-copyright works. As a result of his bankruptcy, he sold it to Oxford University Press in 1905, under which imprint it now publishes Johnson's edition of the 1922 *Ulysses*. (Kenner, *A Sinking Island* 33.)

4. "'First, I never borrowed a kettle from B. at all; secondly, the kettle had a hole in it already when I got it from him; and thirdly, I gave him back the kettle undamaged.'" Freud, *Jokes and Their Relation to the Unconscious* 100; see also 266–68.

5. The briefest outline of such a thematics of the call would have to include the calls which frame *Portrait*. We shall turn to the first of these in chapter 3; at the other end of the novel, Stephen will again be called by "kinsmen":

> *16 April:* Away! Away!
> The spell of arms and voices: the white arms of roads, their promise of close embraces and the black arms of tall ships that stand against the moon, their tale of distant nations. They are held out to say: We are alone. Come. And the voices say with them: We are your kinsmen. And the air is thick with their company as they call to me, their kinsman, making ready to go, shaking the wings of their exultant and terrible youth.
> *26 April:* . . . Welcome, O life! I go to encounter for the millionth time the reality of experience and to forge in the smithy of my soul the uncreated conscience of my race.
> *27 April:* Old father, old artificer, stand me now and ever in good stead. (*P* 275–76)

In *Ulysses*, Stephen's interior monologue is called into being on the page by Mulligan's mirror-games (*U* 1.134–37), but even before that we have the mysterious "long slow whistle of call" to which "two strong shrill whistles answered" (*U* 1.24, 26). Matching and inverting this, in "Calypso" Bloom's first *direct* speech will be in response to another call, this time from the cat (*U* 4.16–17). Two sets of uncanny address structure "Proteus," broadly speaking one of them analeptic and the other proleptic. Stephen is haunted not only by the mute apparition of his mother, as is often commented on, but also—and far more frequently at this point in the text—by the voice of the father by which others recognize him ("You're your father's son. I know the voice" [*U* 3.229]); the two are frequently coupled ("Wombed in sin darkness I was too, made not begotten. By them, the man with my voice and my eyes and a ghostwoman with ashes on her breath" [*U* 3.45–47], and, of course, the famous garbled telegram, "—Nother dying come home father"

[*U* 3.199]). And proleptically, there is Stephen's Haroun al Raschid dream (*U* 3.365–69), which foresees his meeting with Bloom later that day in the "street of harlots" (*U* 3.366). In chapter 3, we shall examine in more detail some of the implications of the *address* of *Ulysses*' characteristic use of free indirect discourse, particularly in those middle chapters between "Sirens" and "Oxen of the Sun," which are so often seen as a series of parodies separating the earlier innovation of interior monologue from the later radical reinventions of style (as, for example, Groden, *"Ulysses" in Progress* 43). In its syntactic ambiguity, the opening "riverrun" of *Finnegans Wake* is like the title both invocation and injunction; at the other end of the *Wake*, Anna Livia's final words are a response to "Far calls. Coming, far!" (*FW* 628.013). Within the *Wake*, calls and invocations abound, from the radio and television which are forever intruding in II.3, to the Howth Hill seance in which Mamalujo eventually raise the giant HCE in III.3, to the morning clamor which opens the final chapter.

6. Sylvia Beach's catalogue lists the date of the surviving pages of *Stephen Hero* as 1903; Herbert Gorman says Joyce had tried to burn the manuscript in 1908 (Spencer 13). The stories of *Dubliners* date from mid-1904 to 1907.

7. Mahaffey points out the elaborate pairings of the names (151):

RIChard   BeatRICe
RoBERT   BERTha

8. "But in fine art it is obvious furthermore that even a rationalistic interpretation of the principle of purposiveness must presuppose that the purposes are ideal rather than real. For the liking that arises from aesthetic ideas must not depend on our achieving determinate purposes (since then the art would be mechanical as well as intentional); and yet fine art, as such, must be regarded as a product of genius rather than of understanding and science, and hence as getting its rule through *aesthetic* ideas, which are essentially distinct from rational ideas of determinate purposes." Immanuel Kant, *Critique of Judgement*, 225. For this and similar points about intention, I am indebted to discussion with Rex Butler, and to his fine *An Uncertain Smile: Australian Art in the '90s*, 19–20.

9. A crudely absurd calculation is useful here. There are 628 pages in *Finnegans Wake*, which for ease of calculation we will take as each having the standard 36 lines (the overrun will soon be swallowed up). This gives some 22,608 lines. Let's err grossly on the side of modesty, and suggest that any single *line* of the *Wake* will have only about 10 different ways of paraphrasing it. (And that *is* modest. An average per line of only 3 to 4 words each with two meanings will do it.) At this minimal rate, the whole *Wake* could be paraphrased in some 10^{22608} ways: 1 followed by some 22,608 zeroes. But it is estimated that there are only 10^{80} elementary particles in the universe: there simply wouldn't be enough matter in the universe to write the paraphrase on. For Joyce to have *thought* of all of these, in the sense of consciously bringing each and every one of them to mind somewhere along the line, even assuming he worked 24 hours of every day of the 17 years it

took to write the *Wake,* then (dividing by the number of seconds in 17 years, which, at somewhat over half a billion, is truly tiny compared to that vast number) every *second* of that time he must have thought of something of the order of 10^{22599} of those paraphrasable meanings: 1 followed by 22,599 zeroes.

10. See Appendix I of the 1992 Penguin edition. Its chronology is based on Don Gifford, *Joyce Annotated: Notes to "Dubliners" and "A Portrait of the Artist as a Young Man,"* 2nd ed., and Michael Groden, "A Textual and Publishing History," in *A Companion to Joyce Studies,* ed. Zack Bowen and James Carens, 78–79.

11. This doubled recollection will be redoubled shortly after: "As I walked along in the sun I remembered old Cotter's words . . ." (*D* 5).

12. Clive Hart's list of leitmotifs in *Finnegans Wake* (Appendix A to *Structure and Motif in "Finnegans Wake"* 211–47) and John Bishop's *Joyce's Book of the Dark* show how the radical circularity of that "book of Doublends Jined" (*FW* 20.16) lies not so much in the formal narrative device of the sentence which opens and closes it—if indeed it is a single sentence—but in the lexical echoes which structure it across sometimes huge textual spans.

13. For a discussion of the revisions, see Bremen, "'He Was Too Scrupulous Always': A Re-examination of Joyce's 'The Sisters,'" and Morrissey, "Joyce's Revision of 'The Sisters': From Epicleti to Modern Fiction." The *Irish Homestead* version of the story is reprinted in Scholes and Litz, *"Dubliners": Text, Criticism, and Notes.*

14. On voice as a loss of signification, filled instead with a nauseous enjoyment, see Millot, in *Joyce avec Lacan* (89–91); Lacan, *Écrits* (315); and Žižek, *Looking Awry* (133–37), and *Sublime Object* (103–104 and 182–85). The phrase "objectal leftover of the signifying operation" comes from *Sublime Object* (104).

15. Or alternatively, when you add a similar parallelogram to one of the edges. (My thanks to Fritz Senn for pointing this out.) Whichever way you take it, an *L,* perhaps skewed. *L*s missing, excessive, or transplanted turn up elsewhere in Joyce: there is the misprint of Bloom's name as "L. Boom" in the *Telegraph* (*U* 16.1260), as well Martha Clifford's "I do not like that other world" (*U* 5.245). As Shari Benstock points out, in *Finnegans Wake* the *L* is associated with Issy's lisp, and thus, like that other speech defect which hides the desire, HCE's stammer, also recalls the forbidden incest ("Apostrophizing" 601–603). And in "The Sisters," Eliza = *L is a* . . .

16. This is the process of logical inference C. S. Peirce calls at various times *abduction, hypothesis,* or *retroduction,* to distinguish it from the more familiar *deduction* and *induction.* Deduction starts with the initial case and the rule which governs its transformations, and infers the final stage; induction starts with the initial and final stages, and infers the rule of transformation. Unlike deduction but like induction, abduction is logically incomplete. Rather than provide logical proof, all abduction can do is provide hypotheses; these can and need to be worked on further from extra-syllogistic, empirical material, perhaps confirmed to ever higher degrees, perhaps *dis*proved by counterexamples, but they can never be fi-

nally proved in the deductive sense of a theorem. In its logical incompleteness, abduction opens out beyond the syllogism into certain *activities* of confirmation or disproof: it leaves the strict realm of logic for the *work* of testing.

Both deduction and abduction assume the generating rule; but where deduction uses that rule to work from a present state of affairs to a future guaranteed by the rule, abduction uses it to work *back* from such a present state to a far-from-certain past which nevertheless might have given rise to that present. A paradox: the deductive future is certain, but the abductive past is uncertain. Abduction is retrospective as well as logically incomplete. On the one hand, it seeks to reconstruct a state of events: something which is *there*, before the reconstructing investigation, as the very possibility of the present from which the investigation takes place. On the other hand, this state of events is now only available *through* the incomplete logic of hypothesis (Peirce 2.623).

17. The most thorough and convincing exposition of this is Leonard Albert's "Gnomonology: Joyce's 'The Sisters.'"

2. The Debt, the List, and the Window

1. The essays are "Doing Things in Style: An Interpretation of 'The Oxen of the Sun' in James Joyce's *Ulysses*" and "Patterns of Communication in Joyce's *Ulysses*," both in *The Implied Reader*, 179–95 and 196–233. Henceforth cited in the text as "Iser."

2. The question of the authorship of the *Odyssey* is doubled by a doubleness in the figure of the hero himself, wily Odysseus, known for duplicity. Samuel Butler argues famously that the Odysseus of the *Iliad* and the Odysseus of the *Odyssey* are quite different figures, and that the *Odyssey*'s concern for the domestic and the feminine against its predecessor's focus on war and statescraft suggests its author is a woman. Graves and others argue further that the *Odyssey* itself conflates two stories and two heroes into one: the Odysseus who fought at Troy and returned home to claim his kingdom, and another older hero to whom the adventures *en route* belong and whom, to differentiate, he calls Ulysses. (See Robert Graves, *The Greek Myths*, II, 365–66.)

3. The names "Odysseus" and "Ulysses" occur only obliquely in *Ulysses*, never with direct reference to the Homeric hero. Stephen brings the Shakespearean and the Homeric together in the library when he asks rhetorically, citing the late romances, "What softens the heart of a man, Shipwrecked in storms dire, Tried, like another Ulysses, Pericles, prince of Tyre?" (*U* 9.402–404). In "Cyclops," John Wyse's list of Irish heroes includes "Ulysses Browne of Camus that was fieldmarshal to Maria Teresa" (*U* 12.1383–84). In "Ithaca," St. Patrick, converter of Ireland, is "son of Calpornus, son of Potitus, son of Odyssus"—a near miss (*U* 17.33). Molly remembers Gibraltar days when "when general Ulysses Grant whoever he was or did supposed to be some great fellow landed off the ship" (*U* 18.682–83). The only two direct invocations of the name of Homer occur in the library episode: first of all, "the auric egg of Russell warn[s] occultly" that "the

desirable life is revealed only to the poor of heart, the life of Homer's Phaeacians" (*U* 9.103–104, 109–10); and then, of course, there is Mulligan's parody on Yeats's reviews of Lady Gregory, which begs to be read as *Ulysses'* comment on itself: "The most beautiful book that has come out of our country in my time. One thinks of Homer" (*U* 9.1164–65).

4. Robert Martin Adams, for example, speaks most broadly of "Joyce's penchant for building his novel around a series of holes in the pattern of reader-information":

> Is a character in *Ulysses* explained when he is fitted into a literary pattern, when he is derived from an historical original, or when his behavior is associated with the emotional attitudes peculiar to James Joyce? Is one principle of "explanation" better than, contradictory to, or just as good as the other? (By *explanation*, I mean simply an accounting for the character's presence and behavior, an understanding of his function or his effect.) . . . [H]ow far can one look for meaning in [Joyce's freely associated images], and how much of what one finds or creates is really relevant to the novel? Evidently there is some limit beyond which the reader is not justified in imposing *his* private associative ingenuities on the novel; did the novelist impose any such limitations on himself? (Adams 26)

5. And first of all by Valéry Larbaud, in the lecture he gave at the Joyce benefit in Adrienne Monnier's La Maison des Amis des Livres, December 1921, in which he both announces the correspondences and points out their attenuation: see Larbaud; Fitch 110–12; Dettmar, "'Working'" 271–91 and *Illicit Joyce* 161–72; French 2; Kenner, *Dublin's Joyce* 225–62. Because of the tenuous nature of these relations, Fritz Senn prefers the term "Homeric dislocutions" to "parallels" (Senn, *Joyce's Dislocutions* 206).

6. To indicate only some of the main points: Ulysses figures in *Troilus and Cressida*, a play from that "hell of time of *King Lear*" in which Shakespeare himself is "[t]ried, like another Ulysses" (*U* 9.403); wandering, errant Ulysses is as Eglinton points out the site of one of Shakespeare's errors ("He puts Bohemia on the seacoast and makes Ulysses quote Aristotle" (*U* 9.995–96); Stephen has already defended Shakespeare against the charge that his marriage to Anne Hathaway was an error ("—Bosh!" [*U* 9.228]), and will later make a quite volitional error of his own (*U* 9.936); George Sigerson is cited as saying that "Our national epic has yet to be written" (*U* 9.309); he bears almost the same name as the bear Sackerson Stephen imagines growling in the pit as Shakespeare walks to the playhouse, at a time when "It is this hour of a day"—this very hour in which Stephen is performing, here in the Library on Bloomsday—"in mid June" (*U* 9.154–56).

7. This is the problem of logical *in*duction this time: given a first and subsequent terms in a series, how do you pick the pattern which links them? Like abduction, it is logically incomplete, as anyone knows who has done any of the standard

pattern-making tasks of IQ tests: it is always in principle possible to account for a given series in at least two different ways, no matter how large the series.

8. On the figure of asyndeton and its relations to the question of the postmodern, see my "Currency Exchanges: The Postmodern, Vattimo, et Cetera, among Other Things (et Cetera)," *Postmodern Culture* 7.2 (http://muse.jhu.edu/journals/postmodern_culture/v007/7.2thwaites.html). In particular, see the first section, "Lists," 1–9.

9. This is the substance of the complaint about *Ulysses* one finds frequently in earlier criticism: Leavis, for example, made it in "James Joyce and the Revolution of the Word," when he complained that for all its virtuosity *Ulysses* lacked organicism; Schutte and Steinberg make it when they argue that the correspondences of style and technique do not grow out of the needs of the narrated material (Schutte and Steinberg 175–76). They are quite correct, though they can see this only as the result of a failure of artistic or moral nerve: what governs the huge and unstable structures of *Ulysses* and then *Finnegans Wake* is increasingly the work of the word.

10. Groden speaks for many critics when he suggests that in the middle chapters of *Ulysses*, between "Sirens" and "Oxen of the Sun," Joyce "turned to a series of literary and sub-literary parodies before he attempted to create new styles in the last four episodes" (Groden, *"Ulysses in Progress"* 43): it is as if, exhausted by the labors of innovation, the book turns to more familiar and less demanding modes before its final burst.

11. See in particular James Van Dyck Card's "'Contradicting': The Word for Joyce's 'Penelope,'" and "The Ups and Downs, Ins and Outs of Molly Bloom: Patterns of Words in 'Penelope.'"

12. John C. Hannay argues that given the distances involved, the timescale, and the ebbing of the tide, this can hardly be the one Bloom threw away ("The Throwaway of 'Wandering Rocks'"); Hart and Knuth agree in their *Topographical Guide* (73).

13. A small and far-from-exhaustive sampling. The postcard: Adams, *Surface and Symbol* 192–93; B. Benstock, "Who P's in U?"; S. Benstock, "The Printed Letters in *Ulysses*"; Byrnes, "'U.P.: up' Proofed"; Ellmann, *Ulysses on the Liffey* 75; Kershner, "More Evidence on Breen's Telegram." M'Intosh: Adams, *Surface and Symbol* 17–18; Begnal, "The Mystery Man of *Ulysses*"; B. Benstock, "The Arsonist in the Macintosh"; Crosman, "Who Was M'Intosh?"; DeVore, "A Final Note on M'Intosh"; Lyons, "The Man in the Macintosh"; Raleigh, "Who Was M'Intosh?" The identity of Martha Clifford: French, *The Book as World* 121; Honton, "Molly's Mistresstroke"; Power, "Why Miss Dunne Was Reading *The Woman in White* in the Middle of 'Wandering Rocks'"; von Phul, "Bloom's Boustrophedontic Alphabet and Martha Clifford"; and for one of the more preposterous suggestions, Begnal, "The Unveiling of Martha Clifford." Milly's absence: Ben-Merre, "Bloom and Milly"; Eggers, "Darling Milly Bloom"; Ford, "Why Is Milly in Mullingar?" and "A Note Duly Noted"; Kimball, "James Joyce

and Otto Rank: The Incest Motif in *Ulysses*." The movement of the furniture: Hampson, "Joyce's Bed-Trick: A Note on Indeterminacy in *Ulysses*"; Honton, "Molly's Mistresstroke"; Kenner, "Molly's Masterstroke." Bloom's measurements: Adams, *Surface and Symbol* 184; Dunphy, "The Re-tailoring of Bloom"; Kenner, "Bloom's Chest"; Kimball, "The Measure of Bloom—Again." Molly's previous lovers: Niemayer, "A *Ulysses* Calendar"; Raleigh, "On the Chronology of the Blooms in *Ulysses*."

14. Stephen, that is, will not grow up to write *Ulysses*. Peter Costello's imaginary biography, *The Life of Leopold Bloom,* makes precisely that point in its attempt to extend the narrative of *Ulysses*. Towards the end, the aging Bloom is told by Simon Dedalus that his son has written a famous book, and "We're all in it, I'm told" (165). But the book is not *Ulysses,* the *Ulysses* we read, as it is signed by another name, in a world in which the name "James Joyce" is unknown. This is no more than the paradox of naturalism. There must be at least one point in the naturalistic narrative at which, as if by some Gödelian economy, there are only two choices: either it develops an infinite stammer as it tries to incorporate itself in its own depiction, or it remains forever incomplete. That blind spot is a condition of naturalism; if it were not there, we would have a sort of parallel-worlds science-fiction. Or perhaps what the blind spot hides is that naturalism itself is already a branch of science-fiction which walks among us without being noticed.

15. With Deasy's mention of the Jews as sinners against the light and wanderers of the earth, Stephen recalls his time in Paris, and the "goldskinned men quoting prices on their gemmed fingers" on the steps of the Stock Exchange: another window opens, onto another series. Or rather, several windows, as the next chapter will make clear. One of the things that lolloping, protean dog on the beach at Sandycove will bring to Stephen's mind is "a pard, a panther, got in spousebreach, vulturing the dead" (U 3.363–64), which in turn will remind him of Haines "raving all night about a black panther" (U 1.57–62), and only then of his own dream:

> After he woke me last night same dream or was it? Wait. Open hallway. Street of harlots. Remember. Haroun al Raschid. I am almosting it. That man led me, spoke. I was not afraid. The melon he had he held against my face. Smiled: creamfruit smell. That was the rule, said. In. Come. Red carpet spread. You will see who. (U 3.365–69)

This is not the first time he has thought of Haines's dream: after all, he complained of the noise to Mulligan quite early in "Telemachus." But it does seem to be the first time he has remembered his own dream: his "Wait" suggests the effort of dredging into memory. Again, it is only a later event from another series altogether—dogsbody Tatters in his own erratic trajectory over the sand—which serves to trigger the memory of the earlier one. But now that it happens, even that harlot's cry from Blake which was earlier pressed into service can be seen to be also something else again, not evident at the time, a figure of the dream. If the surface is Arabian, with its reference to the Haroun al Raschid of the *Thousand and One*

Nights, everything beneath is Jewish. As Gifford points out, the "rule" is that of Deuteronomy (26:2–11): the firstfruits of the land are brought to the holy place of God's choice, where they become the priest's right; and the melons (from Numbers 11:4–6) are the fruits for whose flesh the children of Israel lust in the wilderness. "That man"—though this can only be a meaning which will arrive back onto the dream from the future—can only be Bloom. Later, in Bella Cohen's brothel, Stephen will apparently recognize the place he dreamed about:

STEPHEN
Mark me. I dreamt of a watermelon. . . .
(*extends his arms*) It was here. Street of harlots. In Serpentine avenue Beelzebub showed me her, a fubsy widow. Where's the red carpet spread? (*U* 15.3921, 3930–31)

We have seen it: but it was in one of Bloom's earlier fantasies:

BLOOM
O, I so want to be a mother.
MRS THORNTON
(*in nursetender's gown*) Embrace me tight, dear. You'll soon be over it. Tight, dear.
(*Bloom embraces her tightly and bears eight male yellow and white children. They appear on a redcarpeted staircase adorned with expensive plants. . . .*) (*U* 15.1816–22)

The melons offered him by Bloom, with their "creamfruit smell," are of course in "Ithaca":

He kissed the plump mellow yellow smellow melons of her rump, on each plump melonous hemisphere, in their mellow yellow furrow, with obscure prolonged provocative melonsmellonous osculation. (*U* 17.2241–43)

Bloom has earlier suggested that Stephen could move in as lodger and teacher of Italian to Molly, and even sees the relationship consolidated by a union with Milly, in somewhat ambiguous terms which would indeed see Bloom as procurer:

Why might these several provisional contingencies between a guest and a hostess not necessarily preclude or be precluded by a permanent eventuality of reconciliatory union between a schoolfellow and a jew's daughter? Because the way to daughter led through mother, the way to mother through daughter. (*U* 17.940–44)

And to complete the circle, in "Nausicaa" Bloom will remember ("Wait") an oriental dream *he* had the previous night:

Dreamt last night? Wait. Something confused. She had red slippers on. Turkish. Wore the breeches. Suppose she does? Would I like her in pyjamas? Damned hard to answer. (*U* 13.1240–42)

In Nighttown, Bloom will see an apparition of Molly in Turkish costume, including scarlet trousers, and his dead father will ask him, "[H]ave you made up your mind whether you like or dislike women in male habiliments? . . . Pyjamas, let us say?" (U 15.2397–402). Same dream or was it?

16. Which has already drifted away from the Hebrew of the Promised Land. See, for example, Charles Parish, "Agenbite of Agendath Netaim"; Francis Bulhof, "Agendath Again"; M. David Bell, "The Search for Agendath Netaim: Some Progress, but No Solution."

17. The phrase occurs throughout *Ulysses*, in seven of its eighteen chapters, and its migration is a perfect example of the point. It comes to be associated with Bloom rather than with Stephen, but it belongs first of all to Tom Kernan. In the carriage on the way to the cemetery in "Hades," in Bloom's hearing, Power quotes Kernan's use of the phrase as a way of making fun of his pomposity:

> —Tom Kernan was immense last night, he said. And Paddy Leonard taking him off to his face.
>
> —O, draw him out, Martin, Mr Power said eagerly. Wait till you hear him, Simon, on Ben Dollard's singing of *The Croppy Boy*.
>
> —Immense, Martin Cunningham said pompously. *His singing of that simple ballad, Martin, is the most trenchant rendering I ever heard in the whole course of my experience.*
>
> —*Trenchant,* Mr Power said laughing. He's dead nuts on that. And the *retrospective arrangement.* (U 6.142–50: emphases in original)

On its very first appearance, the phrase seems to be catachrestic. (Can a musical arrangement be retrospective?) Out of place, the phrase seems to have wandered in from somewhere else. In "Wandering Rocks," that chapter of interpolations, Kernan will remember Dollard's song and his praise of it, and will use the phrase in a more logical sense:

> Mr Kernan approached Island Street. Times of the troubles. Must ask Ned Lambert to lend me those reminiscences of sir Jonah Barrington. *When you look back on it all now in a kind of retrospective arrangement.* Gaming at Daly's. No cardsharping then. One of those fellows got his hand nailed to the table by a dagger. Somewhere here lord Edward Fitzgerald escaped from major Sirr. Stables behind Moira house.
>
> Damn good gin that was.
>
> Fine dashing young nobleman. Good stock, of course. That ruffian, that sham squire, with his violet gloves gave him away. Course they were on the wrong side. They rose in dark and evil days. Fine poem that is: Ingram. They were gentlemen. Ben Dollard does sing that ballad touchingly. Masterly rendition. (U 10.780–91: emphasis added)

In "Sirens," its use in free indirect speech now associates it with both Kernan, of whom it is used, and Bloom, who frames the paragraph:

Bloom ungyved his crisscrossed hands and with slack fingers plucked the slender catgut thong. He drew and plucked. It buzzed, it twanged. While Goulding talked of Barraclough's voice production, while Tom Kernan, *harking back in a retrospective sort of arrangement* talked to listening Father Cowley, who played a voluntary, who nodded as he played. While big Ben Dollard talked with Simon Dedalus, lighting, who nodded as he smoked, who smoked. (*U* 11.795–801: emphasis added)

By "Oxen of the Sun," though, it is used exclusively of Bloom:

What is the age of the soul of man? As she hath the virtue of the chameleon to change her hue at every new approach, to be gay with the merry and mournful with the downcast, so too is her age changeable as her mood. No longer is Leopold, as he sits there, ruminating, chewing the cud of reminiscence, that staid agent of publicity and holder of a modest substance in the funds. A score of years are blown away. He is young Leopold. There, *as in a retrospective arrangement,* a mirror within a mirror (hey, presto!), he beholdeth himself. (*U* 14.1037–45: emphasis added)

"Circe" puts the phrase into Bloom's mouth:

BLOOM

(*seizes her [Mrs Breen's] wrist with his free hand*) Josie Powell that was, prettiest deb in Dublin. How time flies by! *Do you remember, harking back in a retrospective arrangement,* Old Christmas night, Georgina Simpson's housewarming while they were playing the Irving Bishop game, finding the pin blindfold and thoughtreading? Subject, what is in this snuffbox? (*U* 15.440–45: emphasis added)

"Eumaeus" uses it to speak of Bloom, and makes it a part of the Bloomian diction which fills the chapter's free indirect discourse:

Looking back now in a retrospective kind of arrangement, all seemed a kind of dream. And the coming back was the worst thing you ever did because it went without saying you would feel out of place as things always moved with the times. Why, as he reflected, Irishtown Strand, a locality he had not been in for quite a number of years, looked different somehow since, as it happened, he went to reside on the north side. (*U* 16.1400–406: emphasis added)

And finally, in "Ithaca" it will migrate again, to speak of migration itself:

What first reminiscence had he of Rudolph Bloom (deceased)?
Rudolph Bloom (deceased) narrated to his son Leopold Bloom (aged 6) *a retrospective arrangement* of migrations and settlements in and between Dublin, London, Florence, Milan, Vienna, Budapest, Szombathely with statements of satisfaction (his grandfather having seen Maria Theresia,

empress of Austria, queen of Hungary), with commercial advice (having taken care of pence, the pounds having taken care of themselves). Leopold Bloom (aged 6) had accompanied these narrations by constant consultation of a geographical map of Europe (political) and by suggestions for the establishment of affiliated business premises in the various centers mentioned. (*U* 17.1905–15: emphasis added)

18. On the relationships between diaspora and return in "Ithaca," see Mahaffey 133–36; and on the tension this introduces into the criticism, whereby "'Ithaca' . . . emerges as . . . a coherent and exemplary work of art, only when its various excesses have been damped down by specific acts of interpretation," see Miller 210.

19. And which Derrida calls "messianic teleiopoesis": "How could I give you my friendship there where friendship would not be in default, if there were already such a thing? . . . If I give you friendship, it is because there is friendship (perhaps); it does not exist, *presently*" (*Politics of Friendship* 235).

20. The *Liliata rutilantium* recurs in "Scylla and Charybdis," when the death of Ann Hathaway recalls Stephen's mother (*U* 9.221–23); and in "Circe," where "a choir of virgins and confessors sing wordlessly as the resurrected corpse of Stephen's mother appears (*U* 15.4161–65). *Heigho! Heigho!* is found in "Sirens," when Bloom, scanning the pages of the *Freeman,* sees Dignam's funeral notice (*U* 11.856–58); and twice in "Circe," once as a peal of bells from George's church when H. Rumbold, master barber, arrives to execute Bloom for sins against the people of Dublin (*U* 15.1185–86), and again as the bracelets of bells worn by the night hours in Maginni's dancing class (*U* 15.4085–86).

21. Brivic's *Joyce the Creator* has a useful list of more than a hundred such triangulations, which he calls by the more Jungian term "synchronicities" (145–53). If I prefer "triangulations," it is because I do not see them as "a principle of psychic causality" or "generated by a mental structure inherent in the book" (68) so much as first of all verbal and stylistic features.

3. In the Language Machine

1. This relation of the subject to a language which is essentially citational is argued in parallel ways in Eloise Knowlton's *Joyce, Joyceans, and the Rhetoric of Citation,* and particularly in her fourth chapter (51–63).

2. Other names also reveal themselves as already scattered out into series. Later, as Bloom is glancing through the *Telegraph* in the cabman's shelter, he will get "a bit of a start but it turned out to be only something about somebody named H. du Boyes, agent for typewriters or something like that" (*U* 16.1238). There is a neat chiasmic symmetry here, for Bloom has of course engineered quite a bit of his day so as to avoid Boylan. But here, in front of the window of *Lemon*'s sweetshop, Bloom is gazing at pineapple rock, *lemon* platt, butter scotch (*U* 8.1) when the throwaway is put in his hand. Almost the same elision of common and proper

name has already occurred in "Calypso," where the Agendath Netaim advertisement and its description of the crops sparks a number of associations:

> Silverpowdered olivetrees. Quiet long days: pruning, ripening. Olives are packed in jars, eh? I have a few left from Andrews. Molly spitting them out. Knows the taste of them now. Oranges in tissue paper packed in crates. *Citrons* too. Wonder is poor *Citron* still in Saint Kevin's parade. . . . Pleasant evenings we had then. Molly in Citron's basketchair. Nice to hold, cool waxen fruit, hold in the hand, lift it to the nostrils and smell the perfume. Like that, heavy, sweet, wild perfume. (*U* 4.201–208)

Only much later, in "Ithaca," will we find out that this already engages a longtime fantasy of Bloom's ("Bloom Cottage. Saint Leopold's. Flowerville" [*U* 17.1580]). Not quite so far away, but several hours and several hundred pages yet, Boylan will savor the perfume of that syntactical elision of Molly with fruit in the hand as he puts together the basket he will send her, walking here and there "about the fruit-smelling shop, lifting fruits, young juicy crinkled and plump red tomatoes, sniffing smells" (*U* 10.307–309), as if it is again Molly herself in the basket; so too will Bloom, home in "Ithaca" once more, as he "kissed the plump mellow yellow smellow melons of her rump, on each plump melonous hemisphere, in their mellow yellow furrow, with obscure prolonged provocative melonsmellonous osculation" (*U* 17.2241–43). And that perfume will provide almost the last words of *Ulysses*, now belonging to Molly's breasts (*U* 18.1607–608).

3. Not only would we have on the one hand the innumerable movements of commodities throughout the book, Bloom's life as an advertising canvasser, and the talking objects of "Circe," and on the other hand Bloom's masochism and voyeurism or his fascination with women's legs and Molly's buttocks. There would also be the entire question of character in the realist novel—not to mention realist psychology—as depending on just such a disavowal. See Žižek, chapter 1 ("How Did Marx Invent the Symptom?") of *The Sublime Object of Ideology*, 11–53, particularly 18ff; and chapter 3 ("Fetishism and Its Vicissitudes") of *The Plague of Fantasies*, 86–126. For a discussion of the double nature of the fetish in *Ulysses*, see Jones.

4. For an elaboration of this, see Topia, "The Matrix and the Echo: Intertextuality in *Ulysses*," 107–108. Much of Topia's argument is already implicit in Bakhtinian dialogism. As Claudette Sartiliot points out, Bakhtin's examples are "derived mainly from nineteenth-century models—especially Dickens and Dostoevski—in which the various idiolects are used to separate the characters at the social level" (18). Dialogism requires not only at least two distinguishable sets of intonations, points of view, and speech acts, but also a reader who can recognize that ultimately social differentiation.

5. It is significant that it should be aesthetic discourse which carries this freight. Apropos of the occurrence of citations or allusions in the analysand's speech, Lacan assures us that

the more these references become strangely sporadic and peremptory . . . , the more they are correlative of something that makes its presence felt at that moment, and that belongs to the register of a destructive drive. It is at the very moment when a thought is clearly about to appear in a subject, as in the narration of a dream for example, a thought that one recognizes as aggressive relative to one of the fundamental terms of his subjective constellation, that, depending on his nationality, he will make some reference to a passage in the Bible, to an author, whether a classic or not, or to some piece of music. (*Ethics* 239)

6. For a discussion of the implications of this implicit personalization of the terms of narratology, see Gibson, *Towards a Postmodern Theory of Narratology* 144.

7. See, for example, Schutte and Steinberg, "The Fictional Technique of *Ulysses.*"

8. Hayman, *"Ulysses": The Mechanics of Meaning* 70; and, to give only two examples of this pervasive trope, Kenner, *Ulysses* (especially chapter 7, "The Arranger," 61–71) and French, *The Book as World.* French speaks of "the invisible narrator of the sections and the commentator visible in the headlines" as "a comedy team, in which neither plays the straight man" (94–95).

9. The chapter also shows that Gerty is familiar with various popular songs (*U* 13.312–15) and romantic poems in newspapers (*U* 13.645–47). The texts we are explicitly told she has read are also surrounded by all sorts of other references and allusions which stop short of saying she has actually read them. When we are told that "None of your spoilt beauties, Flora MacFlimsy sort, was Cissy Caffrey" (*U* 13.34–35), the allusion to William Allen Butler's 1857 poem "Nothing to Wear" does not even need us to attribute it to Gerty: before it is Gerty's familiarity with poetry or perception of her friend, it is a typology, the sort of thing that might be said of a friend within a given idiom. And as if to emphasize that these discourses cannot be read simply as Gerty's, mixed in with them are snippets from others with which it is less easy to see Gerty as being familiar at first hand: echoes of Shakespeare ("Many a time and oft" from *Merchant of Venice* I.iii [*U* 13.10] and the "ministering angel" from *Hamlet* V.i [*U* 13.326]), or Middleton's 1626 *Anything for a Quiet Life* (*U* 13.256). In "Lotus Eaters," part of the comedy of Bloom's church visit was his apparent ignorance of the words and the ritual of the service, even though he appears to have at some stage received confirmation as a Catholic; but in the first part of "Nausicaa," the Latin of the evening service which increasingly intrudes from the nearby Church of Mary, Star of the Sea, appears directly in the text, unshielded by what would surely be Gerty's lack of Latin.

It is even less easy to see Gerty as being acquainted with two other texts which suffuse the chapter: the *Portrait,* which will not be serialized for another ten years, and then in a periodical Gerty is unlikely to read, but whose hero will also encounter a young woman on a Dublin beach; and Joyce's letters to Martha Fleischmann. On these, see Senn, *Joyce's Dislocutions* 166–70.

10. Split Pea Press's Adobe Acrobat facsimile of the late pink edition of the *Dublin Evening Telegraph* for June 16, 1904, is available at http://www.hare-net.demon.co.uk/splitpea.

11. For a Lacanian view of the way the gaze functions in "Nausicaa" and other episodes of *Ulysses,* see Devlin, "Castration and Its Discontents" 135ff.

12. But this is not *quite* Gerty's first entrance. Just as that earlier "Chrysos-tomos" (*U* 1:26) acted as a tiny snatch of Stephen before the event, we have al-ready glimpsed Gerty watching the viceregal coach go by in a single sentence of "Wandering Rocks":

> Passing by Roger Greene's office and Dollard's big red printinghouse Gerty MacDowell, carrying the Catesby's cork lino letters for her father who was laid up, knew by the style it was the lord and lady lieutenant but she couldn't see what Her Excellency had on because the tram and Spring's big yellow furniture van had to stop in front of her on account of its being the lord lieutenant. (*U* 10.1205–11)

Looking back, the awkward "on account of" and the stammer of the lord lieuten-ant in that last phrase, like Uncle Charles's *repair* and *salubrious,* and Lily's *liter-ally,* let us also know Gerty by the style.

13. In the bookstall in "Wandering Rocks" again:

> Flesh yielded amply amid rumpled clothes: whites of eyes swooning up. His nostrils arched themselves for prey. Melting breast ointments (*for him! For Raoul!*). Armpits' oniony sweat. Fishgluey slime (*her heaving embonpoint!*). Feel! Press! Chrished! Sulphur dung of lions! (*U* 10.619–23)

Later in "Nausicaa," almost immediately after the turn, posttumescent Bloom will speculate that Edy Boardman must be close to her period, which will lead him to ponder Molly's, Milly's, and Martha Clifford's menstrual cycles (*U* 13.777–85), the way menstruation makes women feel (*U* 13.822–25), odors (*U* 13.1031–33), the "white fluxions" brought about by sitting on damp or cold surfaces, and how this means "[n]ever have little baby then less he was big strong fight his way up through" (*U* 13.1081–83). In her later appearance in "Circe," Gerty will be men-struating (*U* 15.372–85). As the *Sweets of Sin* passage from "Wandering Rocks" suggests, all this affords a pleasure close to unpleasure, soiling and abjection, from the poses of the women in the mutoscope erotica in Capel street ("I'm all clean come and dirty me" [*U* 13.797]) to the way Bloom once made a prostitute in Meath Street say "dirty things" (*U* 13.868), and with a clear echo back to the physical disgust of "Lestrygonians" and that "[c]hap in the Burton today spitting back gumchewed gristle" (*U* 13.876).

14. On some of the other implications of this shared watching, see Law, "'Pity They Can't See Themselves.'"

15. Devlin's *Wandering and Return in "Finnegans Wake"* is acutely aware of these instabilities elsewhere in Joyce. She points out that the final monologue of

Finnegans Wake can easily be read not only as ALP's, but as that of the husband imagining his wife speaking to him "on the dream's favorite subject—the dreamer himself" (164, 71). In the Tristan chapter of the *Wake*, "the verbal ambiguities and syntactical disjunctions destabilize the scenario, making it difficult to sort out who is watching whom and who (if anyone) is simply being watched" (121). Stephen's argument about *Hamlet* is that there is a sort of ventriloquy going on, with every character harboring a multitude of individuals (71). And she cites Joyce's own notes to show that the jealous gazes of *Exiles* easily invert themselves (at least in principle—the pragmatics of its stagecraft may be another matter) into just the sort of situation I have suggested for "Nausicaa": Richard watches the progress of the dalliance between Robert and Bertha, feeling his control and power over them lies in this knowledge of what they do; but then this may just be the beginning of an overbidding in which, as Joyce says, "Robert can also suggest that he knew from the first that Richard was aware of his conduct and that he himself was being watched and that he persisted because he had to and because he wished to see to what length Richard's silent forebearance would go" (119). Yet even though she speaks of Gerty's "unequivocal countervoyeurism" (138), Devlin does not draw quite the same conclusions in her discussion of "Nausicaa" (136–42), preferring instead to affirm that the chapter is indeed made up of two separate parts, one for the point of view of each character: "If the first half of the episode satirizes blatantly a particular feminine point of view, the second critiques most subtly a particular masculine one" (137).

16. See Hart and Knuth, *A Topographical Guide to James Joyce's "Ulysses"*; Hart, "Gaps and Cracks in *Ulysses*"; Kenner, *Ulysses*; Niemayer, "A *Ulysses* Calendar"; Raleigh, *The Chronicle of Leopold and Molly Bloom* and "On the Chronology of the Blooms in *Ulysses*"; Costello, *The Life of Leopold Bloom*. See also Jorn Barger's claims on his website, *IQ Infinity: The Unknown James Joyce* (http://www.robotwisdom.com/jaj/oldfaq.html): for Barger, Joyce is "pursuing a detailed analysis of *human psychology*, in ways that should prove useful to artificial intelligence theorists as they try to build a *simulated human personality*. (The central character of Ulysses—Leopold Bloom—is a promising candidate to be the *Virtual Adam*.)" (emphases in original).

4. In the Marketplace

1. In "Laughing in His Sleeve," F. C. McGrath argues out that there are three main groupings of sources for Stephen's aesthetics: classical theories, in particular Aristotle and Aquinas; the fin de siècle aesthetics associated with Flaubert, Gautier, Pater, and Wilde; and more directly, but less frequently commented on, the German Idealist tradition of Kant and Hegel (259). The classic study of the sources of Joyce's ideas on aesthetics, drawing on the early critical writings and Joyce's notebooks as well as on the published fiction, is Jacques Aubert's *The Aesthetics of James Joyce*.

2. Haskell M. Block, for example, insists that "The theoretical formulation of

Joyce's aesthetic rigidly followed Thomistic principles" and that "it is remarkable to observe with what degree of likeness and persistency Joyce conformed to his model" (240). But Maurice Beebe argues that "Joyce follows the form of certain scholastic principles, but by denying the premises on which they are based, distorts the meaning" (273), and James H. Druff argues that Stephen's aesthetics "exhibits a series of logical improprieties based on a romantic distortion of Aristotle" (181).

3. For example, A. D. Hope sees Stephen's comments as "form[ing] a connected discussion, a fact which is not quite clear owing to the dramatic form in which they are presented" (184). Diané Collinson thinks Stephen "does not expound his theory in an orderly way" (61): although she does not examine the links in any detail, his exposition is governed by its novelistic and peripatetic setting, so that as crucial a point as the absence of the artist "raises a whole new question about the relationship of an artist to his work; but it is never explored because the rain falls faster, the two students reach their destination, and Stephen finds his beloved sheltering in the entrance to the Academy" (72).

4. The temptation is not easily avoided. A common critical strategy is to admit the problem, and then proceed as if admission were solution. Thus A. D. Hope, in an article boldly called "The Esthetic Theory of James Joyce," can say that, "Of course the theory is presented dramatically. It is put into the mouth of Stephen Dedalus, . . . so that it cannot strictly be attributed to Joyce. But there is plenty to show that Joyce did hold these views at the age at which Stephen is represented to be, and there is no reason to think that he ever changed them" (183). S. L. Goldberg does something similar, beginning his discussion of Stephen's theories by suggesting that if "they cannot supply us with a critical yardstick, or even a useful structure of the author's intentions, they *can* help us, I believe, in another way: if we are prepared to follow them patiently and critically, they lead us directly towards the preoccupations and the forms of his imagination" (41: emphasis in original).

5. By this, I hope it is clear that I do not mean what Benjamin had in mind when, at the end of "The Work of Art in the Age of Mechanical Reproduction," he spoke of Fascism's aestheticization of politics, and socialism's necessary and corrective politicization of the aesthetic (234–35). Here, I mean simply the practice of the aesthetic: what I shall shortly call a comportment. As Kimberly Devlin points out in *Wandering and Return in "Finnegans Wake,"* Stephen's theories may tell us more about the aesthete than about aesthetics as such.

6. On the shout in "Aeolus," see Spoo 126.

7. Breuer's rhetoric here is still inflected by neuroanatomy: he speaks, after all, of an "intracerebral" excitation, though the "energy" involved in this excitation is hardly to be equated with the neural electrical discharges or any other physically observable feature. This excitation functions as a metaphor, but not as a metaphor *for* anything, rather as metaphoricity itself. In the *Studies on Hysteria* (150), Freud will use the term *cathexis* for the first time to describe this necessarily central metaphoricity of Zero for One. (Thwaites, "Cathexis: Metaphorics of Power"; Žižek, *For They Know Not* 50)

8. And just as inside and outside have necessarily become blurred, so it is with the distinction that this supports, between the pleasure of an internal stasis and the unpleasure of a threatening and external kinesis. Freud will state the impossibility of the homeostatic model explicitly for the first time only some four years after *Beyond the Pleasure Principle*—and almost thirty after the *Studies on Hysteria*, where it already lies coiled up in that "tendency to keep . . . excitation constant" (272)—in the opening pages of the 1924 essay on "The Economic Problem of Masochism" (413–15). Pleasure and unpleasure, he declares with more than a touch of regret, can no longer be just a matter of the increase or decrease of a quantity. Perhaps, he suggests, "it is the *rhythm*, the temporal sequence of changes, rises and falls in the quantity of stimulus. We do not know" (414: emphasis in original). Stasis is not the absence of the kinetic: in this rhythm, from the very beginning it has been its infinite acceleration and overbidding. This is a possibility he had opened up in *Beyond the Pleasure Principle*, which had not so much theorized it as performed it everywhere and incessantly, in its own seesawing rhythms of speculation and withdrawal, tentative solution and collapse, the *fort* and *da* of the child's game. See in particular Derrida's thorough discussion of this text in "To Speculate—on 'Freud.'"

9. Here, we recall the arbitrariness of the relationship between signifier and signified in Saussure, whose effect is not to deny that there is any relationship between the two but only that that relationship can give any explanation of how language works. It is a real relationship (signifiers very often do have clear and obvious signifieds), but not a necessary one (quite a lot of perfectly ordinary signifiers, such as most of the little words in this present sentence, don't have any simple signified). Signification doesn't describe a lot of the most common things language does. This means it is not a principle of explanation of language so much as one of its possible and common effects, and thus something which itself needs to be explained. Saussure's argument, of course, is that this vertical relationship of signification comes about only through the multiple horizontal relationships signs have to each other within the system of *langue* in question.

10. It is hardly accidental that, so closely linked as it is to breath and spirit, *wind* should be almost the exemplary case of apostrophe, or that the direction of the apostrophe is always to double back on itself. Shelley invokes the West Wind so that it in its turn can breathe life into him. See Johnson, "Apostrophe, Animation, and Abortion," *A World of Difference* 184–99.

11. On the paradoxes of the gift (the perfect gift, the one which is free from all calculations of exchange, return, debt, or profit, could only be one which is immediately and irretrievably forgotten . . .), see Derrida, *Given Time*, passim, but in particular 23–27.

12. Language as digestion, or peristalsis: here we already have many of the concerns and imagery of "Laestrygonians" and the Shem chapter of the *Wake*. See Clark, "'Legibly depressed'" 462–63, and Devlin, *Wandering and Return* 6–7.

13. This is, of course, a logic whose consequences Joyce will draw out more fully in *Ulysses*. Hugh Kenner has most famously pointed it out in the case of the narrative's failure to register a crucial event: in "Calypso," Molly must have let Bloom know that Boylan is due at four o'clock, but the event itself is something we can only reconstruct, place, and date from the shadows it casts in later chapters. See Kenner, *Ulysses* and "The Rhetoric of Silence"; Wellington, "A Missing Conversation"; McBride, "At Four She Said" and "At Four She Said: II."

14. E—— C—— would not have been a student: neither Trinity nor University College yet admitted women. In *Stephen Hero,* when Stephen first meets Emma Clery she "always signed her name in Irish. She said Stephen should learn Irish too and join the League" (*SH* 51). Taken with her, he makes discreet inquiries about her from his nationalist friend Madden (*SH* 57), and though he does not join the League, he begins Irish lessons (*SH* 61, 64–67). On one occasion, she asks him if he could not "persuade the President of his College to admit women" (*SH* 71); on another, he encounters her at the Library where she has been "working at some old Irish," and walks her home, to be upbraided along the way for his freethinking and lack of dedication to the League (*SH* 157–60). Virtually all that remains of this in the *Portrait* is the pages of the Irish phrasebook with which E—— C—— toys (*P* 238).

15. No doubt the same moocow whose fortuitous appearance in another piece of not-quite-art started off the entire *Portrait*. For the cattle-motif which pervades the *Portrait,* see Robyn Bach, "If a Tuckoo Meet a Moocow Coming through the Green, Which Jumps over the Moon?"

5. The War within Providence

1. Unless otherwise stated, all subsequent parenthetical references in this chapter are to page and line of *Finnegans Wake*.

2. See, for example, Lacan, *Écrits* 313; Žižek, *Sublime Object* 110–13.

3. It is a critical commonplace that the last and first words of the *Wake* join up to make it into a huge circle. As Harry Burrell points out in a short note in *A Wake Newslitter* ("... /riverrun ..."), there have been dissenters for a while. He cites J. Mitchell Morse, who in both Dalton and Hart's 1965 collection *Twelve and a Tilly* (69–70) and in Begnal and Senn's 1974 *Conceptual Guide* (8) argued that these are parts of two different sentences with different narrators (ALP and Shaun); and Margot Norris, who in her 1976 *The Decentered Universe of "Finnegans Wake"* declares that she can "recall no conclusive evidence that the last word of the book connects with the first to form a complete circle. ... The 'the' at the end of *FW* anticipates nothing—a definite nothing, the void, the silence, the death of ALP" (139).

4. This is why I would argue that the features of the letter which Patrick McCarthy sees as working *against* the commonplace equation of letter and *Wake* suggest instead a similar plurability and non-self-identity for the *Wake* itself:

1) No two versions of the document are identical. . . . 2) Even within a single version of the letter, the ambiguity of the language often undermines the writer's apparent intention, so that what seems to be meant as a defense against baseless charges becomes instead an accusation. 3) The narrator's attention is constantly diverted from the epistolary text to the envelope, the handwriting, and other aspects of the letter's existence as a physical artifact. 4) Likewise, it is difficult to separate the text of the manuscript itself from the commentaries that spring up around it. . . . 5) The damage sustained by the letter in the course of its burial and resurrection . . . makes it difficult to reconstruct the original text. Finally, 6) even the letter's authorship is in doubt. (725)

5. "Calling by a name or nickname," says Lanham on prosonomasia; "confused by some rhetoricians . . . with Paronomasia," which is "a play upon words which sound alike" (Lanham 123)—how could one not confuse the two in the *Wake*? But the nickname is often paronomasic anyway, in and out of the *Wake*. What we have here is not just a confusion between two categories which should be clearly demarcated and kept separate from each other, but two terms which are each intimately bound up with the possibility of the other. To call by a nickname is deliberately or otherwise to invoke (by means of) a paronomasic confusion of names: prosonomasia calls up paronomasia, as its nickname. And paronomasia in turn, for it even to be paronomasia, has already called up the name: that is, paronomasia has already called up prosonomasia.

6. Which, as McHugh and Bauerle point out, invokes another song, "There's a Mother Always Waiting."

7. This emptying-out of signification to leave the letter as pure substance of the signifier is, of course, what Lacan has in mind in the famous dictum that "the unconscious is structured like a language": there is no presignificative content to the psyche governing its representations, and it is precisely "empty speech" shorn of its content which shows this most clearly, preserving as it does the entire interpersonal dimension in which subjects recognize one another:

> speech, even when almost completely worn out, retains its value as a *tessera*.
>
> Even if it communicates nothing, the discourse represents the existence of communication; even if it denies the evidence, it affirms that speech constitutes truth; even if it is intended to deceive, the discourse speculates on faith in testimony. (Lacan, *Écrits* 43).

On empty speech as password, see also Žižek, *Tarrying with the Negative* 94–95.

8. On repetition and understanding, see Sartiliot 79ff.

9. The *locus classicus* for this thematics of the call is the work of Emmanuel Levinas, particularly in *Totality and Infinity* and *Otherwise than Being*.

10. See, for example, Žižek, *Sublime Object* 79–84, and *For They Know Not What They Do* 237–41.

11. The Platonic *khora* is "the receptacle, and in a manner the nurse, of all

generation," that "universal nature which receives all bodies [and] must always be called the same, for, inasmuch as she always receives all things, she never departs at all from her own nature and never, in any way or at any time, assumes a form like that of any of the things which enter into her; she is the natural recipient of all impressions, and is stirred and informed by them." "[T]hat which is to receive perpetually and through its whole extent the resemblances of all eternal beings ought to be devoid of any particular form. Wherefore the mother and receptacle of all created and visible and in any way sensible things is not to be termed earth or air or fire or water, or any of their compounds, or any of the elements from which these are derived, but is an invisible and formless being which receives all things, and in some mysterious way partakes of the intelligible, and is most incomprehensible" (*Timaeus* 49a, 50b–c, 51a–b). See also Derrida, "*Khora*" passim, but in particular 96–100.

12. That *nonoun* is tantalizingly gnomonic in its sense as well as its sound. The word "husband," or some such variation on it, is—at least once it is named—an obvious choice: the "nonoun" is marked with the stutter which is his signature. As the later commentary on these names will point out pithily, "Amousin [Arabic for *husband*] though not but" (107.23).

13. One obvious example: even though it is found in the Isabel section the most obvious anchorage for "*My Golden One and My Selver Wedding*" (104.9) is the older Kate, the weary ALP who flows back to the sea in the final pages ("It is for me goolden wending. . . . yea your goolden, silve me solve . . ." [619.24, 30]).

14. And particularly and first of all in *The Interpretation of Dreams*: see, for example, 172–73, n. 1, and Žižek, *Looking Awry* 50–52, *Sublime Object* 12–14. The indications Joyce's notebooks give of the detail of his reading of Freud (see Ferrer, "The Freudful Couchmare of /\ d") suggest that his dismissive attitude to "grisly old Sykos" (115.21) comes not so much from an unbridgeable gap as from an unbearable proximity. Even the proper names which demarcate it, *Freud* and *Joyce*, collapse joyfully into one another.

15. Indeed, *Joyce's Book of the Dark* is a spectacular example of critical work which was unthinkable before what is still one of the truly indispensable tools for *Wake* criticism, Clive Hart's 1963 *Concordance*, which concerns itself almost exclusively with charting the *Wake*an signifier. The *Concordance* does this not only in the signifier's repetitions but also in its distortions, displacements, and condensations, by means of the three indices. Before the personal computer and the word processor, Hart compiled the *Concordance* by typing the *Wake* one word at a time onto a vast stack of index cards. Several online sites now help in *Wake* searches. Tim Szeliga's *Finnegans Web* (http://www.trentu.ca/jjoyce/fw.htm) has searchable HTML versions of *Finnegans Wake* and *Ulysses,* including a search engine which uses fuzzy logic to include certain sorts of pun and distortion. It also has links to Mark Thompson's three search engines:

- the *Finnegans Wake Concordex* (http://shaman.lycaeum.org/~martins/Finnegan/index.html), which, like Szeliga's index, will find passages from

Finnegans Wake containing any or all of the selected keywords, and provide links to the full page for all passages it finds

• *Lexichaun* (http://shaman.lycaeum.org/~martins/Finnegan/lexichaun. html), which is "a pun-organized exhaustive vocabulary gleaned from *Finnegans Wake*"

• *FarFetch* (http://shaman.lycaeum.org/~martins/Finnegan/farfetch.html), which "searches for words in *Finnegans Wake* with a divergent punning and mutation algorithm that approximates Joyce's polyglot brogue." The site describes the results of this engine as "occasionally astonishing."

16. As Derek Attridge points out, dreaming is "one among a number of such contexts which, though incompatible with one another, all have some potential value" ("Finnegans Awake" 26). Like the Homeric correspondences of *Ulysses,* the dream is not a self-evident framework, and depends on a complex and countersigned history of "extratextual commentary, by Joyce and by others" (17).

17. *Bordereau* also suggests *bord de l'eau:* not quite ALP herself (or at least the water with which she is associated), but somewhere on those unhemmed and uneven margins. It will also shortly become a *bordello,* introducing the motif of prostitution which runs through the chapter.

18. That Arabic owl *(pou)* will shortly become the French hen *(poule):* "Bethicket me for a stump of a beech if I have the poultriest notions what the farest he all means" (112.5–6). From being blind, the addition of some vowels makes it another sort of fowl, *Belinda,* the hen who will scratch the letter into the light of day (111.5). She in turn is hidden even in those who complain about her, "those gloom*pou*rers who *grouse* that letters have never been quite their old selves again since . . . Biddy Doran looked at literature" (112.24–27). And as *poule* is also French slang for "prostitute," the hen will also become the *"prostituta in herba"* (115.15) of the chapter's later readings of the letter, or the "con's cubane[s and] pro's tututes" in "Paoli's where the poules go" (117.15, 24–25).

19. Harold D. Baker, in "Rite of Passage: 'Ithaca,' Style, and the Structure of *Ulysses,*" points out how this process of structuring begins in "Ithaca," where what starts as an "inflated and alliterative diction imitative of academic style . . . begins to transcend itself into a musical rhythm of syntax" (282).

20. See Hayman, *A First-Draft Version of "Finnegans Wake"*; Rose, ed., *James Joyce's "The Index Manuscript: Finnegans Wake" Holograph Workbook VI. B. 46;* and Groden et al., eds., *The James Joyce Archive,* vols. 44–63.

21. Which of course, are exactly the domains crossed by the concept of the *fetish:* see note 3, chapter 3. On the logic of the fetish in the *Wake,* see Brivic, "Reality as Fetish: The Crime in *Finnegans Wake.*"

22. On the triviality of the epiphanic incident itself, see Millot, for whom "Center of gravity but also black holes of the Joycean universe, they mark the heart of a radical meaninglessness [*non-sens*]" (87).

23. In this discussion of the letter as rhythm, and its relations to enjoyment and

the subject, I am drawing on Serge Leclaire's invaluable *Psychoanalyzing: On the Order of the Unconscious and the Practice of the Letter,* particularly on chapter 6, "The Unconscious, or the Order of the Letter."

24. On the sigla and their relations to the personages, see in particular McHugh, *The Sigla of "Finnegans Wake"*; S. Benstock, chapter 3, "Apostrophizing the Feminine in *Finnegans Wake,*" of *Textualizing the Feminine,* 49–85; Rasula, "*Finnegans Wake* and the Character of the Letter."

25. See also Leclaire, *Psychoanalyzing,* especially chapters 3 and 5.

26. The name *Humphrey Chimpden* is used at 30.2–3, and *H. C. Earwicker* is used twice shortly after that, at 33.30 and 36.12. *Anna Livia* is used at 128.14, 195.4 (at the end of I.7) and frequently in I.8; at 553.25–26, HCE refers to ALP as his "alpine plurabelle." The phrase "Anna was, Livia is, Plurabelle's to be" occurs at 215.24, and is repeated in distorted versions at 128.1, 140.4–5, 226.14, 277.11–12, and 614.9–10.

27. On other Joycean *c*s, see John Gordon's "'Ithaca' as the Letter 'C.'"

28. The debate continues throughout much of the run of *A Wake Newslitter*: see, for example, Dalton, "Re 'Kiswahili Words in *Finnegans Wake*' by Philipp Wolff" (old series 12); Hart, "The Elephant in the Belly" (old series 13); Senn, "A Test-Case of Over-Reading" (new series 1.2) and "One White Elephant" (1.4); Ritchie, "Awake at the *Wake*" (3.2); and Halper, "The Elephant in the Belly (II)" (13.5).

29. See in particular the tables on pages 17 and 19 of *Structure and Motif.* To a significant extent, Hart's editorial decisions in the *Concordance* work to limit the ruinous effects of the signature. As Adeline Glasheen pointed out in her brief *JJQ* review, the *Concordance*'s omission of 123 common words means that it misses the "special significance" the *Wake* throws "on some of the commonest words in the English language":

a, an often mean Anna Livia
but often means Butt
can often means Cain
he is two-thirds of HCE
I Am is a name of God
is often is Issy
no often is Noah
(Glasheen, review 37)

30. See Derrida, "Two Words for Joyce" 147–48, and "Ulysses Gramophone" 281.

Bibliography

Adams, Robert M. *Surface and Symbol: The Consistency of James Joyce's "Ulysses."* New York: Oxford University Press, 1962.

Albert, Leonard. "Gnomonology: Joyce's 'The Sisters.'" *James Joyce Quarterly* 27.2 (1990): 353–64.

Atherton, James S. *The Books at the Wake: A Study of Literary Allusions in James Joyce's "Finnegans Wake."* London: Faber and Faber, 1959.

Attridge, Derek. "Finnegans Awake: The Dream of Interpretation." *James Joyce Quarterly* 29.1 (1991): 11–29.

———. *Joyce Effects: On Language, Theory, and History.* Cambridge: Cambridge University Press, 2000.

———. *Peculiar Language: Literature as Difference from the Renaissance to James Joyce.* Ithaca: Cornell University Press, 1988.

Attridge, Derek, Geoff Bennington, and Robert Young, eds. *Post-Structuralism and the Question of History.* Cambridge: Cambridge University Press, 1987.

Attridge, Derek, and Daniel Ferrer, eds. *Post-Structuralist Joyce: Essays from the French.* Cambridge: Cambridge University Press, 1984.

Aubert, Jacques. *The Aesthetics of James Joyce.* Baltimore and London: Johns Hopkins University Press, 1992.

Austin, J. L. *How to Do Things with Words.* Oxford: Oxford University Press, 1962.

Bach, Robyn. "If a Tuckoo Meet a Moocow Coming through the Green, Which Jumps over the Moon?" *A Wake Newslitter,* n.s., 6.6 (1969): 83–91.

Baker, Harold D. "Rite of Passage: 'Ithaca,' Style, and the Structure of *Ulysses.*" *James Joyce Quarterly* 23.3 (1986): 277–97.

Bakhtin, Mikhail. *Problems of Dostoevsky's Poetics.* Ed. and trans. Caryl Emerson. Vol. 8 of *Theory and History of Literature.* Minneapolis: University of Minnesota Press, 1984.

Baldick, Chris. *The Social Mission of English Criticism, 1848–1932.* Oxford: Clarendon, 1983.

Barger, Jorn. *IQ Infinity: The Unknown James Joyce.* (http://www.robotwisdom.com/jaj/oldfaq.html).

Barthes, Roland. "Introduction to the Structural Analysis of Narrative." In *Image—Music—Text,* trans. Stephen Heath, 79–124. Glasgow: Fontana/Collins, 1977.

Bauerle, Ruth. *The James Joyce Songbook.* New York: Garland, 1982.

Beckett, Samuel. "Dante . . . Bruno. Vico . . . Joyce." In *Our Exagmination round His Factification for Incamination of Work in Progress*, by Samuel Beckett et al. London: Faber and Faber, 1961.

Beckett, Samuel, et al. *Our Exagmination round His Factification for Incamination of Work in Progress*. London: Faber and Faber, 1961.

Beebe, Maurice. "Joyce and Aquinas: The Theory of Aesthetics." In *Joyce's Portrait: Criticisms and Critiques*, ed. Thomas E. Connolly, 272–89. New York: Appleton-Century-Crofts, 1962.

Begnal, Michael H. "The Mystery Man of *Ulysses*." *Journal of Modern Literature* 2 (1972): 565–68.

———. "The Summerfool in the Elephant's Belly, or Come Back to the Text Again, Peg, Honey!" *A Wake Newslitter*, n.s., 7.1 (1971): 7.

———. "The Unveiling of Martha Clifford." *James Joyce Quarterly* 13.4 (1976): 400–405.

Begnal, Michael H., and Fritz Senn, eds. *A Conceptual Guide to "Finnegans Wake."* University Park and London: Pennsylvania State University Press, 1974.

Beja, Morris. "Synjoysium: An Informal History of the International James Joyce Symposia." *James Joyce Quarterly* 22.2 (1985): 113–29.

Beja, Morris, and Shari Benstock, eds. *Coping with Joyce: Essays from the Copenhagen Symposium*. Columbus: Ohio State University Press, 1989.

Beja, Morris, Phillip Herring, Maurice Harmon, and Davis Norris, eds. *James Joyce: The Centennial Symposium*. Urbana and Chicago: University of Illinois Press, 1986.

Bell, M. David. "The Search for Agendath Netaim: Some Progress, but No Solution." *James Joyce Quarterly* 12.3 (1975): 251–58.

Bell, Robert H. *Jocoserious Joyce: The Fate of Folly in "Ulysses."* Florida James Joyce Series. Gainesville: University Press of Florida, 1996. Reprint of Ithaca: Cornell University Press, 1991.

Benjamin, Walter. *Illuminations*. Trans. Harry Zohn. Ed. and intro. Hannah Arendt. London: Fontana, 1992.

Ben-Merre, Diana Arbin. "Bloom and Milly: A Portrait of the Father and the 'Jew's Daughter.'" *James Joyce Quarterly* 18.4 (1981): 439–44.

Benstock, Bernard. "The Arsonist in the Macintosh." *James Joyce Quarterly* 20.2 (1983): 232–34.

———. *Joyce-Again's Wake: An Analysis of "Finnegans Wake."* Seattle and London: University of Washington Press, 1965.

———. "'The Sisters' and the Critics." *James Joyce Quarterly* 4 (1966): 32–35.

———. "The State of the *Wake*." *James Joyce Quarterly* 14.3 (1977): 237–40.

———. "Who P's in U?" *James Joyce Quarterly* 21.4 (1984): 372.

Benstock, Bernard, ed. *The Seventh of Joyce*. Bloomington: Indiana University Press/Sussex: Harvester, 1982.

Benstock, Shari. "Apostrophizing the Feminine in *Finnegans Wake.*" *Modern Fiction Studies* 35.3 (1989): 587–614.

———. "The Printed Letters in *Ulysses.*" *James Joyce Quarterly* 19.4 (1982): 415–27.

———. *Textualizing the Feminine: On the Limits of Genre.* Oklahoma Project for Discourse and Theory. Norman and London: University of Oklahoma Press, 1991.

Benstock, Shari, and Bernard Benstock. "The Benstock Principle." In *The Seventh of Joyce,* ed. Bernard Benstock, 10–21. Bloomington: Indiana University Press/ Sussex: Harvester, 1982.

———. *Who's He When He's at Home: A James Joyce Directory.* Urbana: University of Illinois Press, 1980.

Benveniste, Emile. *Problems in General Linguistics.* Trans. Mary Elizabeth Meek. Coral Gables, Fla.: University of Miami Press, 1971.

Bishop, John. *Joyce's Book of the Dark.* Madison: University of Wisconsin Press, 1986.

Block, Haskell M. "The Critical Theory of James Joyce." In *Joyce's Portrait: Criticisms and Critiques,* ed. Thomas E. Connolly, 231–49. New York: Appleton-Century-Crofts, 1962.

Boheemen, Christine van. *The Novel as Family Romance: Language, Gender, and Authority from Fielding to Joyce.* London and Ithaca: Cornell University Press, 1987.

Bollettieri Bosinelli, R. M., C. Marengo Vaglio, and Christine van Boheemen. *The Languages of Joyce: Selected Papers from the Eleventh International James Joyce Symposium, Venice, June 12–18, 1988.* Philadelphia: John Benjamins, 1992.

Bourdieu, Pierre. *In Other Words: Essays towards a Reflexive Sociology.* Trans. Matthew Adamson. Cambridge: Polity, 1990.

Bowen, Zack, and James F. Carens, eds. *A Companion to Joyce Studies.* Westport, Conn., and London: Greenwood Press, 1984.

Bremen, Brian A. "'He Was Too Scrupulous Always': A Re-examination of Joyce's 'The Sisters.'" *James Joyce Quarterly* 22.1 (1984): 55–66.

Brivic, Sheldon. "Images of the Lacanian Gaze in *Ulysses.*" In *Coping with Joyce,* ed. Morris Beja and Shari Benstock, 157–167. Columbus: Ohio University Press, 1989.

———. *Joyce the Creator.* Madison: University of Wisconsin Press, 1985.

———. "Reality as Fetish: The Crime in *Finnegans Wake.*" *James Joyce Quarterly* 34.4 (1997): 449–60.

———. *The Veil of Signs: Joyce, Lacan, and Perception.* Urbana and Chicago: University of Illinois Press, 1991.

Budgen, Frank. *James Joyce and the Making of "Ulysses."* 1930. Reprint, Bloomington: Indiana University Press, 1960.

Bulhof, Francis. "Agendath Again." *James Joyce Quarterly* 7.4 (1970): 326–32.

Burrell, Harry. ". . . /riverrun . . ." *A Wake Newslitter,* n.s., 14.5 (1977): 80–81.

Butler, Rex. *An Uncertain Smile: Australian Art in the '90s.* Woolloomooloo, N.S.W.: Artspace, 1996.

Byrnes, Robert. "'U.P.: up' Proofed." *James Joyce Quarterly* 21.2 (1984): 175–76.

Campbell, Joseph, and Henry Morton Robinson. *A Skeleton Key to "Finnegans Wake."* London: Faber and Faber, 1947.

Card, James Van Dyck. "'Contradicting': The Word for Joyce's 'Penelope.'" *James Joyce Quarterly* 11.1 (1973): 17–26.

———. "The Ups and Downs, Ins and Outs of Molly Bloom: Patterns of Words in 'Penelope.'" *James Joyce Quarterly* 19.2 (1982): 127–39.

Chadwick, Joseph. "Silence in 'The Sisters.'" *James Joyce Quarterly* 21.3 (1984): 245–55.

Cheng, Vincent. *Joyce, Race, and Empire.* New York: Cambridge University Press, 1995.

Cixous, Hélène. "Joyce: The (R)use of Writing." Trans. Judith Still. In *Post-Structuralist Joyce: Essays from the French,* ed. Derek Attridge and Daniel Ferrer, 15–30. Cambridge: Cambridge University Press, 1984.

Clark, Hilary. "'Legibly Depressed': Shame, Mourning, and Melancholia in *Finnegans Wake.*" *James Joyce Quarterly* 34.4 (1997): 461–71.

Collinson, Diané. "The Aesthetic Theory of Stephen Dedalus." *British Journal of Aesthetics* 23.1 (1983): 61–73.

Connolly, Thomas E., ed. *Joyce's Portrait: Criticisms and Critiques.* New York: Appleton-Century-Crofts, 1962.

Costello, Peter. *The Life of Leopold Bloom.* Scull, West Cork, Ireland: Roberts Rinehart, 1992.

Crosman, Robert. "Who Was M'Intosh?" *James Joyce Quarterly* 6.2 (1969): 128–36.

Dalton, Jack P. "Re 'Kiswahili Words in *Finnegans Wake*' by Philipp Wolff." *A Wake Newslitter,* o.s., 12 (1963): 6–12.

Dalton, Jack P., and Clive Hart, eds. *Twelve and a Tilly: Essays on the Occasion of the 25th Anniversary of "Finnegans Wake."* Evanston: Northwestern University Press, 1965.

Deleuze, Gilles. *Difference and Repetition.* Trans. Paul Patton. New York: Columbia University Press, 1994.

———. *The Logic of Sense.* Trans. Mark Lester with Mark Stivale. Ed. Constantin V. Boundas. New York: Columbia University Press, 1990.

Deleuze, Gilles, and Félix Guattari. *Difference and Repetition.* Trans. Paul Patton. New York: Columbia University Press, 1994.

———. *Kafka: Towards a Minor Literature.* Trans. Dana Polan. Theory and History of Literature. Minneapolis: University of Minnesota Press, 1986.

———. *A Thousand Plateaus: Capitalism and Schizophrenia.* Trans. Brian Massumi. London: Athlone, 1988.

———. *What Is Philosophy?* Trans. Graham Burchell and Hugh Tomlinson. London and New York: Verso, 1994.

Derrida, Jacques. *Dissemination.* Trans. Barbara Johnson. Chicago and London: University of Chicago Press, 1981.

———. *The Ear of the Other: Otobiography, Transference, Translation—Texts and Discussions with Jacques Derrida.* English edition ed. Christie McDonald. Trans. Avital Ronell and Peggy Kamuf. French edition ed. Claude Levesque and Christie McDonald. Lincoln and London: University of Nebraska Press, 1988.

———. *The Gift of Death.* Trans. David Wills. Chicago and London: University of Chicago Press, 1995.

———. *Given Time: I. Counterfeit Money.* Trans. Peggy Kamuf. Chicago and London: University of Chicago Press, 1992.

———. "Hors Livre: Outwork, Hors d'oeuvre, Extratext, Foreplay, Bookend, Facing: Prefacing." *Dissemination,* 1–59.

———. "Khora." In *On the Name,* ed. Thomas Dutoit, trans. David Wood, John P. Leavey, Jr., and Ian McLeod. Meridian Crossing Aesthetics series. Stanford: Stanford University Press, 1995.

———. "Living On/Border Lines." Trans. James Hulbert. In *Deconstruction and Criticism,* ed. Harold Bloom et al., 73–176. New York: Seabury Press, 1979.

———. *Margins of Philosophy.* Trans. Alan Bass. Chicago: University of Chicago Press, 1982.

———. "Of an Apocalyptic Tone Recently Adopted in Philosophy." Trans. John P. Leavey, Jr. *Semeia* 23 (1982): 63–97.

———. *Of Grammatology.* Trans. Gayatri Chakravorty Spivak. Baltimore and London: Johns Hopkins University Press, 1976.

———. "Otobiographies: The Teaching of Nietzsche and the Politics of the Proper Name." Trans. Avital Ronell. In *The Ear of the Other,* 1–38. Lincoln and London: University of Nebraska Press, 1988.

———. *Politics of Friendship.* Trans. George Collins. London and New York: Verso, 1997.

———. *The Post Card: From Socrates to Freud and Beyond.* Trans. Alan Bass. Chicago and London: University of Chicago Press, 1987.

———. "Signature Event Context." In *Margins of Philosophy,* 307–30. Chicago: University of Chicago Press, 1982.

———. *Signéponge/Signsponge.* Trans. Richard Rand. New York: Columbia University Press, 1984.

———. "To Speculate—on 'Freud.'" In *The Post Card,* 257–409. Chicago and London: University of Chicago Press, 1987.

———. "The Tower of Babel." Trans. Joseph F. Graham. In *Difference in Translation,* ed. Joseph F. Graham, 165–248. Ithaca: Cornell University Press, 1985.

———. "Two Words for Joyce." Trans. Geoff Bennington. In *Post-Structuralist Joyce: Essays from the French,* ed. Derek Attridge and Daniel Ferrer, 145–59. Cambridge: Cambridge University Press, 1984.

————. "Ulysses Gramophone: Hear Say Yes in Joyce." Trans. Tina Kendall. In *Acts of Literature*, ed. Derek Attridge, 253–309. New York and London: Routledge, 1991.

————. *Writing and Difference*. Trans. Alan Bass. Chicago: University of Chicago Press, 1982.

Dettmar, Kevin J. H. *The Illicit Joyce of Postmodernism: Reading Against the Grain*. Madison: University of Wisconsin Press, 1996.

————. "Selling *Ulysses*." *James Joyce Quarterly* 30.4–31.1 (1993): 795–812.

————. "'Working in Accord with Obstacles': A Postmodern Perspective on Joyce's 'Mythical Method.'" In *Rereading the New: A Backward Glance at Modernism*, ed. Kevin J. H. Dettmar, 277–96. Ann Arbor: University of Michigan Press, 1992.

Devlin, Kimberly J. "Castration and Its Discontents: A Lacanian Approach to *Ulysses*." *James Joyce Quarterly* 29.1 (1991): 117–44.

————. "The Romance Exposed: 'Nausicaa' and *The Lamplighter*." *James Joyce Quarterly* 22.4 (1985): 383–96.

————. *Wandering and Return in "Finnegans Wake": An Integrative Approach to Joyce's Fictions*. Princeton: Princeton University Press, 1991.

DeVore, Lynn. "A Final Note on M'Intosh." *James Joyce Quarterly* 16.3 (1979): 347–50.

Donoghue, Denis. "Is There a Case against *Ulysses*?" In *Joyce in Context*, ed. Vincent J. Cheng and Timothy Martin, 19–39. Cambridge: Cambridge University Press, 1992.

Druff, James H. "The Romantic Complaint: The Logical Movement of Stephen's Aesthetics in *A Portrait of the Artist as a Young Man*." *Studies in the Novel* 14.2 (1982): 180–88.

Duffy, Enda. *The Subaltern Ulysses*. Minneapolis: University of Minnesota Press, 1994.

Dunphy, Mark. "The Re-tailoring of Bloom." *James Joyce Quarterly* 20.1 (1982): 129.

Eggers, Tilly. "Darling Milly Bloom." *James Joyce Quarterly* 12.4 (1974): 386–95.

Eliot, T. S. *The Sacred Wood: Essays on Poetry and Criticism*. London: Methuen, 1950.

————. *Selected Prose of T. S. Eliot*. Ed. Frank Kermode. London: Faber and Faber, 1975.

Ellmann, Maud. "Disremembering Daedalus: *A Portrait of the Artist as a Young Man*." In *Untying the Text: A Post-Structuralist Reader*, ed. Robert Young, 189–206. London: Routledge and Kegan Paul, 1981.

Ellmann, Richard. *James Joyce*. New and revised edition. New York: Oxford University Press, 1982.

————. *Ulysses on the Liffey*. New York: Oxford University Press, 1972.

Epstein, Edmund L. "Chance, Doubt, and Coincidence and the Prankquean's Riddle." *A Wake Newslitter,* n.s., 1 (1969): 3–7.

Evening Telegraph. June 16, 1904. Facsimile by Split Pea Press (http://www.harenet.demon.co.uk/splitpea).

Fairhall, James. *James Joyce and the Question of History.* Cambridge: Cambridge University Press, 1993.

Ferrer, Daniel. "The Freudful Couchmare of /\ d: Joyce's Notes on Freud and the Composition of Chapter XVI of *Finnegans Wake." James Joyce Quarterly* 22.4 (1985): 367–82.

Fitch, Noel Riley. *Sylvia Beach and the Lost Generation: A History of Literary Paris in the Twenties and Thirties.* Harmondsworth: Penguin, 1985.

Ford, Jane. "A Note Duly Noted: Bloom and Milly Again." *James Joyce Quarterly* 20.2 (1983): 229–30.

———. "Why Is Milly in Mullingar?" *James Joyce Quarterly* 14.4 (1977): 436–49.

Foucault, Michel. *The Archaeology of Knowledge.* Trans. A. M. Sheridan Smith. New York, Hagerstown, San Francisco, and London: Harper and Row, 1972.

———. "The Order of Discourse." In *Untying the Text: A Post-Structuralist Reader,* ed. Robert Young, 48–78. London: Routledge and Kegan Paul, 1981.

French, Marilyn. *The Book as World: James Joyce's "Ulysses."* Cambridge, Mass.: Harvard University Press, 1976.

Freud, Sigmund. *Beyond the Pleasure Principle.* In *On Metapsychology: The Theory of Psychoanalysis,* trans. and ed. James Strachey, 275–338. Pelican Freud Library 11. Harmondsworth: Penguin, 1984.

———. "The Economic Problem of Masochism." In *On Metapsychology: The Theory of Psychoanalysis,* trans. and ed. James Strachey, 413–26. Pelican Freud Library 11. Harmondsworth: Penguin, 1984.

———. "From the History of an Infantile Neurosis." In *Case Histories II,* trans. and ed. James Strachey, 225–366. Pelican Freud Library 9. Harmondsworth: Penguin, 1979.

———. *The Interpretation of Dreams.* Trans. and ed. James Strachey. Pelican Freud Library 4. Harmondsworth: Penguin, 1976.

———. *Introductory Lectures on Psychoanalysis.* Trans. and ed. James Strachey. Pelican Freud Library 1. Harmondsworth: Penguin, 1973.

———. *Jokes and Their Relation to the Unconscious.* Trans. and ed. James Strachey. Pelican Freud Library 6. Harmondsworth: Penguin, 1976.

———. *New Introductory Lectures on Psychoanalysis.* Trans. and ed. James Strachey. Pelican Freud Library 2. Harmondsworth: Penguin, 1973.

———. "Notes upon a Case of Obsessional Neurosis." In *Case Histories II,* trans. and ed. James Strachey, 31–128. Pelican Freud Library 9. Harmondsworth: Penguin, 1979.

Freud, Sigmund, and Joseph Breuer. *Studies on Hysteria.* Trans. and ed. James Strachey. Pelican Freud Library 3. Harmondsworth: Penguin, 1974.

Gibson, Andrew. *Towards a Postmodern Theory of Narratology.* Edinburgh: University of Edinburgh Press, 1996.

Gifford, Don. *Joyce Annotated: Notes to "Dubliners" and "A Portrait of the Artist as a Young Man."* 2nd ed. Berkeley, Los Angeles, and London: University of California Press. 1988.

———. *Ulysses Annotated: Notes for James Joyce's "Ulysses."* With Robert J. Seidman. 2nd ed. Berkeley, Los Angeles, and London: University of California Press, 1988.

Gilbert, Stuart. *James Joyce's "Ulysses."* Harmondsworth: Penguin, 1963.

Glasheen, Adeline. *A Census of "Finnegans Wake": An Index of Characters and Their Roles.* Evanston, Ill.: Northwestern University Press, 1956.

———. Review of *A Concordance to "Finnegans Wake,"* by Clive Hart. *James Joyce Quarterly* 1.1 (1963): 36–37.

———. *A Second Census of "Finnegans Wake": An Index of Characters and Their Roles.* Evanston, Ill.: Northwestern University Press, 1963.

———. *Third Census of "Finnegans Wake": An Index of Characters and Their Roles.* Berkeley, Los Angeles, and London: University of California Press, 1977.

Goldberg, S. L. *The Classical Temper.* London: Chatto and Windus, 1961.

Gordon, John. "'Ithaca' as the Letter 'C.'" *James Joyce Quarterly* 32.1 (1994): 45–59.

Graves, Robert. *The Greek Myths.* 2 vols. Harmondsworth: Penguin, 1960.

Greimas, A. J., and J. Courtés. *Semiotics and Language: An Analytical Dictionary.* Trans. Larry Crist et al. Bloomington: Indiana University Press, 1982.

Groden, Michael. "A Textual and Publishing History." In *A Companion to Joyce Studies,* ed. Zack Bowen and James F. Carens. Westport, Conn., and London: Greenwood Press, 1984.

———. *"Ulysses" in Progress.* Princeton: Princeton University Press, 1977.

Groden, Michael, Hans Walter Gabler, David Hayman, A. Walton Litz, and Danis Rose, with John O'Hanlon. *The James Joyce Archive.* 63 vols. New York: Garland, 1977–79.

Halper, Nathan. "The Elephant in the Belly (II)." *A Wake Newslitter,* n.s., 13.5 (1976): 100.

Hampson, R. G. "Joyce's Bed-Trick: A Note on Indeterminacy in *Ulysses." James Joyce Quarterly* 17.4 (1980): 445–48.

Hannay, John. "The Throwaway of 'Wandering Rocks.'" *James Joyce Quarterly* 17.4 (1980): 434–39.

Hart, Clive. *A Concordance to "Finnegans Wake."* Minneapolis: University of Minnesota Press, 1963.

———. "The Elephant in the Belly: Exegesis of *Finnegans Wake." A Wake Newslitter,* o.s., 13 (1963): 1–8.

———. "Gaps and Cracks in *Ulysses." James Joyce Quarterly* 30.3 (1993): 427–37.

———. *Structure and Motif in "Finnegans Wake."* London: Faber and Faber, 1962.

Hart, Clive, and Leo Knuth. *A Topographical Guide to James Joyce's "Ulysses."* 5th ed. Colchester: A Wake Newslitter Press, 1981.

Hayman, David. *A First-Draft Version of "Finnegans Wake."* Austin: University of Texas Press, 1963.

———. *"Ulysses": The Mechanics of Meaning.* Englewood Cliffs, N.J.: Prentice-Hall, 1970.

Hegel, G. W. F. *The Phenomenology of Spirit.* Trans. A. V. Miller. Oxford: Oxford University Press, 1977.

Heidegger, Martin. *Being and Time.* Trans. John Macquarrie and Edward Robinson. Oxford: Basil Blackwell, 1962.

Herr, Cheryl. *Joyce's Anatomy of Culture.* Urbana: University of Illinois Press, 1986.

Herring, Phillip. "The Frankforall Symposium." *James Joyce Quarterly* 22.2 (1985): 131–35.

Honton, Margaret. "Molly's Mistresstroke." *James Joyce Quarterly* 14.1 (1976): 25–30.

Hope, A. D. "The Esthetic Theory of James Joyce." In *Joyce's Portrait: Criticisms and Critiques,* ed. Thomas E. Connolly, 183–203. New York: Appleton-Century-Crofts, 1962.

Iser, Wolfgang. *The Implied Reader: Patterns of Communication in Prose Fiction from Bunyan to Beckett.* Baltimore and London: Johns Hopkins University Press, 1978.

Jakobson, Roman. "Closing Statement: Linguistics and Poetics." In *Style in Language,* ed. Thomas A. Sebeok, 350–77. New York: Wiley, 1960.

Johnson, Barbara. *A World of Difference.* Baltimore and London: Johns Hopkins University Press, 1987.

Jones, Ellen Carol. "Commodious Recirculation: Commodity and Dream in Joyce's Ulysses." *James Joyce Quarterly* 30.4/31.1 (1993): 739–56.

Joyce, James. *Dubliners.* Intro. and notes by Terence Brown. Harmondsworth: Penguin, 1992.

———. *Exiles.* In *A James Joyce Reader,* ed. Harry Levin, 527–626. Harmondsworth: Penguin, 1993.

———. *Finnegans Wake.* London: Faber and Faber, 1964.

———. *A Portrait of the Artist as a Young Man.* Ed. Seamus Deane. Harmondsworth: Penguin, 1992.

———. *Selected Letters of James Joyce.* Ed. Richard Ellmann. London: Faber and Faber, 1975.

———. *Stephen Hero: Part of the First Draft of "A Portrait of the Artist as a Young Man."* Ed. and intro. by Theodore Spencer. Revisions and foreword John J. Slocum and Herbert Cahoon. Revised ed. London: Jonathan Cape, 1956.

———. *Ulysses.* London, Sydney, and Toronto: Bodley Head, 1960.

————. *Ulysses*. Ed. Jeri Johnson. The World's Classics. Oxford: Oxford University Press, 1993.

————. *Ulysses*. Ed. Declan Kiberd. Harmondsworth: Penguin, 1992.

————. *Ulysses: A Critical and Synoptic Edition*. Ed. Hans Walter Gabler. 3 vols. New York and London: Garland Publishing, 1986.

Kant, Immanuel. *Critique of Judgement*. Trans. Werner S. Pluhar. Indianapolis: Hackett, 1987.

Kelly, Joseph. *Our Joyce: From Outcast to Icon*. Literary Modernism Series, ed. Thomas F. Staley. Austin: University of Texas Press, 1998.

Kenner, Hugh. "Bloom's Chest." *James Joyce Quarterly* 16.4 (1979): 505–508.

————. *A Colder Eye: The Modern Irish Writers*. London: A. Lane, 1983.

————. *Dublin's Joyce*. Gloucester, Mass.: Peter Smith, 1969. London: Chatto and Windus, 1955.

————. *A Homemade World: The American Modernist Writers*. London: Marion Boyars, 1977.

————. *Joyce's Voices*. Berkeley and Los Angeles: University of California Press, 1978. London: George Allen and Unwin, 1980.

————. "Molly's Masterstroke." *James Joyce Quarterly* 10.1 (1972): 19–28.

————. "The Rhetoric of Silence." *James Joyce Quarterly* 14.4 (1977): 382–94.

————. "Shem the Textman." In *The Languages of Joyce: Selected Papers from the Eleventh International James Joyce Symposium, Venice, June 12–18, 1988*, ed. R. M. Bollettieri Bosinelli, C. Marengo Vaglio, and Christine van Boheemen, 145–54. Philadelphia: John Benjamins, 1992.

————. *A Sinking Island: The Modern English Writers*. London: Barrie and Jenkins, 1988.

————. *Ulysses*. Revised ed. Baltimore and London: Johns Hopkins University Press, 1987.

Kershner, R. B. *Joyce, Bakhtin, and Popular Literature: Chronicles of Disorder*. Chapel Hill and London: University of North Carolina Press, 1989.

————. "More Evidence on Breen's Telegram." *James Joyce Quarterly* 29.2 (1991): 407–408.

Kimball, Jean. "The Measure of Bloom—Again." *James Joyce Quarterly* 18.2 (1981): 201–204.

Knowlton, Eloise. *Joyce, Joyceans, and the Rhetoric of Citation*. Gainseville: University Press of Florida, 1998.

Kristeva, Julia. *Revolution in Poetic Language*. Trans. Margaret Waller. New York: Columbia University Press, 1984.

Lacan, Jacques. *Écrits: A Selection*. Trans. Alan Sheridan. London: Tavistock, 1977.

————. *The Ethics of Psychoanalysis, 1959–1960: The Seminar of Jacques Lacan, Book VII*. Ed. Jacques-Alain Miller. Trans. Dennis Porter. London: Tavistock/Routledge, 1992.

———. *The Four Fundamentals of Psychoanalysis.* Ed. Jacques-Alain Miller. Trans. Alan Sheridan. Harmondsworth: Penguin, 1979.

———. "Seminar on 'The Purloined Letter.'" In *The Purloined Poe: Lacan, Derrida, and Psychoanalytic Reading,* ed. John P. Muller and William J. Richardson, 28–54. Baltimore and London: Johns Hopkins University Press, 1988.

Lacan, Jacques, et al. *Joyce avec Lacan.* Sous la direction de Jacques Aubert. Préface de Jacques-Alain Miller. Paris: Navarin Éditeur, 1987.

Lanham, Richard A. *A Handlist of Rhetorical Terms.* 2nd ed. Berkeley, Los Angeles, and Oxford: University of California Press, 1991.

Laplanche, Jean. *Life and Death in Psychoanalysis.* Trans. Jeffrey Mehlman. Baltimore and London: Johns Hopkins University Press, 1976.

Larbaud, Valéry. "The *Ulysses* of James Joyce." In *James Joyce: The Critical Heritage,* ed. Robert H. Deming, 1:252–62. New York: Barnes and Noble, 1970.

Law, Jules David. "'Pity They Can't See Themselves': Assessing the 'Subject' of Pornography in 'Nausicaa.'" *James Joyce Quarterly* 27.2 (1990): 219–39.

Lawrence, Karen R. *The Odyssey of Style in "Ulysses."* Princeton: Princeton University Press, 1981.

Leavis, F. R. "James Joyce and the Revolution of the Word." *Scrutiny* 2.2 (1933): 193–201.

Leavis, Q. D. *Fiction and the Reading Public.* London: Chatto and Windus, 1932.

Leclaire, Serge. *Psychoanalyzing: On the Order of the Unconscious and the Practice of the Letter.* Trans. Peggy Kamuf. Meridian Crossing Aesthetics series. Stanford: Stanford University Press, 1998.

Levinas, Emmanuel. *Otherwise than Being or Beyond Essence.* Trans. Alphonso Lingis. Pittsburgh: Duquesne University Press, 1998.

———. *Totality and Infinity.* Trans. Alphonso Lingis. Pittsburgh: Duquesne University Press, 1969.

Lyons, John O. "The Man in the Macintosh." In *A James Joyce Miscellany,* ed. Marvin Magalener, 133–38. 2nd series. Carbondale, Ill.: Southern Illinois Press, 1959.

Lyotard, Jean-François. *The Differend: Phrases in Dispute.* Trans. Georges Van Den Abbeele. Manchester: Manchester University Press, 1988.

Lyotard, Jean-François, and Jean-Loup Thébaud. *Just Gaming.* Trans. Wlad Godzich and Brian Massumi. Minneapolis: University of Minnesota Press, 1985.

MacCabe, Colin. *James Joyce and the Revolution of the Word.* London and Basingstoke: Macmillan, 1978.

MacCabe, Colin, ed. *James Joyce, New Perspectives.* Brighton, Sussex: Harvester Press; Bloomington: Indiana University Press, 1982.

Magalener, Marvin, ed. *A James Joyce Miscellany.* 2nd series. Carbondale, Ill.: Southern Illinois Press, 1959.

Mahaffey, Vicki. *Reauthorizing Joyce.* Gainesville: University Press of Florida, 1995. Reprint of Cambridge: Cambridge University Press, 1988.

McBride, Margaret. "At Four She Said." *James Joyce Quarterly* 17.1 (1979): 21–39.

———. "At Four She Said: II." *James Joyce Quarterly* 18.5 (1981): 417–31.

McCarthy, Patrick A. "The Last Epistle of *Finnegans Wake.*" *James Joyce Quarterly* 27.4 (1990): 725–33.

McGinley, Bernard. "Bloom's Other Throwaway and the Writing on the Sand." *James Joyce Quarterly* 24.4 (1987): 474–75.

McGrath, F. C. "Laughing in His Sleeve: The Sources of Stephen's Aesthetics." *James Joyce Quarterly* 23.3 (1986): 259–75.

McHugh, Roland. *Annotations to "Finnegans Wake."* Rev. ed. Baltimore and London: Johns Hopkins University Press, 1991.

———. *The "Finnegans Wake" Experience.* Dublin: Irish Academic Press, 1981.

———. *The Sigla of "Finnegans Wake."* London: Edward Arnold, 1976.

Miller, Nicholas A. "Beyond Recognition: Reading the Unconscious in the 'Ithaca' Episode of *Ulysses.*" *James Joyce Quarterly* 30.2 (1993): 209–18.

Millot, Catherine. "Épiphanies." In *Joyce avec Lacan,* by Jacques Lacan et al., 87–95. Paris: Navarin Éditeur, 1987.

Morrissey, L. J. "Joyce's Revision of 'The Sisters': From Epicleti to Modern Fiction." *James Joyce Quarterly* 24.1 (1986): 33–54.

Morse, J. Mitchell. "Where Terms Begin." In *A Conceptual Guide to "Finnegans Wake,"* ed. Michael H. Begnall and Fritz Senn, 1–17. University Park and London: Pennsylvania State University Press, 1974.

Niemayer, Carl. "A *Ulysses* Calendar." *James Joyce Quarterly* 13.2 (1976): 163–93.

Nietzsche, Friedrich. *"On the Genealogy of Morals" and "Ecce Homo."* Trans. Walter Kaufmann and R. J. Hollingdale. Ed. Walter Kaufmann. New York: Vintage, 1969.

Norris, Margot. *The Decentered Universe of "Finnegans Wake": A Structuralist Analysis.* Baltimore: Johns Hopkins University Press, 1976.

———. *Joyce's Web: The Social Unraveling of Modernism.* Austin: University of Texas Press, 1992.

Osteen, Mark. *The Economy of "Ulysses": Making Both Ends Meet.* Syracuse: Syracuse University Press, 1995.

Parish, Charles. "Agenbite of Agendath Netaim." *James Joyce Quarterly* 6.3 (1969): 237–41.

Peirce, Charles Sanders. *Collected Papers of Charles Sanders Peirce.* Ed. Charles Hartshorne, Paul Weiss, and Arthur W. Burks. Cambridge, Mass.: Harvard University Press, 1935–1966.

Plato. *Timaeus.* Trans. Benjamin Jowett. In *The Collected Dialogues of Plato, including the Letters,* ed. Edith Hamilton and Huntington Cairns, 1151–211. Bollingen Series LXXI. Princeton: Princeton University Press, 1961.

Power, Mary. "Why Miss Dunne Was Reading *The Woman in White* in the Middle of 'Wandering Rocks.'" *James Joyce Quarterly* 13.2 (1976): 237–41.

Prince, Gerald. *A Dictionary of Narratology.* Aldershot, England: Scolar Press, 1988.

Proust, Marcel. *Remembrance of Things Past.* Trans. C. K. Scott Moncrieff and Andreas Mayor. 12 vols. London: Chatto and Windus, 1957.

Rabaté, Jean-Michel. *James Joyce, Authorized Reader.* Baltimore and London: Johns Hopkins University Press, 1991.

———. *Joyce upon the Void: The Genesis of Doubt.* Basingstoke, England: Macmillan, 1991.

Raleigh, John Henry. *The Chronicle of Leopold and Molly Bloom: "Ulysses" as Narrative.* Berkeley: University of California Press, 1977.

———. "On the Chronology of the Blooms in *Ulysses.*" *James Joyce Quarterly* 14.4 (1977): 395–407.

———. "Who was M'Intosh?" *James Joyce Review* 3 (1959): 59–62.

Rasula, Jed. "*Finnegans Wake* and the Character of the Letter." *James Joyce Quarterly* 34.4 (1997): 517–30.

Reichert, Klaus. "Towards the Sublime." In *The Languages of Joyce: Selected Papers from the Eleventh International James Joyce Symposium, Venice, June 12–18, 1988,* ed. R. M. Bollettieri Bosinelli, C. Marengo Vaglio, and Christine van Boheemen, 223–28. Philadelphia: John Benjamins, 1992.

Ritchie, A. M. "Awake at the *Wake,* or How to Tell When Not Seeing What Is Not Is Seeing What Is." *A Wake Newslitter,* n.s., 3.2 (1966): 39–42.

Rose, Danis, ed. *James Joyce's "The Index Manuscript: Finnegans Wake" Holograph Workbook VI. B. 46.* Colchester: Wake Newslitter Press, 1978.

Sartiliot, Claudette. *Citation and Modernity: Derrida, Joyce, and Brecht.* Oklahoma Project for Discourse and Theory, vol. 13. Norman, Okla.: University of Oklahoma Press, 1993.

Saussure, Ferdinand de. *Course in General Linguistics.* Ed. Charles Bally and Albert Sechehaye, with Albert Riedlinger. Trans. Roy Harris. London: Duckworth, 1983.

Scholes, Robert A., and A. Walton Litz. *"Dubliners": Text, Criticism, and Notes.* New York: Viking, 1971.

Schutte, William M., and Erwin R. Steinberg. "The Fictional Technique of *Ulysses.*" In *Approaches to "Ulysses": Ten Essays,* ed. Thomas F. Staley and Bernard Benstock, 157–78. Pittsburgh: University of Pittsburgh Press, 1970.

Seidel, Michael. *Epic Geography: James Joyce's "Ulysses."* Princeton: Princeton University Press, 1976.

Senn, Fritz. "'He Was Too Scrupulous Always': Joyce's 'The Sisters.'" *James Joyce Quarterly* 2.2 (1965): 66–72.

———. *Inductive Scrutinies: Focus on Joyce.* Ed. Christine O'Neill. Baltimore: Johns Hopkins University Press, 1995.

———. *Joyce's Dislocutions: Essays on Reading as Translation.* Baltimore and London: Johns Hopkins University Press, 1984.

———. Letter to the Editor. *James Joyce Quarterly* 24.1 (1986): 115–16.

———. "Linguistic Dissatisfaction." In *The Languages of Joyce: Selected Papers from the Eleventh International James Joyce Symposium, Venice, June 12–18, 1988,* ed. R. M. Bollettieri Bosinelli, C. Marengo Vaglio, and Christine van Boheemen, 211–22. Philadelphia: John Benjamins, 1992. Reprinted in Senn, *Inductive Scrutinies,* 226–37.

———. "One White Elephant." *A Wake Newslitter,* n.s., 1.4 (1964): 1–2.

———. "A Test-Case of Over-Reading." *A Wake Newslitter,* n.s., 1.2 (1964): 1–8.

Serres, Michel. *Hermès.* 5 vols. Paris: Éditions de Minuit, 1968–80. (1. *La Communication,* 1968; 2. *L'Interférence,* 1972; 3. *La Traduction,* 1974; 4. *La Distribution* 1977; 5. *Le Passage du nord-ouest,* 1982.)

Slote, Sam. "Nulled Nought: The Desistance of Ulyssean Narrative in *Finnegans Wake.*" *James Joyce Quarterly* 34.4 (1997): 531–42.

Spencer, Theodore. Introduction to the first edition of *Stephen Hero: Part of the First Draft of "A Portrait of the Artist as a Young Man,"* by James Joyce, 13–24. Revised ed. London: Jonathan Cape, 1956.

Spoo, Robert. *James Joyce and the Language of History: Dedalus's Nightmare.* New York and Oxford: Oxford University Press, 1994.

Staley, Thomas F., and Bernard Benstock, eds. *Approaches to "Ulysses": Ten Essays.* Pittsburgh: University of Pittsburgh Press, 1970.

Szeliga, Tim. *Finnegans Web.* (http://www.trentu.ca/jjoyce/fw.htm).

Thompson, Mark. *Finnegans Wake Concordex.* (http://shaman.lycaeum.org/~martins/Finnegan/index.html).

———. *Finnegans Wake FarFetch.* (http://shaman.lycaeum.org/~martins/Finnegan/farfetch.html).

———. *Finnegans Wake Lexichaun.* (http://shaman.lycaeum.org/~martins/Finnegan/lexichaun.html).

Thwaites, Tony. "Cathexis: Metaphorics of Power." In *Foucault: The Legacy,* ed. Clare O'Farrell, 279–86. Brisbane: Queensland University of Technology, 1997.

———. "Currency Exchanges: The Postmodern, Vattimo, et Cetera, among Other Things (et Cetera)." *Postmodern Culture* 7.2 (http://muse.jhu.edu/journals/postmodern_culture/v007/7.2thwaites.html). 42 paragraphs.

Tindall, William York. *A Reader's Guide to "Finnegans Wake."* London: Thames and Hudson, 1969.

Topia, André. "The Matrix and the Echo: Intertextuality in *Ulysses.*" Trans. Elizabeth Bell and André Topia. In *Post-Structuralist Joyce: Essays from the French,* ed. Derek Attridge and Daniel Ferrer, 103–25. Cambridge: Cambridge University Press, 1984.

van Caspel, Paul. *Bloomers on the Liffey: Eisegetical Readings of Joyce's "Ulysses."* Baltimore and London: Johns Hopkins University Press, 1986.

Volosinov, V. N. (Mikhail Bakhtin). *Marxism and the Theory of Language.* Trans. Ladislav Matejka and I. R. Titunik. New York: Seminar Press, 1973.

von Phul, Ruth. "Bloom's Boustrophedontic Alphabet and Martha Clifford." *James Joyce Quarterly* 14.3 (1977): 357.

Walzl, Florence L. "A Book of Signs and Symbols: The Protagonist." In *The Seventh of Joyce*, ed. Bernard Benstock, 117–23. Bloomington: Indiana University Press/Sussex: Harvester, 1982.

Wellington, Frederick. "A Missing Conversation in *Ulysses*." *James Joyce Quarterly* 14.4 (1977): 476–79.

Wohlpart, A. James. "Laughing in the Confession Box: Vows of Silence in Joyce's 'The Sisters.'" *James Joyce Quarterly* 30.3 (1993): 409–17.

Young, Robert, ed. *Untying the Text: A Post-Structuralist Reader.* London: Routledge and Kegan Paul, 1981.

Žižek, Slavoj. *Enjoy Your Symptom! Jacques Lacan in Hollywood and Out.* New York and London: Routledge, 1992.

———. *For They Know Not What They Do: Enjoyment as a Political Factor.* London and New York: Verso, 1991.

———. *Looking Awry: An Introduction to Jacques Lacan through Popular Culture.* Cambridge, Mass., and London: MIT Press, 1991.

———. *The Metastases of Enjoyment: Six Essays on Women and Causality.* London and New York: Verso, 1994.

———. *The Plague of Fantasies.* London and New York: Verso, 1997.

———. *The Sublime Object of Ideology.* London and New York: Verso, 1989.

———. *Tarrying with the Negative: Kant, Hegel, and the Critique of Ideology.* Durham: Duke University Press, 1993.

Index

Tony Thwaites teaches and researches Joyce, modernism, literary theory, and cultural studies in the School of English, Media Studies and Art History at the University of Queensland, Brisbane, Australia.